T0198580

The Girl From Number 7, Windsor Avenue

A memoir

Vivienne Grilliot Worthington

THE GIRL FROM NUMBER 7, WINDSOR AVENUE
A MEMOIR

iUniverse books may be ordered through booksellers or by contacting:

iUniverse
1663 Liberty Drive
Bloomington, IN 47403
www.iuniverse.com
844-349-9409

Because of the dynamic nature of the Internet, any web addresses or links contained in this book may have changed since publication and may no longer be valid. The views expressed in this work are solely those of the author and do not necessarily reflect the views of the publisher, and the publisher hereby disclaims any responsibility for them.

Any people depicted in stock imagery provided by Getty Images are models, and such images are being used for illustrative purposes only.
Certain stock imagery © Getty Images.

ISBN: 978-1-6632-4876-3 (sc)
ISBN: 978-1-6632-4878-7 (hc)
ISBN: 978-1-6632-4877-0 (e)

Library of Congress Control Number: 2022922703

Print information available on the last page.

iUniverse rev. date: 01/11/2023

In memory of my parents, Bob and Doreen Grilliot

If I should die, think only this of me:
That there's some corner of a foreign field
That is for ever England. There shall be
In that rich earth a richer dust concealed;
A dust whom England bore, shaped, made aware,
Gave, once, her flowers to love, her ways to roam;
A body of England's breathing English air,
Washed by the rivers, blest by the suns of home.
Rupert Brooke, "The Soldier"

Prologue

The afternoon sun glided down toward the horizon, painting stripes on the floor as it seeped between the venetian blinds, which weren't quite closed all the way. My parents stood near the door of the hospital room, engaged in a murmuring conversation with Major Walters. My brother lay under an oxygen tent. Except where it was bruised, his skin was a scary white—whiter than I'd ever seen it before. He got bruises all the time now, but at seven years old, I didn't yet know the term *spontaneously ruptured capillaries*. A tube ran from a bottle of clear liquid hanging from a pole—it ended at his left ankle. I knew that meant they couldn't find a place on his arms to give him his blood transfusion. I also knew that since he had been unable to eat or drink for two days before he had to come to the hospital, the liquid in the bottle was giving him water so he wouldn't be thirsty. Someone had put Vaseline on the crusty sores on his lips, and when I slipped my head under the oxygen tent, I could see the greasy sheen. Lately, he'd been getting more sores in his mouth, and in the mornings, Mummy had to swab his lips and tongue with warm salt water before he could even sip his chocolate milk through a straw. He was wearing his favorite Howdy Doody pajamas, and somehow, that made me feel a little better. I'd hated it when he came to the hospital last time in his shorts and T-shirt and been put in a green gown that tied in the back. It had looked like a dress. I pulled my head out of the heavy clear canopy of the oxygen tent and slid my hand under, taking hold of his. I gave it a soft squeeze every so often. He didn't squeeze back. This time, he was even sicker than usual.

My mother was sobbing softly into her hankie; my father was standing with his head bowed. Major Walters walked over to me. She had curly red hair and freckles. She was Johnny's favorite nurse, and whenever he had to be admitted to the children's ward at Fitzsimons Army Hospital for blood transfusions, she always took care of him. She put her arm around my skinny shoulders and gave me a squeeze. Normally, she didn't do that. Normally, she had a big grin on her face and said things like "Well now, let's see what we need to do to get this brother of yours back home so he can watch *The Lone Ranger*, and you two can play Chutes and Ladders! Who's winning this week?"

"Do you see what is on the nightstand, Vivienne?" she asked me now.

I looked at the bedside table and saw a long cardboard box wrapped in cellophane. Through the clear front packaging, I could see four metal army soldiers in various fighting stances.

"Did Johnny get to go upstairs and see Ike?" Briefly, my spirits lifted, and hope soared through me.

When Johnny had been admitted two days ago, Major Walters had told him President Eisenhower was on a private ward upstairs. Ike was Johnny's hero. Around our house, it was "Ike this" and "Ike that"–of course, we were a military family, which explained that. Last year, our father had received an award from the president. We had a picture above the desk in the dining room that showed Daddy and two other airmen standing at attention while President Eisenhower pinned a medal onto our father's chest. Daddy assured us that the other men had received medals too, and two more pictures had been taken to show them receiving their medals. They all had done a good job during something called the Berlin Airlift.

"No, hon," said Major Walters. "Johnny was too sick to be able to be wheeled up to see him. President Eisenhower was discharged this morning, but he had been waiting for a visit from Johnny. He asked me to give him the soldiers and tell him that Ike is pulling for him."

"Does Johnny know?" My voice was barely a whisper.

"Not yet. He's been sleeping all day."

I waited for Major Walters to say that she was sure he'd wake up by dinnertime, and then she'd give the gift to him. Or that she would be there until eleven o'clock that night, so there would be plenty of time for her or Mummy to surprise him with the toy soldiers from Ike, his hero.

Her head was tilted to the side a little, and I thought her eyes looked wet.

I wasn't sure anyone heard me, because I thought maybe the words were just in my head. But I was telling them what Johnny had told me just last week: *I'm going home soon. I don't mean to this house here on Fulton Street after I've been in the hospital for my blood transfusion. I mean to my real home. To Jesus and Mary, my parents in heaven.*

I had pondered that for a bit. I had climbed down from the top bunk that night to lie next to my brother. I often did that at bedtime. I could make up the most fantastic stories of all measure of things–England mostly. I told him stories about the elves and fairies I used to see from Nanna and Granddad's bedroom window at twilight. They lived at the bottom of our garden, and I had to be very quiet, kneel on Nanna's stool, and look down from the open window to see them. Everyone knew you could only see fairies in that special light that Nanna called *the gloaming*. My favorite story to tell Johnny was about Prince Charles, who was exactly five months younger than I and who would want to marry me when we were old enough.

"But if you marry Prince Charles, won't they make you live in England?" Johnny had asked once in a worried voice.

"Oh no. I'll be a princess and will be able to choose to live wherever I want. I'll just visit Buckingham Palace and the queen when I go home to England to visit Nanna and Granddad."

"Oh, good. I would miss you if you had to live in England again!"

But one night less than a week ago, John had asked me to tell him again about heaven and about Jesus and Mary, our heavenly parents. I was good at describing heaven. Just last year, I had made my First Holy Communion at Saint Mary's Catholic Church in Muncie, Indiana. I had memorized every catechism lesson that Sister

Philathea had taught. I was convinced that heaven was at least as wonderful as Flixton, the little town in Lancashire where I had lived with my grandparents—and sometimes my mother—since I was born.

John's hospitalizations had become more frequent since Christmas, and it was now the week after Easter, so perhaps he was right. Suddenly, while telling him about heaven, I'd thought of something Sister had said during catechism class: "Nothing you ask in the name of his mother will Jesus deny. He does everything Mary asks of him, so pray your rosary every day."

"Don't worry," I'd said to Johnny, "because when you die and go to heaven, I'm going to ask Mary to bring me up to visit you. All the time. I'd come up there to live with you and Jesus and Mary, but I would worry about Mummy and Daddy. They would be so sad if we both went to heaven at the same time."

"I know," John had answered, "Just visit me. That will be fine. And bring Chutes and Ladders in case they don't have things like that up there." He'd paused for a minute then added, "Now, don't be sad, but I'm going very soon—probably next week or the week after. Jesus told me last night."

John Charles Christopher Grilliot, aged four and a half, slipped into a coma and died in the early morning of April 18, 1956. His disease, aplastic anemia, had ravaged his small body for more than a year. He had had so many blood transfusions that toward the end, the only veins that could be accessed were those in his feet and ankles. He had suffered greatly; not until many years later would I understand how much. He never knew that his hero, Ike, had sent him toy soldiers. Somewhere in a battered old suitcase filled with memorabilia, there was a newspaper clipping dated a few days before Johnny died. A front-page article about President Eisenhower's hospitalization was featured, and there was a picture of David Eisenhower, the president's grandson, arriving at Fitzsimons Army Hospital with the package of toy soldiers in hand as a gift for his grandfather.

The year following Johnny's death, I had an epiphany. My mother and I were coloring eggs on Easter Saturday. Connie, the baby, was one and a half and, with help, would have fun looking for hidden Easter eggs, we thought. As usual, the eggs would be left in a bowl on the kitchen counter for the Easter Bunny to hide, along with a carrot for him to snack on. Suddenly, I stopped to focus on the implausible scene unfolding in my head: a rabbit so large it could carry Easter baskets filled with hard-boiled chicken eggs–because there wasn't such a thing as rabbit eggs–all over the world, depositing them in various nooks and crannies and throwing in lots of chocolate for good measure. The thought made me giggle. It also made me immediately think of Father Christmas–or Santa Claus, as he was called in America–flying around the world in a sleigh pulled by flying reindeer on Christmas Eve and working his fat little body with a huge sack of toys down fireplace chimneys near and far.

And just like that, I grew up.

Just like that, I knew I could stop asking Mary to ask Jesus to take me up to heaven for a visit with Johnny.

Coming to America

One

SOMETIMES, OUT OF NOWHERE, WHILE DOING ORDINARY tasks, tasks of repetition that require no real thought, a memory pops into my head, and a surge of nostalgia sweeps through my veins like the first sip of fine wine. Suddenly, I find myself transported back to Windsor Avenue. I have been picked up as though I am Dorothy in *The Wizard of Oz* and planted right down on the pavement in front of my grandparents' house. If I look to my left, I can see Kenny Ainsworth and the other boys on our street kicking a football in the distance. If I look the other way, I can see the stone wall that conceals the garden of the house with the apple tree. Once again, I smell the ordinary smells of Windsor Avenue, and my ears hear the familiar sounds echoing down through the decades since I lived there. I heard a lecture at college once and learned that sound stays in the universe forever; it never goes away. I like to ponder that. I like knowing that out there somewhere in the infinity that is space are the voices of all the people I have loved, saying all the words I loved to hear. In my daydream, I turn around and face number 7. I can see Nanna's front-room curtains–Belgian lace, of course–blowing through the open windows as she lets the brisk breezes of northern England sweep through the house, and once again, I'm in my childhood home.

My name is Vivienne Dempster, and I live with my grandparents–and sometimes my mother–at number 7 Windsor Avenue in the small town of Flixton, seven miles from Manchester in Lancashire, England. I think Flixton is the most wonderful place on earth, and our street is the most exciting in the whole world.

Every week, the rag-and-bone man, with his tired old horse, comes slowly clip-clopping down the street, shouting, "Bring yer rags! All rags! Rags needed!" He never does call for bones, and once, when I asked Nanna if we should save our chicken bones from Sunday dinner for the rag-and-bone man, she said no, he only wanted rags. She said not for years had he collected bones of any sort. But she does save old rags for him, and in exchange, he gives her the hard, brick-like yellow soap that she scrubs our front steps with every Monday. Granddad says Nanna is house-proud. I think that means she cleans too much.

Right across the street from our house is an air-raid shelter. It looks like a small hill on the outside, with grass sprouting between its rounded bricks. It has a heavy wooden door with iron hinges that creak when it's pushed open, and inside are steps that go down to a big room with wide wooden seats fastened to the walls. Granddad says that during the war, when the sirens went off at night, the women and children and very old men went down into the shelter because the German planes dropped bombs on the factories all around Trafford Park, which is near Flixton. At night, Nanna says, no lights were allowed to shine from any windows, so all the houses all over the British Isles had to hang heavy curtains to black out the house lights. Now the air-raid shelter is not used by any grown-ups, since the war ended before I was born. The boys on our street play in it whenever they play war, and sometimes, if we girls feel like it, we go along with the boys' game and go down into the shelter to escape the bombs that they pretend are falling from airplanes in the sky.

At the end of our street, next door to the house Nanna calls a bungalow, just where Windsor Avenue connects with Whitelake Avenue, there is a house with an apple tree that pokes its top above the tall stone wall that goes around its garden. The boys dare each other to climb the wall and steal apples, which is difficult because there really isn't anywhere to stick your feet or to hold on to the stones. I tried it once and fell and scraped my knees, and Nanna said it served me right, as it was wrong to steal anything, even if the apples go to waste because the people in the house with the apple tree never pick them.

The best thing about our street is its name. It is named for the family of our queen, Elizabeth Windsor. Last year, after her father, the king, died, she was crowned in June. It was called a coronation, and there were parties and parades all over England. I remember it because June is my birthday month. Mrs. Murphy and Nanna set up a table in the street, all the ladies baked cakes and made biscuits, and we had lemonade. Elizabeth is the most beautiful queen in the world, and whenever her picture is in the newspaper, Nanna lets me cut it out after Granddad's finished looking to see if he won on the ponies. He bets on the races and sometimes wins money, and when he does, he goes to his pub on Moorside Road, the Garrick's Head.

Mummy told me that when she was expecting me, Granddad's horse came in, and he took his winnings to Manchester and bought my pram. It's a Silver Swan, and it's the most beautiful pram in our whole town. Nanna said it's the kind of pram that Queen Elizabeth used for Charles and Ann. Of course, I'm five now and much too big to ride in it. Nanna keeps it in the box room, the tiny room at the end of our upstairs landing. When I'm bigger, Nanna says, I will be allowed to have my bed in the box room, and she'll let me sleep in there by myself. Now, though, I share a room with Auntie Barbara, Mummy's little sister. Apart from the horses, Granddad's favorite thing to do is play dominoes at the Garrick. He's going to teach me how to play dominoes when I'm six. When I was four, he said he'd teach me when I turned five, but when I did, he changed his mind and said he'd teach me when I turned six.

All in all, next to living with the queen in Buckingham Palace, living at number 7 Windsor Avenue with Nanna, Granddad, Auntie Barbara, and sometimes Mummy is the best place in the whole world to live.

One day I overheard Nanna talking to Mrs. Murphy, who is Irish and lives next door at number 9 Windsor Avenue. Nanna told her she'd helped the midwife deliver me. That sounded quite reasonable, as our coal and milk are delivered right to our house too, and everyone on our street knows that midwives deliver babies. I suppose Nanna and the midwife went and got me from Park Hospital, which is where all babies round here seem to come from, although I heard Nanna's friend Edie Faye say that Mrs. Brickles's daughter went away to somewhere near London for hers. It certainly makes more sense than what Granddad says: that I was found by fairies, and they put me under the hedge in the back garden. He always says it in his jokey way, and he always follows up with the rhyme he made up for me: "There once was a man who lived in a can down at the bottom of the garden. Then came the day he had to go away; now the fairies rent the can and pay a farthing!"

"How do the fairies find him to pay the rent, Granddad?"

"Oh, you know what fairies are like. They know everything that goes on everywhere. They know where to find him, by gum."

One day, Granddad said, after the fairies moved in, he was tending to his tomatoes and heard them laughing in their fairy way, so he bent down to see if he could catch them out for once, and what do you know? There I was, under the hedge. When I was little, I believed him. But now I'm five–and in ten and a half months, I'll be six–and while I do know we have fairies in the back garden, because I saw them once in the twilight when I was upstairs looking out Nanna and Granddad's bedroom window, I realize even a tiny baby would be too large for fairies to carry from anywhere and hide under our back hedge. So it makes perfect sense that the midwife and Nanna brought me from Park Hospital and delivered me to Mummy.

One day something most exciting happened on our street, something even more exciting than usual. The lady who lives in the bungalow next to the apple tree house bought an icebox–the sort like Americans have, we think. It makes ice from water out of the tap. Two of the boys saw it being delivered this morning by a man with a lorry. None of us really know what an icebox is, but it sounds exciting, because Kenny Ainsworth's older sister said Americans all have them in their houses. One of the big girls from up Whitelake Avenue said she has a sister who married a Yank, and they moved to America. She lives in a place called Hoboken, and she has her very own icebox.

One of the bigger boys from Moorside Road said, "So what? It's not only Americans that have iceboxes." He said his auntie who lives in Manchester has one, and he's seen the man with a lorry full of blocks of ice who comes round once a week to put the ice in the icebox. It is a huge frozen block that comes from the ice factory, he said, and the man must use a giant pair of tongs—like fireplace tongs, only much bigger—to carry it up the path, through the back door, and into the scullery. His auntie makes meat pies and Cornish pasties for some of the pubs in Manchester and needs to be able to keep the meat from spoiling. She has pounds and pounds of it, which is why she needs an icebox. He said that some of her neighbors think she's putting on airs—getting a bit airy-fairy and trying to act posh—but she isn't really. He said he's never heard of ice being made at home and not delivered by the ice lorry man, at least not here in England.

Another boy said his dad said that certain American iceboxes make tiny blocks of ice called ice cubes to put in drinks, but nobody in England waters drinks down with frozen water, not even in the pubs. His dad said of everyone in the entire world, only Americans want their drinks to be cold enough to freeze balls, so didn't it stand to reason that the icebox came from America? We all nodded in agreement, puzzled in unity at the thought of anyone wanting to freeze a rubber ball. I left my ball out in the back garden one cold night last winter, and it was frozen solid the next day. It wouldn't bounce for hours, and when it finally thawed, it never again bounced as high as it used to.

We were all quite in awe of the two older boys' superior knowledge. "How does it work," we asked, "if the ice isn't being delivered by the ice lorry man?"

"Electricity," they said, "or perhaps gas." They aren't quite sure. That's the exact opposite of what those two things usually do inside our houses: instead of providing hot water, they think, it freezes water from the kitchen tap, but it's anyone's guess how it turns the water into little squares of ice.

One of the other boys said he didn't believe it. "I'll believe it when I see it, by gum," he said in a grown-up manner. (Once, when I said *by gum* just like Granddad does sometimes, Nanna scolded me. Nanna is from a posh family, and I am never allowed to use *common* words.) Soon we tired of talking about something so abstract that we had difficulty understanding it, and we returned to our games in the street.

It was a particularly hot summer day a week or so later, and most of the boys who lived on Windsor Avenue and a few from Whitelake were playing the boys' favorite game: war. The boys were shouting that the girls needed to get into the air-raid shelter because the sirens had just sounded, and the Huns were coming, but the shelter was stuffy and dusty inside, and we girls were ignoring them. We had just decided to take our dollies on a walk in their prams, when one of the older girls noticed the lady with the icebox–she was no longer called the lady in the bungalow–kneeling by her flower bed, pulling weeds. I'm not sure which of the girls suggested it, but given that we were all obsessed with the marvel of a gas or electric box that turned water into ice, and joined by a few of the boys, we gathered ourselves into a tight little group and marched down the pavement until we were standing at her gate.

When she looked up quizzically, one of the girls stepped forward. "Please, missus, could we see one of those little square ice things Kenny said your icebox makes? Me mum said she heard if you ask for them at Lewis's Tea Room in Manchester, they'll bring you some to put in your lemonade to make it really cold."

Smiling, the lady got up, went into the house, and came out with a bowl of small clear cubes that looked just a bit bigger than chocolates from a box of Cadbury's Milk Tray. They were perfectly square, and they were colorless–just like tap water. She held the bowl out, and we took one each and looked in wonder at this marvel she called an ice cube. One of the children asked if she could lick it like an ice-lolly. Of course she could, said the lady. Tentatively, I licked mine. My tongue stuck to it for a second, and when it loosened, I realized it tasted like plain tap water, which it was quickly turning into as it melted in my hand. I popped mine into my mouth to savor the iciness as long as possible. It had no flavor; it was just lovely and cold and melted into water.

"'Ow did you make them square?" one boy asked.

"I have a special tin that came with the refrigerator, which is what an electric icebox is called. I pour water into the tin, which is divided up into small square compartments, and put it in the top part of the refrigerator, which is called a freezer—where it is so cold you can see your breath if you breathe into it! Hours later, or overnight, the water will have turned into ice—you know, just like icicles that hang from the roof in the winter. The tin has a little lever attached to it, and when the water has completely frozen, you pull the lever up, and voilà! Out pop the ice cubes!"

I had only a vague idea of what a miracle was. Our Sunday school teacher at Saint Michael's Church talks about the miracle of baby Jesus's birth, but babies come from Park Hospital all the time. It isn't every day that a person can turn ordinary tap water into ice in the scullery! The Miracle of the Ice Cubes. Now I was sorry I had eaten mine—I should have run home with it to show Nanna and Granddad!

Granddad was in the garden, admiring his tomatoes, when I ran home to tell him about the lady with the icebox that we think must have come from America.

"It's called a refrigerator, Granddad, and she gave us little squares of ice that are frozen water! They are called ice cubes, and the top part of the icebox magically makes them. Do you think we will ever get an icebox, Granddad? Don't you think it must be a miracle?"

"How do you think frozen lollipops are made that you get from Mrs. Walsh's Top Shop?" he asked. "And how do you think Grimwood's makes the ice cream they bring round in the ice cream van?"

"I don't know, Granddad. I just thought they were made at the ice-lolly factory or the ice cream factory. Like Cadbury Flake bars at the chocolate factory or like bread from the bakery. But, Granddad, this is ordinary tap water that is turned into real ice. It *is* a miracle!"

We never did get any sort of an icebox at number 7 Windsor Avenue. For her entire life, my grandmother did her shopping several days a week at the village shops or at the shops at the farthest end of our street, near the Red Lion Public House in Woodsend.

Our house had a larder off the kitchen, built of brick and overlaid with a thick layer of plaster to keep its interior temperature cool, in which both the perishables and the nonperishables were stored. Milk was delivered daily to the doorstep by the milkman; bread was bought fresh from the bakery on days when my grandmother and I walked to the village; and in the summertime, I still got my ice-lollies from Mrs. Welsh's Top Shop. And, years after, whenever I visited my grandparents—and well into my teens—I still got my ice cream cones with raspberry vinegar from the Grimwood's ice cream van as it made its way round our plebeian streets.

Two

MY EARLY CHILDHOOD IN ENGLAND WAS IDYLLIC—AT least it remained so in my memories. Although my vocabulary in those days didn't extend to describing it as such and although we were far from wealthy, I knew nothing but the security of being cared for by loving grandparents. My grandfather worked what he referred to as the "two-ten shift" at Turner's Asbestos in Trafford Park, and my grandmother worked part-time cleaning the surgery of our family physician. Granddad also had a share of the allotment behind our house, the borders of which were defined by the back gardens of the semidetached houses along both Windsor and Whitelake avenues. Often, I would help him weed the plot in which he grew his vegetables, always on the lookout for fairies I was sure were hiding amid the cabbages. My mother's sister, my aunt Barbara, got married before she turned seventeen, and I was a flower girl. True to the simplicity of our lives, it changed nothing, other than I finally got to have my own little bed in the box room. Then, suddenly, my life was completely uprooted.

On October 11, 1954, I boarded a Royal Sabena Airlines flight at Ringway Airport and flew from Manchester, England, to New York. I was not quite six and a half years old. Apparently, a child flying unaccompanied across the Atlantic Ocean at that time was a newsworthy event, because when the plane landed, I was met by my parents, my brother, and the *New York Times*. Somewhere also is a newspaper clipping of an article that appeared in the *Manchester Evening News*. It is dated the day I departed, and it refers to me as Flixton's youthful and feminine Gulliver and relates the story of my journey from my grandparents' house in Lancashire, England, to New York City and from there to Muncie, Indiana. My father had recently been transferred from Patrick Air Force Base on the east coast of Florida to Muncie, so it must have seemed to my parents as good a time as any to bring me to America.

I soon learned that my father was a staff sergeant in the United States Air Force and that he had been transferred to Ball State Teachers College to teach something called ROTC. My parents rented an old farmhouse that belonged to the Ball family, and life on the Ball estate was much as I imagined living in Buckingham Palace would have been. There were no narrow streets and semidetached houses like those in Flixton, and everything in America seemed to me to be very big. The house had a huge back garden separated from an even larger pasture by a wooden fence. The pasture was green and lush, even though the cold of autumn had turned the leaves on the trees red and yellow, and when Mummy or Daddy was outside with us, my brother and I were allowed to feed carrots and apples to the horses that galloped up to the fence whenever they saw us playing in the yard.

I had been in America for about two weeks, when we went to something called a drive-in movie. Going to a drive-in movie was one of the most amazing things ever; it was almost as amazing as flying in an airplane up above the clouds. Mummy said England had no such thing as films that you could watch while sitting in your car. In fact, no one we knew in England had a motorcar. Once, though, my auntie Barbara took me to the Curzon in Urmston to see a Shirley Temple film. Even though there were pretty girls in short frocks carrying trays of chocolate and ice cream in wafers and walking all around the seats to sell the sweets during something called intermission, it wasn't nearly as exciting as sitting in the backseat of Daddy's car and sipping Coca-Cola through straws that were pushed down into the bottles of pop. I was sure Nanna would never let me drink a whole bottle of Coca-Cola, and even if she did, she'd never let me drink it out of the bottle. She would say that wasn't polite, and she would make me pour it into a glass. Mummy was much better about things like that–perhaps because Daddy told her that was how it was done in America.

At first, I spent a good deal of time wondering how the people who showed the films on the huge outdoor screen managed to separate the voices of the people and the music in the movie and send those sounds down the wires to the all the boxes that hung on the windows of the cars. I noticed that when we went to the toilets during intermission, there was no sound at all coming from the screen. The huge people onscreen were moving their mouths, but nothing was coming out. Daddy said the boxes on the poles outside the cars were called speakers, and they worked just like radios. Did I not remember Nanna and Granddad's radio in their front room? All the music and voices on their radio came from far away at the BBC. It was the same thing, said my father. That made me wonder: When the people at the BBC sent their voices down the wires to all the people who had radios, how did they get them back? For that matter, how did the actors on the screen at the drive-in movie get theirs back? One thing was certain: I was never going to speak into something that sent my voice somewhere else until I was sure I would still have it! I thought of our next-door neighbor in number 5 Windsor Avenue, who couldn't speak. When Nanna and I passed him sometimes while going to the shops, he would nod and tip his hat, but he couldn't say hello or anything. Perhaps he'd once made the mistake of sending his voice somewhere on the wireless.

I had never seen any American movies before, except for Shirley Temple, of course, but the boys of Windsor Avenue had occasionally played something called cowboys and Indians. They had used sticks for guns, and the boys who were supposed to be Indians had made bows and arrows out of sticks and string. I had no idea where the boys on Windsor Avenue had ever seen a cowboy movie, but I could see now that they made better German soldiers than they did American cowboys.

Gary Cooper was everything I had imagined an American film star would be. He was tall, handsome, and brave—and to the relief of his wife, all the townspeople, and me, he got rid of the horrible, villainous men who were trying to take over the town. That was exactly why I wasn't scared to live in America—because there were brave men here like my daddy and Gary Cooper. However, Nanna was worried about gangsters in some place called Chicago, which was why she had kept me in England for so long.

I wished my grandparents could come live here with us. We had a television, a motorcar, a refrigerator that made magic ice cubes, and hot running water all the time, not just when we put a shilling in a gas meter like at number 7. Living here in America was just like living in a film. When I asked Mummy if she thought Nanna and Granddad would ever come to America to live, she said no, probably not. Nanna would have missed walking to the shops every day and having a natter with the neighbors as she made her way up Whitelake, and Granddad would have missed his pub. They would come for a visit someday, though, she said.

I found I quite liked my parents, who, up until then, had not been a consistent presence in my life. My mother had sometimes been part of my world; I remembered her going out to work every day and coming home at teatime when I was small. After she moved to America with my father, I remembered her coming back to England with my brother, who was just a baby, and she stayed for quite a long time. But then she returned to America. I never admitted it, as I thought it might hurt his feelings, but I had no memory of my father at all. We had a picture of the three of us—Mummy, Daddy, and me—taken in the back garden at number 7, so one would have thought I would remember him. In the picture, I was sitting in the pedal car I'd gotten for my third birthday. It was light blue, and all the other children on Windsor Avenue wished they had one. Nanna said I must let everyone who wasn't too big have a turn driving it. I thought Daddy must have bought it at his American base, because the steering wheel was on the wrong side—just like our motorcar in America.

Still, I didn't dwell on the fact that I felt as if I'd just met my father. I figured it must have been because when we were all in England, he was stationed at a base called Burtonwood—a long way from Flixton—and probably did not live much at number 7 with Nanna, Granddad, Mummy, and me.

I found that the only thing about America I didn't like was American food. I didn't go hungry, but it meant Mummy had to fix me different things, which annoyed Daddy. Things I'd never heard of seemed to show up at every meal, and most of the time, I lived on soft-boiled eggs and toast. I watched in amazement as my little brother ate peanut butter, canned corn, popcorn, bologna, and something called hot dogs, which looked like sausages but tasted horrible. On Fridays, Mummy made something called salmon patties, but they were nothing like the salmon sandwiches Nanna used to make from little tins of red salmon mashed with vinegar and spread on lovely buttered English bread and sometimes topped by a thinly sliced cucumber. Even though Nanna and Granddad ate their bread crusts, I didn't like them, so Nanna used to cut mine off. I only liked my sandwiches cut into triangles, not squares, but I learned not to bother about that in America—my fussiness annoyed Daddy. Even worse than salmon patties was another Friday dinner: tuna and noodle casserole. While I sometimes tried to swallow teeny bites of salmon patty, I couldn't even begin to put mushy fish-flavored noodles anywhere near my lips.

Mummy understood how I felt about American food, because she said she used to feel the same way. After she'd lived here for a while, though, she had gotten more used to things we didn't eat in England. Luckily, the soft-boiled eggs, jam sandwiches, beans on toast, and cornflakes she mostly fixed me tasted almost the same as they did in England, and I liked Sunday dinner, because it was almost just like Nanna used to make—roasted meat, potatoes, and two vegetables. I just avoided eating the horrible yellow creamed things that came out of a tin.

"Why do Americans eat corn, Mummy?"

"They just do. It's an American thing."

"Do you just pretend to like it when you eat it?"

"Well," replied my mother, "once you get used to it, it really isn't too bad. And Daddy doesn't much like cauliflower or peas, so I make him corn."

Almost immediately upon arriving in Muncie, I was enrolled in school. Now, Mummy said, I had to use my correct last name: Grilliot.

"But my last name is Dempster, like Nanna and Granddad's," I said, puzzled that my mother was saying it wasn't.

"No, your real last name is Grilliot, but it was just easier to enroll you in school in Flixton as a Dempster since Nanna was taking you. It saved any problems that might have occurred if you'd had a different name. Remember when you had to go to Park Hospital because you had stomach pains, and Nanna thought it was appendicitis?"

I nodded.

"So that's why Nanna and Granddad just listed you as Vivienne Dempster whenever your full name was needed for anything. It was just easier all around."

So I was Vivienne Grilliot, and my parents enrolled me in the first grade at Saint Mary's Catholic School.

At first, I was properly offended that I had to start over. I had, typically, started school in England–year one–when I was four years old. Now I was six, and I expected to be put in year three, as I had been in Flixton. Of course, that was in infant school, but only four-year-olds went in the first year.

"First grade is the same as the third year," my mother explained.

"It can't be! What do they call the second year?" I asked.

"Kindergarten," said Mummy.

"Well then, where do the infants go?"

Around and around we went to no avail. First grade it was, and with nuns at that.

"We're Church of England, Mummy!"

"No, we're Chapel. But that doesn't matter, because now we're Catholic."

Soon, though, I overcame my frustration at being stripped of my rightful academic position—and of my Church of England or Chapel upbringing as well—and thoroughly embraced the newly imposed Catholicism. I loved my teacher, Sister Philathea, and liked school in general. Before long, I was the most enthusiastic Anglican-Catholic English American girl in my First Communion class. I believed there was nothing in the entire world that praying to Jesus and his mother, Mary, could not bring about, resolve, or save.

Shortly after I arrived in America, my parents took me to Illinois to introduce me to my American grandparents. I was surprised to learn that I had another set of grandparents; up to a dozen or so weeks ago, the nucleus of my world had been Nanna; Granddad; Auntie Barbara; and other various aunts, uncles, and cousins, all of whom had lived within walking distance of Windsor Avenue. Now I found that far away in a place called Freeport, I had a set of American grandparents. They were nice and, to my surprise, different in every way from my English grandparents. They thought every word I uttered with my accent was charming—although I couldn't hear how I sounded, so I wasn't sure why they liked it so much—and there were no rules. Of course, I was expected not to play in traffic and not to wander away from the house—a huge house, even bigger than our house in Muncie—but anything else I wanted to do or not do, eat or not eat, and explore or not explore was perfectly acceptable. Did I want ice cream before bed? Did I want a root-beer float? I didn't like root beer. No problem. "Open the little icebox that's kept just for soda pop," said my new grandfather. "The one near the cellar stairs, and choose whatever pop you would like." And he advised that almost any pop tasted better with a scoop of ice cream in it. So charmed was I at being indulged that for the entire long weekend, I forgot to miss Nanna and Granddad.

Soon, though, my life would not revolve around the charming attention of new grandparents, the wonder of the miracles Sister Philathea said Jesus could perform, or my enchantment by cowboys in white hats and their ability to tame the wild and scary West. Soon our happy family and the idyllic world we lived in would be torn asunder.

One Saturday night at bath time, after Christmas and about two months after we had returned from Illinois, Mummy noticed bruises on Johnny's legs—a lot of them. Had I seen him fall outside? No, I hadn't. Maybe he'd fallen out of bed, I suggested. He still slept in his crib, so he couldn't have, could he? Our parents worried about what possibly could have caused the bruising. Johnny climbing perhaps? Riding his rocking horse? Playing cowboys and Indians and jumping off the furniture that was the mountain he'd been hiding behind? Suddenly, a thought seemed to appear to both Mummy and Daddy: Johnny's holster and guns. Except at nap time, and sometimes even then, he wore them from the time he got up in the morning until he went to bed at night.

Mummy lifted Johnny out of the tub, dried him off, and slipped his underpants on him. Daddy knelt and put the holster belt around his skinny little waist. The two holsters exactly covered the bruises. "That's that," said Daddy. "No more wearing your holster and guns all day long!" They obviously were the cause of all the bruises.

For the next few weeks, I became a bossy older sister and, when necessary, a tattletale.

"Mummy! Johnny's wearing his holsters again, and he already had them on once this morning! I told him to take them off, but he's ignoring me!"

Before long, though, our parents started noticing bruises on John's arms and torso also, and one day they took him to visit a pediatrician in Muncie. That visit was to be the first of what became a year of physician appointments, treatments, and hospitalizations for a dreaded blood disorder known as aplastic anemia—for which, in 1955, there was no cure. Shortly after the diagnosis was confirmed, the air force transferred our family to Lowry Air Force Base in Aurora, Colorado, so that Johnny could be treated by specialists at Fitzsimons Army Hospital.

Three

THE MOVE TO COLORADO WAS SCHEDULED FOR THE FIRST week of May 1956, which happened to be the week before my First Holy Communion. The decision was made to leave me with family friends in Muncie, and my father would escort my mother and brother to Colorado and then return for me as soon as school ended for the summer.

There must have been much stress and uncertainty upon my parents' arrival at Lowry Air Force Base, because when my father returned to Indiana, he drove me to Illinois instead of Colorado and left me with his parents, those doting people who seemed only to want to spend entire days indulging me.

To my delight, I learned I had an aunt, an uncle, and two girl cousins around the corner from my grandparents. Within a few weeks, I was spending many of the long summer days with Aunt Babe, Uncle Dick, Linda, and Terri. I loved my aunt and uncle; I loved their house, their clothes, and their accents; and I was thrilled that I had American cousins. Most of all, I loved their dog, Fluffy.

We had never had a dog in England, but for the brief time I'd lived in Muncie, we'd had a cat. That cat was a terror, and I thought it must have come with the farmhouse. It didn't have a name–my mother just called it Pussy Cat–and it was pure evil. At night, it waited until I was asleep and then jumped onto my face, letting out a fierce meow. I learned to sleep with my head under the covers, until finally, my parents realized the cat and I would never bond, and my father started putting it out at night. But Fluffy was different. Fluffy was the dog I'd dreamed of having when I lived at number 7 Windsor Avenue.

I longed for a dog so much that once, when Nanna entered me in a talent contest in Urmston, I soulfully sang "How Much Is That Doggy in the Window?" Somehow, I thought Nanna would relent upon hearing such pleading in my voice and would let me have a dog. Instead, she bought me tuppence worth of Dolly Mixture and seemed shocked that the contest judges failed to recognize my talent. I thought Nanna had hoped I had inherited her voice. Nanna had a lovely voice. She sang "I'll Take You Home Again, Kathleen" whenever she went with Granddad to the pub. I never got to go to the pub, but I had heard her singing it lots of times when she cleaned the brasses or scrubbed the front steps, and I thought her voice was beautiful.

"I do believe you have been gifted with my voice," my grandmother said as we left Mrs. Welsh's Top Shop, where she'd bought my sweets. "And I also believe those three judges were tone-deaf. The girl who won did not sing half as well as you!" When Nanna was annoyed, her voice sounded even more posh than usual.

Tuppence provided quite a lot of sweets–at least as many as would fill a teacup–and Mrs. Welsh had measured them into a paper cone she'd made by rolling a piece of paper and twisting the end. I always loved to watch her make them. When my friends and I played shops, Nanna would cut up old newspaper for us to roll into paper cones. We filled them with whatever we could find–pebbles, leaves, and dandelion petals mostly.

As Nanna and I walked along, I picked out the pink sweets from the Dolly Mixture. They were marshmallow and tasted like strawberry. Suddenly, I had a thought: "If I had won, Nanna, would you have let me have a dog?"

If there was a chance she would change her mind, I would practice singing daily. Then she would see how in earnest I was!

"No. And I've told you: stop mithering for a dog. They shed hair in the carpets, they eat much more than cats, and they get muddy footprints on my clean steps, not to mention they aren't even good mousers!"

I could always tell when my grandmother said no and meant it. I sighed. "Well, then I think I'd rather be a rag-and-bone lady than a singer. At least I'd have a horse!"

There were other children on the street my cousins lived on, and one sunny afternoon shortly after I arrived in Freeport, several of us were outside playing hopscotch on the pavement in front of my cousins' house. Linda threw her stone, and it landed right on the line between numbers four and six.

"You must either reroll or miss a turn, Linda," I said. "Since you were trying for the six, it really didn't land squarely in the proper box."

"How come you talk funny?" asked Tommy, one of the other children. Tommy had scabbed knees and a perpetual runny nose.

What did he mean? Did I really talk funny? No one else had mentioned that they thought I talked funny.

"She's English," answered Linda.

"What's English?"

"It's a country far away across a big ocean," she replied.

"The Atlantic Ocean," I said. "I flew by myself on an airplane because my mummy, daddy, and brother already got here before me."

"Why is English so far away, and why do they talk like that?"

"It isn't En*glish*; it's Eng*land*," I said. "Just like this is Amer*ica*, not Amer*ican*."

"I am too American," responded the boy.

I looked at Linda, who, as a real American, was much more likely to be able to argue the point I was trying to make. I couldn't begin to form an explanation; it was out of my depth. I had heard Aunt Babe tell Grandma that Linda was smart and had gotten all As in the first grade. (I didn't know what I had gotten, because we'd left Muncie before I got my report from the headmistress—that was, the head nun, who I now remembered was called a principal here in America.)

"Well, we are American," said Linda, "because we live here in America all the time. My cousin is English because she used to live in England all the time."

The boy just shrugged and wiped his nose on his sleeve–satisfied, I supposed, that my cousin's explanation had not challenged his nationality. Still, the conversation bothered me. Was I really that different from my cousins?

For the next few days, I worried that I didn't really fit in, and I stood in front of my grandmother's dressing table mirror and scrutinized myself. Then I spoke out loud in the privacy of her bedroom to see if I could hear how I sounded. I wasn't sure how I sounded, but I could tell that the girl looking back at me from the mirror did not look American: pale skin; braided hair with a part in the middle; and a dress–or frock, as it was called in England–that was too English-looking. I had to do something with myself.

I decided Linda was exactly the American girl to copy. She not only had a perfect American accent but also looked American: shorts, sleeveless blouses, tanned skin, and a cute haircut with a fringe that she called *bangs*. I was going to ask my American grandmother why I had to wear my dresses every day. All the girls on Windsor Avenue wore dresses and, usually, because of English weather, cardigans, but girls in America wore shorts when they played outside. Also, I was going to ask Aunt Babe to cut my hair just like Linda's–because long braids with a part in the middle and no fringe looked too English.

Just like that, it came to me what else I needed to do: I not only needed to practice looking like an American girl but also needed to start speaking American! Even though I couldn't hear how I sounded, I must have sounded odd–why else would someone have asked me why I talked "like that"? I would practice every day, and when I had to go to yet another new school, I would sound so American that no one would even think to ask me why I talked funny.

That summer, one idyllic day melted into another. My new grandmother took me shopping and bought me shorts, sleeveless blouses, and sandals that didn't need socks, but she said I couldn't have my hair cut unless my mother said so. She would ask her the next time they spoke on the phone, she said. In the meantime, she would put my hair in a ponytail instead of braids. Ponytails were, she assured me, very American.

I spent most of my time with my cousins at my aunt and uncle's house, and although we had rules to follow, there was such a vast difference in the structure of our daily lives that in years beyond, I would forever think of it as my American summer. We played outside all day, got sunburned, went barefoot (I was never going to tell Nanna about that!), ate Kool-Aid powder mixed with sugar out of the palms of our hands, and caught lightning bugs in jars at dusk.

On Sundays, my new aunt and uncle, my new cousins, and I, along with our grandparents, went to Mass at Saint Mary's Catholic Church. On my first Sunday there, I asked if all Catholic schools and churches in America were called Saint Mary's. Grandma Grilliot said no, it was just a coincidence that the Catholic church and school in Muncie were named after Jesus's mother, as were those in Freeport.

August arrived. Long days of sunshine, summer rain, and the fertile soil of the prairies had worked their magic, and Grandpa's corn and tomatoes were ripe and brimming with flavor. Linda, Terri, and I were in the backyard at our grandparents' house, sitting at the picnic table, eating hot dogs that Grandma Grilliot had just roasted on the grill. I didn't know why I hadn't liked hot dogs when I first came to America, because these tasted wonderful. I reached for a roasted cob of corn and spread butter over the kernels, just as my cousins did. I took a tentative bite and then a bigger one. The taste surprised me: it was nothing like the canned creamed corn that Daddy ate.

Someone took a picture of me with corncob in hand and butter dripping down my chin and mailed it to my mother. She couldn't believe I was eating corn. Not only did I think it was delicious, but more importantly, it was a symbol of my newfound Americanism: I knew of no English children who had ever eaten corn, on or off the cob, or, for that matter, any who had eaten a hot dog.

Through the years, I would think back to that summer and would realize what a truly wonderful American experience it was, full of laughter and family warmth. What a wonder to me to fall into bed completely spent at night, to imagine my body so filled with golden sunshine that I was sure it was oozing out of my pores, and to have no worries that day or the next or the next.

Throughout that whole summer, I practiced my American accent. I was sure that by September, when I had to start yet another new school, I would sound as American as everyone else.

Four

MY FATHER HAD DRIVEN TO FREEPORT AND PICKED me up the week before school started. Now it was September 1955, and I was enrolled in the second grade at the public elementary school in Aurora, Colorado. It was nothing like Saint Mary's in Muncie, a small parochial school supported by families who all shared a common thread. In Muncie, children rode to school together in various carpools, studied together for their First Holy Communions or their confirmations, and gathered for sporting events and other extracurricular activities on the school grounds or at the local park. Whenever Mummy had taken my brother and me to watch Daddy umpire a Little League game, one or two of my school friends always had come to watch an older brother play ball.

In Aurora, my parents had rented a bland-looking house on a dreary street. There were no children of my age in our new neighborhood, and the two teenage girls who lived on the corner went to the high school that was in the other direction—so at seven years old, I found myself walking the five or so blocks to and from the elementary school. My father had to be at work earlier than I had to be at school, and my parents decided it would be safer for me to walk by myself through our neighborhood than to be dropped off in an empty schoolyard an hour early.

My parents referred to our house as *living on the economy*–which meant not living in base housing, whatever that was. As I had never lived in base housing, I wasn't sure if this was better or worse. There were no trees or flowers growing in either our front or our back garden, and both the house and the street were devoid of any of the beauty of the Ball estate. Neither the house nor the neighborhood had any of the charm of Windsor Avenue or of my cousins' street in Freeport. Still, plain as it was, it was clean and fairly new, and the next-door neighbor turned out to be a godsend.

I wasn't exactly sure what a godsend was, but I heard my mother speaking on the phone to my American grandmother, and that was what she told her. I thought it meant that when she and Daddy had to take Johnny to the hospital in the middle of the night, God sent the neighbor over to stay with me if it was a school night. (If it was a weekend night, I got bundled up and taken next door to her house.) I wished I could go back to Windsor Avenue or even live with my cousins in Freeport, but Mummy would have been left all by herself with Johnny when Daddy went to work, and she needed my help. Plus, Mummy said we were getting a new baby in November, and she was counting on me to be there when she had to be at the hospital with Johnny. I was to take care of the new baby, even if we were at a neighbor's house.

It was now October, and the autumn had turned cold. That morning, I pulled a kitchen chair up to the sink to look out our kitchen window at Pike's Peak. It looked different from our kitchen window than it looked up close. Last month, we had taken a car ride to the mountains. We had gone to something called a saloon, which Daddy said was the same as a pub, where a long time ago, a cowboy had painted a huge picture of his girlfriend on the wooden floor. After Johnny and I had drunk our Roy Rogers and Dale Evans soda pops, we had gone to an Indian village where there were teepees, and the Indians who lived in the village had done something Daddy called a traditional dance. They wore beautiful clothes and feather headdresses, and their movements had made me feel light and happy, a feeling I hadn't felt since being with my cousins in Freeport. I decided that never again would I think the Indians in any cowboy and Indian movies we went to were bad, not even if all the cowboys wore white hats.

I had a place inside me now that felt uncomfortable all the time. The funny sensation wasn't really in my stomach and didn't feel like it was in my heart, but it was in there somewhere, and I noticed it at different times during the day. If I was walking to school, I felt worried about being in the classroom. What if Johnny had to go to the hospital suddenly? I never knew if Mummy was going to be home when I got there or if she would have had to call Daddy to come take Johnny and her to Fitzsimons. When I got home, even when Mummy was there, I felt anxious in case I woke up during the night and found God had sent a neighbor to sleep on the couch because my brother had gotten sick and had to go to the hospital, no matter what time it was. That was called a crisis, and it meant he could hardly breathe. I hoped when Johnny got better, the scary feeling inside me would go away.

Constance Marie Grilliot was born on November 21, 1955.

"I wonder if Mommy will be home for Thanksgiving," Johnny said as we climbed into our bunk beds. Daddy had just told us we had a new baby sister.

"Probably," I replied. "Mummy's always saying that having a baby is just about the easiest thing in the world to do." No longer did I think that families simply went with a midwife to the hospital to pick out a baby; I knew now that babies grew in their mothers' tummies and had to be taken out by a doctor or a midwife. "Mummy said she'd rather stay home to have the baby, but she doesn't think you can do that in America. That's why you were born in a hospital."

"Which one?" asked Johnny. "Fitzsimons?"

"No. We didn't live here then, remember? I think Mummy said she and Daddy lived in Florida when you were born, but I'm not sure. You were already born when I met you in England."

Mummy and our new baby sister were not home for Thanksgiving, and Daddy, Johnny, and I ate chicken noodle soup with crackers for dinner. I thought it was good, and secretly, I was glad Daddy didn't know how to make salmon patties.

"It's not very Thanksgivingy," said Daddy. "Sorry, kids."

"What is Thanksgiving, Daddy?" I asked. "Teacher said it was when the Indians and the Pilgrims all got together and celebrated America being discovered, and they called it the First Thanksgiving. Hadn't the Indians already discovered it? I wonder how they thought up the name Thanksgiving, and I wonder why they didn't call it the First Picnic. The picture that Teacher put up showed everyone sitting around a picnic table, eating a big chicken."

"Turkey. They were eating wild turkey–at least that's what historians think. And they called it Thanksgiving because the two different cultures–the English and the Native Americans–wanted to get together to give thanks for the bountiful food and for their friendship. Don't you remember Thanksgiving last year right after you came to America? Mom cooked a turkey and stuffing."

"I think so. Anyway, Daddy, this chicken noodle soup is very nice. It's lovely. The best I've ever, ever had," I said, and Johnny nodded in agreement.

My father looked at me quizzically, but I decided to leave well enough alone; I didn't tell him I would rather have eaten chicken noodle soup every day for a year than have to eat salmon patties or tuna and noodles. I didn't think he knew how to make either, but I didn't want to give him any incentive to learn. I thought if I complimented the soup enough, he might fix it every time Mummy had to be at the hospital with Johnny. Usually, he just fed me cereal, which was OK too, but this was nice for a change.

"When do you think Mummy and the new baby will come home?"

"Tomorrow, I hope."

Our mother came home on Friday, November 25, 1955, and brought our new sister, Connie Marie, with her.

The whole next month was a blur in my memory amid fixing my own breakfast, walking to school, and taking care of Connie at the neighbor's across the street on the two occasions when my parents had to take Johnny to the hospital. I couldn't keep track of the days on the calendar, as I used to do.

Finally, it was Christmas Eve, and early that morning, it began to snow. All day, I prayed to Mary and Jesus to please let Johnny be there for Christmas and not have to go to the hospital. Most of the day, Johnny lay on the couch, watching television or playing Chutes and Ladders with me. Between us, we were trying to keep Connie entertained.

"Why can't we get her to laugh or smile?" asked Johnny.

"She's still too little," answered Mummy. "After another month or so, she will."

Johnny, Mummy, and I decorated the Christmas tree after Daddy strung the lights on its branches, and afterward, Daddy tacked lights around the living room's picture window. Johnny and I placed our stockings on Daddy's chair near the tree since we didn't have a fireplace. I'd never lived in a house without a fireplace before, and I wasn't sure if it was going to be a problem as far as Father Christmas was concerned.

Later, when we were in our bunk beds, Johnny asked, "What do you think Santa will bring us?"

"Well, I didn't ask for anything. Did you?"

"I think I remember asking for a train set, and I'll pretend the engineer is Grandpa Grilliot. But anything will be OK."

"I couldn't think of anything I wanted," I said, "but I just hope Santa Claus can find us. Mummy said Santa Claus and Father Christmas are the same person, just called different names in different countries. But what if he thinks I still live in England? Or what if he thinks we all still live in Muncie? How can he possibly keep track of all the people in the air force who move around all the time and all the other people in the world too?"

"I think Jesus probably tells him where he needs to go," said Johnny.

Sometime after Johnny and I fell asleep, I woke up suddenly. I sat up in bed, listening to the sounds of a sleeping house. I wasn't sure what had wakened me, but the house felt different. It still felt like a house covered in snow, but something was noticeably different. Suddenly, I heard a noise: a dull sound coming from the roof. *Oh no!* Santa was on the roof! How could Rudolph not have noticed that we didn't have a chimney? Daddy had left the front door unlocked and assured me that Santa would know it was unlocked, because Santa knew everything.

"Like Jesus and the Virgin Mary?" I had asked.

"Not quite. But enough to know to come in the front door," he'd replied.

I listened for quite some time. I listened until I was sure that if it was Santa I had heard, he must have figured out he needed to come in the front door. But what if he had simply abandoned our house because he hadn't found a chimney? I was stricken with anxiety: if he had left because he hadn't thought to come in the front door, this would be the first time Daddy ever had been wrong about anything. Finally, unable to stand the tension any longer, I crept out of bed and tiptoed down the hallway.

There was a night-light on in the living room, and in the weak light, I could see outlines of objects clustered around the tree that hadn't been there when I went to bed. One of the outlines looked just like a train set. I breathed a sigh of relief: Santa had found the unlocked door, and Johnny would not be disappointed. I crawled back into bed, and as I drifted off to sleep, I suddenly realized I had forgotten to ask Santa to please ask Jesus for the thing I wanted most: all I wanted for Christmas was for Johnny to get well. I figured Santa might have a special relationship with the people who ran heaven.

On Christmas morning, Mummy was wearing her sad smile: her mouth was smiling, but her eyes were sad. I opened my presents, and Johnny and I emptied our stockings. Johnny said, "Look–Santa left me more soldiers. See? These ones are littler than my others. And look–Santa left me a log cabin set. Now I can build a fort for my soldiers, and the army can send them to the fort on the train." Before Johnny finished building his fort, he crawled up onto the couch and fell asleep.

I wished Mummy and Daddy had looked happy. I was not sure why I felt so sad on Christmas morning. I never had before.

Five

JOHNNY HAD DIED TWO DAYS AGO. THE WEEKS SINCE Christmas had been dismal gray days filled with grief and despair–unlike anything my seven-year-old self had ever experienced or could even fathom. They were weeks filled with hospital admissions and discharges and, since Connie had arrived, nights of more than one neighbor taking turns sleeping on our living room couch.

I understood why Mummy and Daddy were sad, because I was too. I was not sure if I should tell them about the arrangement I'd made with Mary for me to go up to heaven for visits now that Johnny was up there. I thought once we put it to the test, if it worked out OK, I'd ask Mary to take our parents up for a visit–one at a time, of course, because I didn't think I could manage Connie completely on my own. Besides that, though, I wasn't sure why I still felt so sad. I thought it might have been because even though I planned on visiting Johnny, it just wasn't the same here on earth without him. I felt like crying all the time.

We took a train to Freeport, Illinois, so that Johnny could be buried with all our American relatives at Calvary Catholic Cemetery. I was worried because I had no idea where Johnny was. I was afraid maybe they had left him at Fitzsimons in all the confusion of the last few days.

"How is Johnny getting to Freeport to be buried, Mummy?"

"Johnny is in a special compartment here on the train," my mother answered. "When someone dies, he or she is placed in something called a casket, and that has to go in a different place on the train."

I had an idea of what a casket was—a special box, I thought. But now I was worried that Johnny would be afraid in something dark like that, all by himself. And what if he hadn't really died but had just gone into a really long sleep? What if he was just really tired from being sick all the time? What if he woke up in that box? I had been praying to the Virgin Mary that he would wake up. At least if he were in this compartment with us, we would hear him.

Daddy stood up suddenly and said he was going to the dining car. "I'll be back in half an hour."

Mummy hugged me and said Johnny was not just sleeping. His soul was in heaven with Jesus. She said I was not to worry. Mary was right there in the special compartment with him, watching over his earthly body so he wouldn't feel alone and scared.

I reached into my pocket and felt the rosary that Sister Philathea had given me when I made my First Communion. *Hail, Mary, full of grace, please stay with Johnny until we get to Freeport. Hail, Mary, full of grace …*

We arrived in Freeport and went to Grandma and Grandpa Grilliot's. I gave Mummy a letter to put in Johnny's pocket when she and Daddy went to the funeral home for something called visitation. My cousins and I were not allowed to go. In my letter, I reminded Johnny that I had been praying to Mary to ask Jesus to bring me up for a visit, and I told him if he saw either one of them, he should remind them of that. I wasn't sure I'd be bringing the Chutes and Ladders game, I told him, because I'd tried to carry it everywhere—just in case the visit Mary arranged was a sudden thing—but it had become awkward, and I didn't know if I was going to get any sort of message in advance, such as "Be ready at seven o'clock tonight." I'd let Mary figure that part out, I wrote.

The next day, there was a funeral mass at Saint Mary's Catholic Church, followed by a burial at Calvary Catholic Cemetery. No sooner was the funeral over than we were back on the train, returning to Colorado.

There wasn't much conversation anymore in the evenings. My father worked at Lowry Air Force Base, and he told me he was no longer teaching college students about the military, as he had at Ball State. He liked his new job—he said he was learning something called computer programming—and he promised he would take me to his office one Saturday to show me the computers. I asked if they were like his typewriter, but he said no. In Muncie, Daddy used to let me sit at his typewriter sometimes in the evening after he finished typing things for work, and he'd shown me how to push the keys down to make words.

I thought a lot about Muncie, when we all had been so happy—when the time after dinner had been for playing board games, watching television together, or going to drive-in movies. Sometimes Mummy, Johnny, and I had gone to watch Daddy play baseball or referee a basketball game. Now Daddy just sat and read the paper after dinner, and Mummy just read her books. I thought all the stories in Mummy's books must have been sad. She cried when she read, but then again, she also cried when she cleaned the house. She cried when she rocked Connie in the rocking chair to stop Connie from crying. Between Mummy and Connie, I felt like crying myself most of the time, and every night when I went to bed, I asked Mary to please ask Jesus to hurry up and bring me up to heaven for a visit with Johnny. I missed him so much, and I didn't like being down here anymore without him.

School ended for the summer, and the tedium and loneliness of second grade was finally over. I had made no friends and participated in no after-school activities. On Friday, June 8, my father came home from work with the news that our name was next on the list for base housing. "We will likely be moving in less than two weeks," he said. Suddenly, things felt different in the house—there was some normal conversation around the dinner table that evening, and Mummy cheered up a bit.

In the days that followed, as my mother cleaned and packed in preparation for the move, I spent hours walking Connie in her stroller just to keep her happy. Up and down our dismal little avenue in Aurora I pushed her, the avenue that was devoid of children. Although I didn't know the words to describe it, my heart recognized that the neighborhood had neither the intimacy nor the community of Windsor Avenue, despite the kindness of our immediate neighbors during Johnny's illness. Nor did it have any of the pastoral beauty of the Ball estate. The grayness that encompassed our family, our house, and the street, I would say in later years, felt in all ways like a shroud. We moved from Fulton Street to Lowry Air Force Base on June 20, 1956. It was my eighth birthday.

To me, the base housing was like the typical British neighborhood. Each building had multiple two-story units called town houses, and they stood in rows facing one another. On our street were eight buildings—four per side, divided by a shallow grassy swale with a narrow path running along its bottom. The clusters were replicated dozens of times and, in total, were known as *the housing area*. At the end of our street was a playground, and the entire residential area was connected by sidewalks, with cul-de-sacs for parking.

I awakened early on June 21 and lifted Connie out of her cot, where she was bawling her head off.

Connie was a fussy baby. She rarely slept for more than two hours at a time, even during the night, and I had learned when we lived on Fulton Street that the best routine for quieting her down in the morning was to change her diaper and give her a bottle to suck on while I heated her mushy cereal. Then I would shovel the pap into her little mouth as quickly as she could swallow it. With that done, I would put her in her stroller and then spend hours walking her up and down the sidewalk as far as I was allowed in either direction.

That day, as I pushed her out our new front door, I looked with wonder at our surroundings: sidewalks everywhere and not a busy road in sight. Thus began a morning routine that lasted the entire summer: within five minutes of being pushed, Connie would fall asleep. As long as I kept pushing, Connie kept sleeping. Mum slept,

Connie slept, and I marveled at a sense of freedom I hadn't felt since Windsor Avenue. Somehow, things were changing, and the mantle of gloom that had been present since Johnny died was lifted slightly.

Afternoons were mine, and there were enough children in our section of the housing area to ensure that I was constantly entertained. I learned games I had never heard of before: checkers, which I realized were what we called draughts in England; pick-up sticks; jacks; badminton; and a card game called Old Maid. Although I still couldn't stand peanut butter and jelly sandwiches, one day Mum and I decided to try a peanut butter and banana sandwich–she said she'd heard it was Elvis's favorite. In the end, we decided we still had an intense dislike for peanut butter and went back to the plain banana sandwiches on buttered bread–sometimes sprinkled with sugar–we used to eat in England.

I had been jumping rope outside with some of the other girls and had come inside for a drink. I was making a pitcher of Kool-Aid, and as I reached into the fridge for a tray of ice cubes, I had a flashback to Windsor Avenue and the lady with the new icebox. I giggled that I had thought frozen water was magic. What a baby I had been! *Nanna and Granddad should see me now!* I fixed my drink and went into the living room.

"Mum, I've been thinking," I said.

"What, love?"

"I'm really American, aren't I?"

"Well, half. I am English, you know," said my mother in that British way she had of saying something that she knew someone knew.

"Well, that makes me half American anyway. And the other kids look at me funny when I call you Mum or Mummy. One boy asked me if you were a dead Egyptian. Anyway, would you mind very much if I called you Mom or Mommy? I've been practicing my American accent almost every day when I remember, and I think it's coming along quite well. Don't you?"

"I happen to think you have a lovely British accent. Not too broad, and it is very nicely modulated. Remember those friends of

Nanna's from Yorkshire? Even Nanna could hardly understand them! But if you are intent on speaking like an American, I don't mind. I'll be a bit sad, mind you, but no doubt I'll get over it."

"Thank you, Mummy! I mean Mom! And I can't wait to tell Granddad that I know how to make my own magic ice cubes!"

My mother smiled and tilted her head in the way she used to do when she was happy before Johnny died, and I hoped we were both finally beginning to heal.

That summer, I thought my new accent continued to develop nicely, and it was with great anticipation that I started the third grade. It would be years, though, before I would find out I was not half English.

Six

WHEN I CAME TO AMERICA AND, LATER, WHEN WE MOVED to Colorado, I was too young to be excited or, for that matter, dismayed about moving. Nor did it cause me any anxiety–Daddy was in the air force, and that was what military families did, said my mother. And after all, if I could fly all the way to America from England by myself, moving to another state with my family seemed easy enough.

In February, a little less than a year after Johnny died and after we moved to the base housing on Lowry Air Force Base, my father came home with a big grin on his face–one such as I hadn't seen in a long while. Daddy was wearing his before-Johnny-died face, and it gave me a light and happy feeling.

"Guess where we're going!" he said to Mom.

"Surprise me!" she said with a smile lighting up her face.

"Nope! You gotta guess."

"Is it England?" she asked excitedly.

"Not Britain, but close!"

"Scotland?"

"Nope. That would be Britain also, so no."

"Well, Hawaii then! No, wait. That's not close. Germany?"

Dad shook his head.

"France? Are we going to France?"

"Bingo! We're going to Phalsbourg Air Force Base in Alsace-Lorraine!"

"I don't know where Alsace-Lorraine is, but people have told me that you can see the White Cliffs of Dover from Calais!" Mom put a hand over her heart, and with a smile that reached her eyes for the first time in a long time, she asked, "When do we go?"

My parents' excitement was electric, and at that moment, I realized that being a military family was the best thing in the whole wide world. From that moment on, I was smitten, and I looked forward to every move we ever made.

The first thing my father wanted to do–to ensure once and for all that we would always travel as a family–was to make sure my mother and I became American citizens. I reminded him that I was already half American, but he said I must be recognized by America, because I had been born in England. That meant studying for the citizenship test.

He brought study materials home from the courthouse in Denver, and he drilled us every evening when he got home from work. I had learned the Pledge of Allegiance in school, of course, but now my mother and I had to learn about the Constitution–the preamble and the amendments–and be prepared to answer questions about why we had applied for citizenship. Daddy told me not to worry about the *why.* He said, "That will be evident to the judge. If asked, just tell the judge, 'Because my father is a natural-born American, and he is in the air force.'" I tried to understand what an amendment was, and I tried to understand why the revolution had been fought–something about the colonists throwing lots of tea overboard rather than paying the taxes on it. I wondered what a tax was. I also wondered if the tea had been PG Tips. That would have been a terrible waste.

Mommy was a mess; she was nervous, afraid she would say something wrong. "You are the wife of an American serviceman," Daddy told her, "and you have nothing to worry about. It is just a formality." He didn't tell me that, though, and he helped me study.

Besides studying for our citizenship appointment, Mommy said we had to get inoculated. I might have had to get shots to come to

America, but I didn't remember. In any case, my parents didn't have a shot record for me. On the day we went to the base dispensary, I was aware I was to get vaccines, but I had no real concept of what that meant. Once the nurse started giving me shots, I felt as if they were going to be never ending. I received one jab after another in my upper arms and my bottom. I was determined not to cry. I thought of my brother and the days and months he had been stuck with needles when he was in the hospital, and he never had cried. I squeezed the tears back into my eyes and realized the nurse was saying something.

"It's over, Vivienne. We're finished!" she said.

Connie was still screaming from getting hers, and I felt bad, because how could one explain to a baby why she was being stuck? Mommy said that because Connie had been born in America and America was different from England, Connie already had had most of her shots during the past months. She just needed two that babies didn't ordinarily get unless they were leaving America. Still, it was impossible to explain that to Connie. The nurse gave us each a lollypop, and that finally shut my baby sister up.

The dreaded day finally arrived. We went as a family to the courthouse, and we were all taken to a room called the judge's chambers. Daddy was told to sit in the back of the room with Connie. The judge was stern, and I didn't think he liked us much. I knew deep inside in the place that warned me about things–things I didn't know why I was being warned about–that he didn't think people born in England should be allowed to become American citizens. I wanted to tell him I was already half American, but I didn't, because what would that have said about my mother, who wasn't? A lady at a desk with a funny-looking little typewriter handed me a paper with questions I had to answer. She didn't hand one to my mother. Maybe, I thought, grown-ups didn't need to take a written test, because they were already out of school.

After I finished, the judge called me to the front of his desk and asked me questions about the Constitution. I was worried I would answer wrongly, but I did my best. Then he told my mother and me to stand together, face the flag, and say the Pledge of Allegiance.

Afterward, the judge called my dad up to his desk, and Mom and he signed some papers together. When they were finished, the judge stamped the papers; handed them to my father; and, without looking up, said, "You may see yourselves out."

My father hugged us and said, "My two beautiful Yankees!"

He told us he was taking us to a proper restaurant for lunch—not the NCO club—to celebrate. After lunch, we went back to the base, and my mother, Connie, and I sat and had our picture taken together for our passport. We three would be on the same one, although I reminded my mother that I had my own passport from when I had flown to America by myself.

"Yes, but that is a British passport, and today you became an American citizen."

I started to say, "Haven't I always been half an American citizen, and why is everyone ignoring that?" but after what my mother and I had been through, I supposed the American judge didn't think so, and I let it rest. It had been too busy a day for me to be argumentative.

For the next two weeks, maps were brought out, towns and cities were circled, and letters were written to grandparents in England and Illinois. Boxes were packed with out-of-season clothes, kitchen utensils, and all knickknacks. We would be traveling with suitcases only. A footlocker of medium size that contained what my mother called *necessary essentials* would be shipped separately from our household goods and, hopefully, would be waiting for us at our new base. Until we were assigned base housing, Daddy said we would be living in temporary quarters and would have to get by on just a few things. Once we had a permanent address, our household goods would be delivered.

For the umpteenth time, I asked my mother, "Will we see Nanna and Granddad as soon as we get to France? England looks close to France on the map. Can they come over right away if we can't go there?"

"If I've told you once, I've told you a million times: probably not right away. We'll have to see how long it will take to get settled. Now, stop mithering about it!"

"The other day, I told that boy down the road to stop mithering me, and he said there's no such word! He said only silly English girls use that word. Is that true, Mum–I mean, Mom? There are other words that the kids ask me what they mean sometimes too. They don't know what a car bonnet is or a car boot! Do you think *mither* is one of them? What would I use instead?"

"Bother," said my mother, laughing. "You would use the word *bother*. Now, we've just over a week until we leave for Illinois to visit Grandma Helen and Grandpa Leo and all the other Grilliots and then four weeks before we leave Illinois for France. If you don't calm down, you're going to be so worn out you'll be too tired to enjoy any of it. Now stop *bothering* me, and go look through your closet one more time to make sure there's nothing else that can go in this box!"

When the moving company arrived, the men began loading all the furniture and cardboard boxes into enormous wooden crates that took up most of the moving van. Daddy said the crates would be driven to New York and shipped across the Atlantic Ocean. I realized something: the excitement, the anticipation, and the thrill of a new adventure made moving day almost as wonderful as Christmas! Most of the day, I pushed Connie in her stroller to keep her quiet and out of the way as I made the rounds in the housing area. My friends were unimpressed that I was leaving–after all, most of them were accustomed to moving from one base to another too. Just before the last of the furniture was loaded into the second crate, an airman stopped by and inspected the house. He looked at everything, even the top of the refrigerator, and finally handed Daddy a piece of paper and said everything looked fine. When I asked why the man had worn white gloves and wiped his hands over everything, Daddy said it was because some people would have left their houses dirty if they knew they didn't have to pass inspection.

As soon as the moving van left and the car was loaded with suitcases, blankets, and pillows, we departed Lowry Air Force Base for good. I noticed Daddy didn't take the usual road. He instead took the road that led to the hospital in Aurora. As we drove near

Fitzsimons, he slowed the car down. To me, it seemed like a long time ago that Johnny had been there.

One day I had heard my mother telling her friend over tea about arriving with my brother at his last admission.

"They had the elevators blocked off that day–or, rather, guarded by men in suits. Bob hadn't gotten there yet from work. Our neighbor Lois had driven us, and I was carrying Johnny myself. I wasn't sure what I was going to do if I had to carry him up flights of stairs to the children's ward. Then one of the men showed me his badge and took Johnny from me. He said he was a Secret Service agent, and he would escort us on the elevator and up to the ward. We found out later that President Eisenhower had been admitted for his six-month checkup after his heart attack. All the elevators, all the stairs, and probably all the wards were being guarded by agents."

Now, as Daddy stopped on the shoulder of the road across from the front of Fitzsimons Hospital, he put his arm around Mommy. They were quiet for what seemed to me to be a long time, and then Mommy blew her nose. Daddy slowly pulled out and back onto the road, and soon we were heading to Illinois. I realized how much I was looking forward to being indulged by my American grandparents. For the first time, I thought how wonderful Daddy's life must have been while growing up in Freeport and living with two such amazing people.

"Daddy," I asked, leaning over the back of the front seat, "was it really, truly wonderful for you and Uncle Dick and Aunt Sally to live all your lives with Grandma and Grandpa? Did you get to eat all the ice cream and drink all the soda pop you wanted every single day?"

"Honey, you have no idea," he answered. "Life in Freeport was grand, and life with Grandma and Grandpa was terrific. It was one halcyon day after another, and I was so sick of ice cream and root beer by the time I left home that I thought I'd never like either again!"

"Wow. What's halcy–whatever?"

"It means close to perfect," said Daddy.

My mother just rolled her eyes and said, "You'll need to go to confession for that one, Robert."

I was married with children before my grandmother told me about the October 31 when the Freeport police came to 103 East Empire Street and took Dad and his best friend, Don, into custody just after school let out for the day.

According to Grandma, it was a precaution based on their antics the previous Halloween. Apparently, someone had siphoned gas out of a police car in the parking lot of the Freeport police station and written some sort of inappropriate note, leaving it under the windshield wipers. Dad and Don so vehemently denied it was their doing that my grandmother said it left little doubt in anyone's mind that they were the culprits. So, said Grandma, she was more than happy to have them safely in jail for the night the following Halloween. That way, regardless of what pranks occurred that October 31 in Freeport, nobody in town would be able to blame Bob Grilliot or Don DeMong.

By the next Halloween, Don was in college, and Dad was in the Army Air Corps.

Seven

IT WAS ALMOST ONE YEAR TO THE DAY SINCE JOHNNY DIED when we left America for France aboard the USS *John C. Butler* in April 1957.

The *Butler* was a naval destroyer escort ship commissioned in World War II from 1944 to 1946. After the war, she was decommissioned and then, shortly after, recommissioned–primarily to transport American military families back and forth between the United States and destinations in Europe. At eight years old, I had not one shred of knowledge about transatlantic ocean travel and had no expectations. In fact, prior to our sailing to France that spring, the only open water I had ever seen had been the Irish Sea on rare outings to Blackpool with my grandparents. If I had any notion that traveling aboard a naval military ship would be remotely like flying across that same Atlantic Ocean on a commercial airliner–attended by pretty stewardesses–I quickly realized there was not one shred of similarity. On that blustery spring morning, we walked up a wooden gangway, with the planks shifting and slightly swaying under our weight, and into the belly of a warship.

Our cabin was sparse. Daddy explained that when the ship was in the war and filled with sailors, the cabins were called crews quarters or bunk rooms. Now two sets of bunk beds with drawers under the bottom bunks and a small nightstand between the two took up the entire room. The cabin had no bathroom, which my father said was called the head, nor was there anything as frivolous as a dressing table for Mom to put her toiletries on or in. There was no telephone, television, or radio. Daddy pointed out a square box on the wall next to the door and explained that it was an intercom.

"What is it used for?" I asked.

Just then, static issued forth from the box, and a voice said, "Attention, all passengers. This is your captain ..."

When the announcement was finished, Daddy said, "That's what it's used for!"

The first night was the worst. I threw up twice, and Mom and Connie threw up all night long in the bucket Daddy had placed between the bunks. Twice, Daddy walked Mommy outside to get fresh air–he thought standing up in the briskness of the night might make her feel better. She said it did temporarily. I felt considerably better on day two, and even though Mom still felt sick to her stomach, she was no longer vomiting. She said it was because she had nothing left in her stomach; she couldn't even keep down a cup of tea.

"It wouldn't be so bad," she said, "if it weren't for the constant rocking motion of the ship. When I went back to England on the White Star Line, I was a little nauseous for two days, but nothing like this!"

I thought she was talking about the time she had gone back to England to get me but ended up leaving me with Nanna and Granddad again after being there for a long time. I'd heard her tell her friend Millie that she'd left without me again because something called her visa was getting ready to expire, and Daddy wasn't sure he could get it renewed once it expired. I didn't understand how all that worked, but I was glad we had gone to Denver before we left for Illinois and gotten an American passport so that Mommy and I wouldn't be separated again.

Initially, I did not understand the naval vernacular that was spoken all around the ship: *starboard, port, mess deck,* and more. But by day three, I was spouting navy words–jargon, Daddy called it–like a sailor. Despite my being seasick during the first thirty-six hours or so, my sense of adventure had forced me to nibble soda crackers to get through the worst of it and carry on. I was afraid I would miss something, and I wanted to memorize every detail of the journey. After all, the boys of Windsor Avenue deserved to be duly impressed that I had the supreme good fortune to travel across the Atlantic Ocean on a ship that had been in the war. To my way of thinking, when I announced that, the status of the Windsor Avenue air-raid shelter would be significantly diminished.

Many years later, my good friend Bob Peterson would make a casual remark about his family's voyage from New York to France on the RMS *Queen Elizabeth* in 1958.

"It was amazing," he would say, "even for a kid."

"Wait!" I would respond. "Our dads were stationed at the same air force base in France, and your family went over on the world's most famous luxury liner, while our family went on a bare-bones naval ship from World War II? How on earth?"

"Luck of the draw, I think. The military uses whatever means is most expedient and most available," Bob would reply. "Just a guess."

Daddy took me all over the ship, explaining its details to me. He let me sit and listen to conversations he had with other soldiers, sailors, and airmen about where they had been stationed during the war and since, what adventures they had encountered, and which bases they were traveling to. Mom rarely ventured from the cabin—or, rather, bunk room—with Connie.

Early in the morning of the fifth day, the White Cliffs of Dover emerged in the mist as we entered the English Channel. Suddenly, we all—men, women, and children—were on the outside deck.

"This is called the weather deck," I told my mother. "I learned that from the sailor who showed Daddy and me around the ship the other day."

Through the misty chill of the damp air, we stood silently as we gazed upon the famous cliffs that were part of England. Although I had never seen them before—we'd lived in the north of England, and the cliffs were in the south—as I stood on the ship's deck, it felt as though I had carried them in my heart forever. Vera Lynn sang a song about them. In fact, it was one of Nanna's favorite songs. Vera

Lynn was a famous singer, and during the war, she had sung lots of songs about England and our soldiers. Nanna said that was patriotic of her, and what she had done for the war effort had been every bit as important as what any other civilian had done.

Now, standing on the ship's deck in the misty cold of the English Channel and looking at the cliffs, I wished with my whole body and my whole heart that I were able to fly, as I sometimes did in my dreams. I'd have flown over the channel and across the valleys, hedgerows, and moors straight to Windsor Avenue. I'd have run up the entryway where I used to bounce my ball against the side of the house, opened the back door, and stepped into the scullery.

"Nanna, I'm home!" I would have called out. "Granddad, I've come back! I flew through the trees just like the fairies do!"

Daddy's voice cut through my musings. He was explaining something to us. "Look," he said. "See the little boat there? That's the pilot who is guiding our ship through the narrow part of the channel to our port."

I saw what looked like a little tugboat, and it was flying the Union Jack. "I thought pilots only flew planes, Daddy!"

"There are airplane pilots and boat pilots. A boat pilot guides big ships into harbors. Watch—when this ship is safely in the harbor, the pilot boat will turn around and head back out to sea, and our captain will blow the ship's whistle to say all's well and thank you!"

Soon, at the sound of the ship's whistle, a cheer went up from the passengers and crew who were on the deck, and then we slowly dispersed, with each passenger returning to his or her quarters.

The next several hours were hurry-up-and-wait ones. We went down to breakfast together—Mom and Connie finally were completely over their seasickness. Having learned that I was ravenous when not seasick, I inhaled the reconstituted scrambled eggs and drank the powdered milk. Connie banged her spoon on her high-chair tray and spit out the eggs. Daddy seemed to be able to eat anything at any time—he said that one could learn to appreciate anything that wasn't a K ration and that if we had been starving and had no other food, we would even have appreciated K rations. Without a doubt, I was sure I'd rather have eaten K rations than tuna and noodles. Mommy just nibbled her toast and drank two strong cups of tea. There was a steady hum of conversation on the mess deck, and a current of excitement ran up and down the long tables. The ocean journey was at an end. Now the passengers would embark on the various last legs of their travels–all of us were military families, and most of us were going to bases in France and Germany. Although bound by a common thread, we likely would never meet again. But who knew? On board, my father had encountered a friend of his from Patrick Air Force Base!

Our ship docked in Cherbourg, and after we gathered our suitcases and disembarked, we took a taxi to the train station and boarded the train that would take us to Sarrebourg, France, and our new base.

France

Eight

DADDY ENROLLED ME IN THE THIRD-GRADE CLASS AT Phalsbourg Air Force Base Elementary School. It was the fifth school I had attended in my eight years of life, and that was not counting the month of March we'd just spent in Illinois before traveling to France. There, I had attended Saint Mary's Catholic School for four weeks with my cousins.

My new school was located on the base, and like me, everyone in my class had a parent in the military—we all had that in common. For the first time, I became aware that some of my schoolmates' mothers were European or Asian, and for once, I was not considered odd because of how many times I had moved, how many schools I had gone to, or how I spoke. At my new school, neither my accent nor my newness aroused any curiosity. Although Phalsbourg Elementary was not a parochial school, I soon found that being part of a military family was similar to the community spirit I had felt at Saint Mary's in Muncie.

While waiting for a three-bedroom unit in base housing to become available, we lived temporarily in a trailer park on the base. Two trailers down from us was a girl from my third-grade class named Mary Sue. She had lived in the park for three years. Because Mary Sue was an only child, her family had been allowed to stay in the two-bedroom trailer, which was called a mobile home. Not only was Mary Sue an only child, she was also adopted, which explained why her parents doted on her. In my mind, I thought it would have been hard to come up with a better combination for being petted, as Nanna called it. I'd never had an adopted friend before, and I noticed whenever I was at her house, some of the doting drifted my way. I liked it. In fact, knowing without a doubt that there was no chance my parents would suddenly start doting on me, I spent as much time after school at Mary Sue's as I was allowed, for whatever short amount of time we would be living in the trailer park.

I had recently started getting an allowance. Daddy said now that I was almost nine and would be in the fourth grade next school year, I needed to learn to manage money. The twenty-five cents a week I received was enough to go to the Saturday matinee and buy two comic books, with a nickel left over for either a candy bar or popcorn.

One day Mary Sue and I lay on her pink-ruffled bed, reading my two new Archie comics and discussing the fact that Veronica was annoyingly obnoxious. How on earth, we wondered, could Archie not see that it was Betty he should have been in love with? Betty was obviously nice and kind and not conceited at all. Veronica was really conceited.

"You know, I think," said Mary Sue, "that Archie better be careful. If he doesn't pay attention, Betty might just decide she likes Jughead better!"

We looked at each other and burst out laughing. Betty and Jughead? Not a chance!

"Oh, I almost forgot! I'm moving to base housing next week!" I said.

"Oh, I'll really miss you," said Mary Sue, "but I'm moving too! We're going back to the States in a few weeks."

We promised to write to each other every month at least, and before I went home, I tacked a note on Mary Sue's pretty bulletin board crisscrossed with pink ribbons: "Vivienne and Mary Sue–best friends forever!"

Moving day came and went, and it required hardly more than packing our suitcases and repacking the footlocker we had collected when we arrived at the base.

It was Thursday afternoon, and my mother was ironing one of Daddy's fatigue shirts, using the kitchen counter as an ironing board. I was amazed that she was managing to iron on the tiny surface; it was the smallest counter I had ever seen. It was tinier even than Nanna's at number 7, and it was wedged between the sink and the fridge. As yet, our only furniture consisted of bedroom furniture and a small dinette set, all of which my father had secured from the place on base that loaned household goods to families while they were waiting for their own furniture to arrive from America or from wherever it had been warehoused since it arrived in France.

Connie was napping, which meant the toilet couldn't be flushed, and no light switches could be flipped. Daddy was at work, and I was in the kitchen with Mom. I had just finished pouring grape Kool-Aid into an ice cube tray to make popsicles, and I was careful to close the fridge door as quietly as possible.

"What would you like for your birthday?" my mother asked me as she hung Daddy's fatigue shirt on a hanger and unplugged the iron.

"I guess I would like for our furniture to hurry up and get here, so I can have my bicycle!"

"That would be nice, and I'm sure the van will arrive any day, but that's not going to be a surprise. What would you like that would be a surprise?"

It must have escaped her that if I thought of something and told her, then that wouldn't be a surprise either.

"Well, I don't know," I said. "New comic books. Or Chinese checkers like some of the kids have. I learned how to play at Lowry, and they're more fun than regular checkers."

"Hmm," said my mother, "you're quite easy to please, aren't you?"

I would never, even before Johnny's death, have asked for anything that I thought might burden my parents financially. Even though they had received no bill from Fitzsimons Hospital–the military had covered all the expenses related to Johnny's admissions–other costs had spilled over into the family finances. I'd overheard a conversation between my parents one evening regarding the bills they had accumulated during Johnny's long illness. They had been sitting at the kitchen table, sorting through the pile. They had received insurance money for John, which they'd used to pay for things that were our family's responsibility, such as the long train ride from Denver to Chicago to take Johnny home to Freeport for burial and the funeral expenses. A small amount had been left over, and my parents had decided to donate it to an organization that assisted families with terminally ill children. Neither had felt as though they could use it for anything else.

"It would be like making a profit on John's death," Dad had said, and Mom had agreed.

"Chinese checkers? Really?" asked Mom now. "If you could have anything you wanted, that's what you'd ask for–Chinese checkers?"

"Anything? Like magic anything?" I asked.

"Anything," she replied.

"Johnny. I would ask God to give us Johnny back. But that's just pretend. So I guess I'll just ask for Chinese checkers."

My mother grabbed me suddenly and hugged me tightly. "I love you. You know that, don't you? You are a good girl, and I love you so much. Don't ever change–not one bit."

"I love you too, Mum–I mean, Mommy."

It was June 18, and the day was bright and sunny and not yet too warm. It was eight o'clock in the morning, and last evening Daddy had announced that he was taking us for a drive today.

"Early to bed tonight," he had said. "I've taken tomorrow off work, and we're going on an outing."

That was unusual, as it was a Tuesday, and Daddy was hardly ever off during the week. Never in my memory had we ever gone for a drive that early either. The windows in the Plymouth were down, and I could smell the new-mown hay as we drove along. Men with scythes were busy cutting tall grasses in the cool air before the hot midday sun beat down on them. The edges of the roads were full of wildflowers–France had as many as England–and I was glad to see the men were not cutting those. Daddy was telling Mommy once again that he was going to teach her to drive. As he was telling her, he was braking and swerving to miss a farmer's cows as they clustered in the road. The animals were oblivious to the car that was trying to avoid them. Clearly, they had the right of way, and I did not for one minute think Mommy was going to agree to learn to drive in France; after all, she had refused to learn in America, where there were nice, wide roads and no cows wandering around.

"Where are we going, Daddy?"

"Guess," said my father.

My mother shot him a "Now, Robert, be careful" look. That meant she was afraid he'd slip up and tell me. I knew any "be careful" looks were always meant for me, because Connie never noticed anything except what was going on in her immediate surroundings. At her age, she wasn't much interested in anything else.

"Moo cow! Moo cow!" said Connie as she stuck her chubby hand out the open car window.

"Are we going to that little bakery where we went for lemonade and croissants the other weekend?" I asked as I suddenly realized we were close to that part of town.

"Nope," said Daddy. "We are taking a ride to the seaside to get some fresh salt air."

"The seaside? Really?" I asked, jumping up and down in the backseat. "Like Blackpool, where I went with Nanna and Granddad?"

"Well, not really the seaside. More like the seaport. We're going to watch the boats and ferries come in."

"Oh."

Mom looked at Daddy again and gave him her serious "Robert, will you just be quiet?" look. She said, "I just feel like a ride to the seaside. You know, to see the boats that are coming across the English Channel from Dover. It will make me feel less homesick."

I understood that. In some ways, Mommy and I were very alike. Upon hearing certain songs on the radio or a mention of certain British foods, we both became immediately homesick for Flixton and Windsor Avenue.

At noon, we stopped in a grassy area near some trees, and Mom spread a blanket on the ground while Daddy lifted the picnic basket out of the car. No sooner had we finished our sandwiches than we packed up the car and got back on the road. It was an odd picnic–I would have liked to walk around a bit.

Although we hadn't lingered, the trip seemed to be taking a long time. Finally, we saw a sign that announced we had arrived in Calais. It was a busy town, by the looks of things, but within minutes, we were at the seaport. Daddy parked the car, and Mom and I got out with Daddy to stretch. He looked at his watch.

"Just on time," he said, and he looked at Mom. "Wait right here."

It was the oddest day out I could ever remember taking. There wasn't much of a view from the parking lot. We couldn't really see the wide span of the English Channel from the car; we could see only ferry boats coming and going out of the dock area. We could not see the White Cliffs of Dover from where we were either. It seemed to me like a very long drive just to sit in a car in a parking lot. We couldn't even see England, and I was pretty sure that had been the whole point. I said that to Mom, but she didn't answer me. We got back in the car. Connie had fallen asleep, and I asked my mother how sitting there was helping her homesickness. "And did Daddy go to the loo? If there is one, can I go too? Because I need to wee."

Suddenly, Mom opened her door again and jumped out. She started to run toward the port's main building, and I could see Daddy walking from the building back toward the car. He was carrying two suitcases, and two people were walking with him. They looked familiar.

"Nanna! Granddad!" I shouted, and I jumped from the car and, like Mom, ran toward them.

I hurled myself into the two of them and began laughing and crying at the same time. Granddad picked me up and held me tightly. My heart was full, and my world was complete–at least as complete as it could have been now that Johnny was up in heaven.

"Happy birthday," said Mommy, and she kissed me on the cheek.

Nine

THE MONTH FLEW BY. THE SUN WASN'T UP YET, AND MOMMY was making a pot of tea to put in the thermos. Nanna was buttering bread for sandwiches–cheese butties, she called them–to take on the boat. Granddad was shaving. Within half an hour, the sun rose, and my grandparents gathered their belongings. We said our goodbyes at the house as I blinked back tears.

Nanna said, "Now, no tears!" She wrapped her arms around me and added, "In just a month, you'll be back in school. Then it will be Christmas and then Easter, and before you know it, it will be summer again. And who knows? Perhaps you'll be able to come to England!"

She was right, of course. Between playing baseball and checkers and trading comic books with the other kids in the housing area, I hardly noticed when July became August. Soon Mom was making me try on last year's school clothes to see which could have the hems let down or the seams let out and which would be given away. One of her American friends had a saying: "Use it up, wear it out, make it do, or do without." During the war, even though the United States' mainland hadn't been attacked, there had been food and dry-goods shortages, and people had had victory gardens and been every bit as proud of contributing to the war effort as people in England.

Thank goodness my American grandmother–that wonderful, generous, indulgent parent of my father–sent us what she called "the Monkey Ward catalog" and said I must pick out three outfits. I was in heaven. She said girls going into the fourth grade needed spiffy new clothes to wear. She said fourth grade was not third grade, and fourth-grade girls noticed things like wardrobe. She was so American–and she understood American girls. On the contrary, my mother often prefaced her sentences with "When I was your age ..."

"When I was your age," said my mother as she picked the hem out of one of my skirts from last year, "I had two dresses: an everyday dress and one that was just a bit nicer that I had to save for the few places your nanna and granddad took your uncle Jackie and me, like to take the bus to visit Nanna's sister, our auntie Dot, or on the occasional Sundays we went to church."

I had heard that many times, and I had a hard time believing it. In my mother's memories, Nanna and Granddad always sounded unlike the two people I knew. I thought my mother sometimes exaggerated.

I was feeling nervous about the fourth grade. Daddy brought home some paperwork from the school that had to be filled out, and I couldn't believe it: we were to have French class three days a week. I still struggled with American, so I was more than a little worried about French. Marguerite, our French cleaning lady and babysitter, said she would help me. Actually, she didn't say, "I'll help you." As I was voicing my concerns to Mom, she pointed to herself and said something in French with a lot of gestures that I thought meant she'd help me.

"Next week will come soon enough," said my mother, "and there's no use in worrying about it today." I decided it was a good day to see if any of the boys were playing outside. It was hot, but it was never too hot for baseball.

The days passed quickly, and before I knew it, it was September 9. The school bus picked me up at the corner of our street, along with two boys who lived in our cul de sac: another fourth grader name Mike Winston, and Tomas Sagett. Tomas was a sixth grader, and his brother, Uri, was in the ninth grade and went to the American boarding school in Verdun, which was closer to Paris than Sarrebourg was. Uri was as handsome as a movie star. Uri and Tomas's mom was

German, which was why Uri had such an odd name, I thought. What was it that made some English and German mothers choose such awful names for their kids? Tomas—we called him Tommy—was a normal name, and my sister, Constance, was lucky because she got to be called Connie. Everyone knew that Connie Francis was beautiful and popular, so who wouldn't have wanted to be named after her? Even though my sister was named for Nanna Dempster, whose middle name was Constance.

"But you're named for Vivien Leigh, the movie star who played Scarlett O'Hara in *Gone With the Wind*," said my mother for the hundredth time. "I saw the film at the Curzon a few months before you were born."

As if that mattered. I didn't want to remind her that it might have been tolerable if I'd had a cute American middle name I could use. I couldn't even bear to say my middle name in my head, so I didn't want to hear her defend it. I blamed my father as much as my mother. His sister was my aunt Sally, and my American cousins were Linda and Terri. Why hadn't he put his foot down when they were thinking of a name for me? He could have suggested any one of at least a dozen cute American girls' names.

Oh well. When I'm an adult, I will find out how much it costs to legally change my name. In the meantime, I'll concentrate on what I'd like to change it to.

On the first day of school, standing against the back wall of the classroom were cubes for the storage of lunch pails and such—Miss White, our teacher, called them *cubbies*—and rows of hooks for our coats in the winter. We all had to find our desks, cubbies, and hooks, which were tagged with our first names and the first letter of our last names.

Miss White had arranged the desks by alternating the boys and the girls so that we were staggered, sort of like a checkers game board. She had to make some last-minute adjustments, though, because she hadn't taken into account that there were three really tall boys and one girl who was taller than most of the boys in the class; they had to be moved to the back. Still, it didn't mess up her nice arrangement too much—it just meant that now there was a girl on my right.

Organizing the class took nearly half an hour: students were rearranged, cubbies were identified, and lunch boxes were stored. Miss White then called roll. As was customary with Americans, she mispronounced my last name. She sounded out the *t* on the end (the French never did, and even the English usually didn't).

When the teacher got to the name of the girl sitting next to me, she said, "Well, look at that! Two young ladies who have very similar French names: Vivienne and Vivica!"

I was confused. My mother was English and had named me after an English actress. My last name was French, but I was sure my first name was English. Still, when asked by other kids, "What kind of name is that?" I thought it might not be so awful if I could just shrug and say, "It's French. My grandparents are French." That wouldn't be a lie, because Grandpa Grilliot had said his family had come from France more than a hundred years ago, and Nanna's granddad had been French; her last name used to be Chapelle. If I could blame it on old family from hundreds of years ago, I could perhaps tolerate my name for another nine years, until I was eighteen and could legally change it.

Miss White was explaining something about Vivica, and I dragged my attention back to what she was saying.

"Vivica's mother is French, and her father is an American businessman. Isn't that right?" the teacher asked, looking at the pretty girl sitting next to me. "Until this year, Vivica attended a local school on the French economy, but her parents thought it might be nice if this year she experienced an American school."

We all murmured agreeably.

At 10:00 a.m., the recess bell rang, and Vivica and I walked outside together. We found a sunny place and sat down on the grass. I was burning with curiosity, wondering about my new French American friend and how she managed to sound so American if she had always gone to French schools.

"Teacher said your mother is French, Vivica, and that you've always gone to French schools, so you obviously can speak French without an accent, but how come you don't have a French accent when you speak English?"

"Well, I guess it's because my father is American. When I was little, if I mixed up my sentences with some French and some English, he would correct me. And he would correct my pronunciation too. Not like I was being punished or anything, but like he wanted me to speak English without an accent just like I speak French without an accent. My mother speaks pretty good English, but she has a very heavy French accent."

Vivica Arquette and I, it turned out, had a lot in common. We both had American fathers and foreign mothers, and we both spent a considerable amount of time trying to be more American. We agreed it was hard work sometimes. I had been born and raised in England in a very British home; Vivica had been born and raised in France in a very French home. Our customs, restraints, and insecurities were not so different. Our lifestyles, however, were.

On the first Thursday in early October, Vivica asked if I would like to spend the weekend at her house.

"Mama said of course when I asked her!" said Vivica. "And she'll make sure my annoying little brother doesn't bother us too much. Please say you'll come! There are absolutely no girls at all on my street—it is very boring! And Mama said she would teach us to bake proper French éclairs, and she'll take us to her favorite boutique."

The feeling her invitation created was one I had never experienced: I suddenly had an inkling of a world so remote from living in base housing and shopping occasionally in the base exchange or ordering clothes from the Montgomery Ward catalog that I was unsure how to even identify the sensation of awe coursing through my veins. *Proper French éclairs. A boutique.* (I thought that was a fancy shop.) I had no point of reference—not Muncie, not Freeport, not Aurora, and definitely not Flixton!

I couldn't wait for the end of the school day, and when the dismissal bell finally rang, I ran to the school bus. I practically bounced up and down with excitement the whole way home. My mother was having her cup of afternoon tea when I walked in the door, and I spilled out in an excited jumble of words that I had been invited to spend the weekend at my new friend's house.

"Oh, Mom, puh-leeze say yes! I promise I'll do my homework, and Vivica said she would help me with my French lesson, and just think–I'll be in a real French house where everybody speaks French! Think about that! I'm sure it will help me to be able to speak better French!"

"Why is there a French girl going to school on the base?" asked Mom.

"Her father is American. But he isn't in the air force; he's in business."

Mom asked Marguerite about the location of the Arquettes' address, which took a painful amount of time and the aid of a local map, and eventually, Mom said she supposed it wouldn't hurt. After all, Vivica's father was American, and that should count for something. Mom's response made me realize she was still a bit iffy about the French–leftover feelings from the war, I supposed. Nanna was the same.

"But mind," my mother said, "you might not like what Mrs. Arquette fixes for dinner. The French are known for not being plain meat-and-potatoes people, and if you don't like what is served, you must eat it anyway. No asking for a piece of toast instead of eating a proper meal. You might get away with that here, but that would be a very rude thing to do as someone's guest."

"I promise," I said, throwing my arms around my mother. "Thank you!"

Vivica's mother drove. Probably, I thought, being French, she was not afraid of the narrow streets, the frequent presence of farm animals, or the constant honking of horns as little French cars wove in and out on the cobbled roads. Mrs. Arquette seemed to me to be an expert driver, as she was able to keep up a steady chatter of conversation despite the distractions, and she didn't complain about the cows in the street or the other drivers who drove so fast it was a wonder that anyone had any nerves left at all.

I was mesmerized by Mrs. Arquette. My mother generally wore her hair in a ponytail, seldom wore skirts or dresses around the house, and never wore makeup, unless she and Daddy were going out. Most of Mom's friends were as casual about their appearance as she was. It was not unusual for me to get home from school and find a group of women drinking tea and smoking cigarettes in our kitchen, and no one was ever dressed up. If it was a bingo night at the club, they would be in bobby pins and hair curlers and oftentimes polishing their nails in between sipping and puffing.

Mrs. Arquette was wearing a flared black skirt and a white blouse with its top button open and the collar turned up. A red leather belt circled her tiny waist. She had her hair done up in what I thought my mother would have called a *French twist*, and around her neck, she was wearing a pearl necklace. She also had tiny pearl earrings in her pierced ears. I loved pierced ears! When I turned sixteen, I was going to beg my mother to let me get mine pierced.

Soon we were pulling into the driveway of a large two-story gray stone house. A wall made of the same stone separated the front lawn from the narrow street, and over the wall, some flowers tumbled in purple profusion.

"What are those purple flowers?" I asked. "They're beautiful!"

"Boog-something," answered Vivica.

"They are called bougainvillea," said Mrs. Arquette. "The last owners of this house must have loved them, because they are growing around and over the greenhouse in the back garden and over the back wall also. But be very careful. Don't get too close to them. They have very sharp—how do you say *epines*, Vivi?"

"Thorns," said Vivica.

Beautifully tended flower beds bordered the front of the house, and I thought of the little strip of weed-filled dirt under our living room window in base housing. I made my mind up right then and there to ask my mother if we could plant some flowers. I would promise her I'd water them and pull all the weeds so she wouldn't need to worry about it for one minute.

I looked up at the front of the house from the backseat of the car. There were wide stone steps leading up to the red front door, which had a half circle of stained glass above it. The place looked even bigger than my grandparents' house in Freeport; to me, it looked like a mansion.

Vivica's mother parked at the end of the driveway, near the back door. "You girls run upstairs and change your school clothes. *Je vais preparer une collation!*"

I looked at Vivica.

"She's fixing us a snack," said my friend.

Everything about Mrs. Arquette was charming: her beauty, her style, and her accent. When she said *Vivica*, it sounded like *Veevee-ca*, and when said *Vivienne*, it sounded like *Veevee-enne*. Suddenly, I was thrilled—at least for that weekend—to have a name that sounded so French.

Vivica's bedroom was right out of a Hollywood movie. I imagined Debbie Reynolds or Shirley Temple having a room like that. It had a full-sized canopy bed; two dressers, plus a dressing table; a full-length mirror on a stand that swiveled when one pushed on it; and a long span of windows overlooking the back garden, with ornate built-in bookcases at either end. The walls were papered with gold-and-cream-colored wallpaper patterned with scenes of people, animals, and bridges spanning narrow streams. I did not know the term *toile*, but I decided I liked it. Later, I would describe it to my mother, and she would tell me it sounded like toile.

"Vivica, your bedroom is really, really, beautiful," I said.

Vivica shrugged and said, "It's OK, I guess. I'd rather have a blue bedroom, but Mama said this house is very old, and it would be a shame to paint over walls and stuff that she thinks are lovely. She thinks it would lower the value, and when Papa's company transfers him back to the States, we will be selling this house. So I guess it doesn't really matter."

"I think your mom is beautiful too; she kind of looks like Sophia Loren. One of my mom's magazines had some pictures of Sophia a couple of months ago. She's Italian, you know. You look like your mom. Your hair is a bit darker, but your eyes are green just like hers."

"I think so too. But I think I look more like my father," she replied. "At least that's what my grandparents think. Anyway, let's go get our snack so we can go outside and explore. We have an old greenhouse out back that Mama is trying to fix up, and we have a creepy old shed filled with stuff. The next-door neighbor said the shed is haunted because someone got killed in it years ago."

Vivica's mama said we could only play outside until dinnertime, and after dinner, we had to do our homework. She said, "You must get it done and out of the way because tomorrow we are going shopping, and when we get home, we are making éclairs. And you won't enjoy yourselves nearly as much if you know you have beaucoup homework left to do."

I was so mesmerized by her beauty and charming accent that I nodded in agreement with everything she said.

Vivica's father was a businessman. From experience, I knew that meant a civilian–just like Mr. Anderson in *Father Knows Best*, the television show we had watched every week before we came to France. We military children were quite cavalier in our knowledge of different types of businesses: we were members of a close-knit community whose parents had jobs that covered every sort of work imaginable. I wasn't sure what type of businessman Mr. Arquette was, but I did have an idea of what to expect: he would be wearing a suit. Mr. Anderson always wore a suit. And I thought Mr. Arquette would definitely have on a tie. He might come in with the evening paper rolled up under his arm, and he would probably be carrying a briefcase. Yes, I was positive about the briefcase; all businessmen carried them. I thought he might smoke a pipe, because I had seen one on the fireplace mantel. He would have dark hair and green or blue eyes. I was sure he'd be handsome, because Vivica's mama was so pretty that she would certainly have picked a handsome husband. I would have if I had been as pretty and vivacious as Mrs. Arquette.

"Dinner is ready, *mon petits!*" called Vivica's mama from the back door an hour later.

"That means Papa is home," said Vivica, and we ran across the yard and into the house.

"Well now, princess," said Mr. Arquette as he lifted up Vivica and gave her a bear hug and a kiss on the cheek, "what have you been up to?"

He was tall—much taller than my father. He put Vivica down and then bent toward me and extended a hand. I put my hand in his, and he gave it a gentle squeeze.

"I understand you are to be our houseguest this weekend. It is very nice to meet you, Vivienne! Are you having fun so far?"

I found my voice and remembered my manners. "Oh yes, sir, Mr. Arquette. Thank you very much for allowing Vivica to invite me."

I suspected he was used to people being surprised upon meeting him for the first time, because Vivica's father looked—and, with his American accent, sounded to me—exactly like Nat King Cole. My mother had an album titled *Moonlight Serenade*, and the picture on the back cover looked just like Mr. Arquette. And whenever Nat King Cole had been on television when we lived in the States and had a television, we had watched his program, so I knew exactly what Nat King Cole looked like.

I suddenly realized I was staring, and that was a rude thing to do. He must have been used to having that effect on people, because he leaned down a little closer and said, "If you ever heard me sing, you would know for sure I'm James Arquette—I've been told my singing voice sounds much worse than a gaggle of geese all honking at once!"

With that, he chuckled, took Vivica and me each by the hand, said "Mademoiselles, may I?" and he led us into the dining room to dinner.

Ten

OCTOBER TURNED BLUSTERY, AND BY THE MIDDLE OF THE month, the temperature dropped. The days would grow shorter, and before we knew it, it would be Halloween, followed soon enough by the holidays. This would be our first Thanksgiving and our first Christmas in France. I liked France–it was quaint and friendly, and last summer, it had been much warmer and sunnier than England. But now the air had become brisk and chilly, and the turning leaves announced the coming of autumn, my favorite season.

"Just wait until winter really sets in," said Mom. "Winters in France can sometimes mean snow up to your waist!"

"I can't wait! I love snow!"

At school, Miss White asked if we thought any of our moms would like to be room mothers. She needed two volunteers. None of us knew for sure, but we said we would ask. At recess, Vivica said she would ask her mother, who would probably say yes because she could drive and because she didn't have a job where she had to go out to work.

My mother didn't drive and was English, and I had a two-year-old sister at home–three reasons I doubted Mom would consider being a room mother, even though I wasn't sure exactly what a room mother had to do. On the bus ride home, I practiced several scenarios in my head and finally settled on the one I thought might possibly sway her: if she hesitated, I would tell her all my classmates had heard she looked like Elizabeth Taylor and couldn't wait to meet her.

"Vivica's mom is going to be a room mother. Please! Oh, please be the other room mother! I know you would love being a room mother," I blurted out as soon as I got home. I couldn't explain why it was so important to me—perhaps because I was so proud of my beautiful mother and wanted to show her off or perhaps because I wanted her to be just a little bit more American.

"What does a room mother do?" she asked. "British schools have no such thing as far as I know."

"Mostly, I think they just bake cupcakes and cookies for the holiday parties, like Halloween and Christmas. And make Kool-Aid. And be at the party to help the teacher."

"Well, that sounds easy enough."

And just like that, before I even had to go into the Elizabeth Tayler thing, my mother was going to do something so very American. I was thrilled.

Claudette Arquette and Doreen Grilliot were stars from the first moment they stepped into Miss White's fourth-grade room. They charmed the fourth graders with their accents, their beauty, and their culinary talents. Much to my delight, for the fourth-grade Halloween party, my mother wore her Katherine Hepburn trousers, and she wore her gorgeous hair in a pageboy. She could have been in films. As the fourth graders gathered around her, asking her to pronounce different words so they could hear how they sounded when she said them, I basked in the popularity my beautiful mom was generating. Mrs. Arquette, with her high heels, flared skirt, and pierced ears, was every bit as charming and just as popular. Vivica and I agreed we had the most beautiful mothers in the whole of Alsace-Lorraine and probably in all of France, and I never again wished my mother was more American.

Fourth grade was a magic year in my life, and Thanksgiving, Christmas, and Valentine's Day provided me with epic memories of my childhood, redeeming for me, as it were, a normalcy that had long been absent. Vivica and I were best friends, sisters in our similarities and conspirators in our vivid imaginations.

Vivica loved coming to my house, which always seemed to be full of Mom's tea-drinking British friends and their young children. In a way, our neighborhood was Vivica's neighborhood too, because she was American and went to school with all of us who attended Phalsbourg Elementary. At our house, she learned to play baseball and Chinese checkers. She helped me with my French, and when I went to her house, she and her parents spoke conversational French in an effort to move me beyond just reciting memorized words and sentences.

The months and seasons of my fourth-grade year came and went, as fluid and fulfilling as any nine-year-old could possibly have hoped for. Rife with imagination, invention, and intrigue, I was sure that any day, a French gendarme would knock on our door and ask for my help with a troubling, challenging case, and I would be ready.

One lovely Saturday in late spring, Vivica and I got out our notepads, the prop most needed by every sleuth, and ticked off our detective notes, preparing to venture into the garden and broaden our investigation. Mr. Arquette heard us–I doubted for the first time– describing and noting what had evolved into a murder and burial of the body of the handyman in or under the dilapidated greenhouse. No one, our keen sleuthing had deducted, would demolish that structure, because it was hiding clues that would reveal the identity of the murderer. That person and his or her accomplices could still have been alive and well and living nearby, plotting yet another dastardly deed. It was deliciously macabre.

Vivica's papa, who had been quietly reading his newspaper, suddenly interrupted us, saying, "OK, girls, enough! There is no body buried anywhere on this property, because there was no murder. The old man who died in the toolshed suffered a heart attack while he was changing a bicycle tire. He was eighty-four years old, and he worked for the people who owned this house at the time. They gave him a very respectable funeral, and he's buried at the old cemetery in Sarrebourg."

My friend and I looked at each other, shrugged, sighed, and

went into the beautiful old kitchen, with its fireplace hearth and its collection of copper pots hanging on an iron rack suspended from the ceiling.

Vivica's mama stood at the massive oak baking table, kneading bread dough. Smiling, Mrs. Arquette gave us each a glass of lemonade and told us she would make us lunch as soon as she put the loaves in the oven.

"So, my *petite filles*, your adventure to find the missing body is *finis, oui?*"

"I guess," said Vivica, sighing. I nodded.

"Well," said Mrs. Arquette, "there are many other interesting things about this old house—things far more romantic. Many, I am told by Madam Perriot the *épicerie*—the grocer. You know who I mean, Vivi? The old lady who wears the big—how do you say *tablier vert?*"

"Green apron," said Vivica.

"Oui, that's it," said Mrs. Arquette as she expertly worked the dough and flipped it over and over. "She tells me that during the war, a daughter of this house—her name was Giselle—and a resistance fighter fell in love. Her papa forbade her to have anything to do with the young man and locked her up in the attic. For the whole last part of the war, she was not allowed to go out of the house. The girl's mother was very distraught, but nothing she could say would make her husband relent."

As Vivica's mother told the story, she occasionally struggled with an English word, and Vivica quickly filled it in. For me, that made the intrigue almost palpable. The story was thrilling: a resistance fighter; a beautiful, lovestruck young woman; and a wicked father. With bated breath and hands over our hearts, we hung on every word.

"But the odd thing, thinks Madam Perriot, is that after the war, when France was liberated, no one ever saw the young woman around the village. People think maybe she escaped her strict papa and ran away with her lover. Or maybe she died of a broken heart. One cannot know these things," said Vivica's mama, shrugging in a French way.

"But," I asked, "if she died of a broken heart, wouldn't she be buried in the cemetery?"

"Oui, I think she would. But if she ran away with her lover and got married, of course"–she frowned at us as she emphasized of course–"she might never have been seen around here again."

"Or maybe," said Vivica, "they changed their names, and maybe they are living in this very town, laughing because they have kept the very best secret of all!"

"That very well could be so." Mrs. Arquette nodded.

Vivica and I agreed that would have been exciting. We imagined, we said to her mama, they had dyed their hair; the handsome resistance fighter had grown a mustache and a beard; and they probably avoided going to any of the local shops in town where they would be recognized by people who still lived there from before the war. The possibilities of how they had managed to evade discovery were endless–and thrilling.

Vivica's mama made us each a sandwich, refilled our lemonade glasses, and told us to take our lunch outside and have a picnic.

As Vivica and I went out the back door and into the garden, Mr. Arquette walked into the kitchen, and I heard him say to Vivica's mama, "That should keep their imaginations busy for a while." At least I thought that was it. I heard *occuper leur imagination*, and I realized suddenly that my French was getting better.

Suddenly, Vivica turned to me and said, "But maybe, if she died of a broken heart, her papa felt really, really guilty for locking her up and didn't want to suffer the disdain of the townspeople, so he might have–probably would have–buried her under the greenhouse!"

"Vivica, you are so right! That is exactly what could have happened!"

Vivica and I spent the afternoon contemplating the possibilities of the demise of Giselle and her handsome lover–disposed of by the mean papa, of course–and considered whether they might have been buried together under the greenhouse or in the nearby garden, under, of course, the bougainvillea.

Eleven

CHILDREN IN MILITARY FAMILIES LEARNED TO ACCEPT CHANGE and loss as normal or at least inevitable, and if possible, we accepted the inevitable with grace. Vivica announced the week before the end of fourth grade that she and her family would be moving to America the second week of June. Her papa's firm was transferring him to Chicago. I was sad because I felt I was part of her family, and she was part of mine. We promised to stay best friends forever, and however far apart we lived, we would think of each other every day and write often.

That was the beginning of the summer of 1958, and in June, I turned ten. Johnny had been gone for a little more than two years, Connie was two and a half, and my mother and father seemed happy or at least happier. In any case, I found I now worried less about them than I had since Johnny died.

Summer in Alsace-Lorraine was lovely. It was warm, sunny, and fragrant with the scent of wildflowers growing in the large meadow on the playground side of the base housing. Besides the baseball field Daddy had made behind our house, there were three places where we children usually gathered: the playground, the main entrance, and the meadow. That was how we all referred to the different areas, because just like in England, it was hard to know compass directions. The roads were not straight; every road in France seemed to wind, and if one were to give directions using compass points, the directions would confuse everyone. Daddy had taught me that the sun rose in the east and set in the west, but it was anyone's guess what location that made the meadow or the playground. My father gave me a compass from his Boy Scout camping supplies, but I wasn't sure how that was supposed to help me find my way around base housing, which I didn't need help doing anyway. Still, when school started again, I would be in the fifth grade, and I was going to join the Girl Scouts, so I figured maybe the compass would come in handy if we went on hikes.

It was our second summer in Phalsbourg's base housing near the town of Sarrebourg, which made it the second summer since my father had created the baseball diamond in the back of our section of houses. Throughout the housing area, there were single-story rows of two-, four-, or six-unit homes. Our row of four units formed one side of a square. Three other rows of four units whose backs faced the grassy field completed the square and made a perfect place to play baseball. Each family was supposed to mow the section of the field directly behind their house, but Daddy always mowed the yards that got overgrown; he was passionate about baseball and wanted us kids to be able to play whenever we could get enough of us together to make a game. We could play baseball whenever we wanted throughout the year if the field was dry and not snowy or icy, but summertime was the best time–it was when baseball was played in America. Daddy and I listened to baseball games aired from the States whenever he was able to pick one up on Radio Luxembourg. I loved baseball. I liked to play shortstop, but I would play any position except catcher. I was a bit scared of getting hit in the face with a baseball or, for that matter, a bat, and from what I had observed, the catchers seemed to get hit more than the other players.

Baseball was not the only thing we did for fun in our housing area. On the weekends, when the weather was nice, and on warm summer evenings, a group of French children from the nearby village gathered in the meadow near our playground. The meadow was bordered by a small forest, and we played hide-and-seek among the trees. At other times, we played soccer or red rover. My French was still iffy, but we somehow communicated, and there was a lot of laughter, along with a jumble of English and French words that, to an onlooker, must have sounded like a conversation taking place in outer space. Like a sponge, I soaked up as much of their culture as I could. Their ruddy, rough, and charming personalities intrigued me, and I realized their lives were as far removed from mine as mine was from Vivica's.

My best friend in base housing was Bob Peterson. He had moved into the housing area at the end of the fourth grade, and in September, we were going to be in the fifth grade together. Bob taught me how to play Chinese checkers the proper way, because apparently, those of us who had been playing it since last summer had been playing it wrong. This summer, among the nine- to twelve-year-old kids, a riveting game took place on a grand scale daily. Unlike regular checkers, the Chinese version took much longer and was far more complicated. Bob said it was a lot like football: it required strategy. We played the game with a passion, and I was hooked. Every summer morning, I woke up, did my chores, and headed outdoors with my tin game board and marbles. Sometimes I had to take Connie in her stroller, but there were always other girls around who loved toddlers and begged me to let them push her around the cul-de-sac. And always there was someone up for the challenge of a checkers game.

Most importantly, though, that was the summer when I finally met my guardian angel. Well, I didn't exactly meet him or her, but I had an encounter that resolved any confusion I might have had regarding Sister Philathea's explanation of the roles of our guardian angels.

One day in our first-grade class, Sister had told us about the different kinds of angels. There were archangels, the highest ranking of all the angels, and there were cherubs, who were baby angels. Then there were guardian angels.

"The guardian angels are divine beings who are constantly in your presence and whose job it is to keep you from harm," Sister had said.

The class had murmured positive sounds, and we all had nodded.

Kathleen had raised her hand. "Didn't Jesus have a guardian angel?"

That was a question I'd understood. Why hadn't Jesus's guardian angel saved him from the Romans? Why hadn't he stricken the soldiers with bolts of lightning or something? I'd held my breath, waiting for Sister's answer.

"Well now," Sister had said, "let us just think about what a guardian angel can and can't do, shall we? We cannot know what God has planned for our lives. Only he knows. But when something is about to happen to you and it isn't something that God wants to happen right then, he sends your guardian angel to protect you. Because God knows everything, and he watches over you constantly. The angels are his celestial workers here on earth—workers who have special powers they use when God directs them to do so."

I'd thought I understood, and since then, I had been on the lookout to see if I could find any evidence of angels of any sort. Grandma Grilliot had told me when Johnny died that God had sent his angels to lift Johnny's spiritual body out of his earthly body and carry it up to heaven to be with Jesus and Mary. Mommy had told me to write a letter to Johnny when he died and had promised she would put it in the pocket of his shirt, so he would have it with him. I worried to no end that the angels had already taken Johnny's other body up to heaven before the letter was put in the pocket of his shirt on his earthly body. If so, he wouldn't have gotten it. On the other hand, I liked to think his guardian angel would have been on the ball and noticed; if so, I was sure he or she would have made a second trip back to retrieve the letter before Johnny was buried—if Sister Philathea and Grandma Grilliot were right, that was.

One lovely, sunny June day in France, I was to finally understand the role of my guardian angel. Never again would I doubt his or her existence.

Two of the mothers in base housing had arranged an outing for us children: they were taking us to a public swimming pool in one of the neighboring towns. A private city bus called a coach came to the housing area to pick us up and deliver us to the pool under the supervision of those mothers. I counted fourteen of us, including Bob and me, and we ranged in age from the youngest three, who were eight, to the eldest boy, who was twelve. I hadn't been swimming since I lived in England, and I was excited. In England, in the summertime, my auntie Barbara used to take me to the Urmston Baths, our local swimming pool.

When the coach arrived, the chaperones checked their list for our names as we boarded. The boys had their swimming trunks rolled up in towels, and we girls had our bathing suits and towels in various shopping bags or overnight cases.

Adrenaline ran high on the short ride, and upon arrival, our bus got in line for a parking space. There were buses everywhere–arriving, parking, and departing in a continuous stream up and down both sides of the road. As passengers got off, buses moved out, while other buses filled with people of all ages took up the vacated spaces. Our driver found a space, we filed off the bus, and the mothers gathered us together in a group and gave us our instructions. We were to form a double line: one mother would be at the head; the other mother would bring up the rear. We were to stay together while crossing the road. Our entry fees had been paid in advance, and we each had a little paper pass that looked like a movie ticket. We were to go through a turnstile, where we would deposit our tickets, and a man on the other side would stamp our hands. Did we all understand? We did. In an orderly fashion, we crossed the street at the first break in traffic.

Once on the other side, I realized immediately that I had left my bag with my swimsuit on the bus, and I was in a panic, afraid the bus would pull out before I could retrieve it.

"I've left my bag on the bus," I said, almost in tears. "It has my swimsuit in it!"

"Calm down," said one of the moms. "Look both ways, and run across and get it before the driver leaves." She walked me to the edge of the sidewalk and gave me a gentle push when the road was clear.

With a sigh of relief, I reached the bus just as the driver was closing the door.

"I've left my bag on the seat!" I shouted.

He nodded and motioned for me to get on the bus.

I grabbed my bag, said *merci*, climbed down, and waited while he pulled into the traffic, not wanting to take a chance that he wouldn't see me crossing in front of him. As soon as he cleared the space, I started to run across the street. I heard my friends across the street scream, and above all the other voices, I heard Bob shout for me to stop. I realized I had run in front of a different moving bus. Simultaneously, I heard the bus's horn, the loud sound of the bus's squealing brakes, and my friends shouting. I froze and then felt myself lifted upward and backward until I was standing back on the sidewalk. The incident took all of five seconds.

I turned around, expecting to see an adult, probably a man, standing behind me. I looked down at my legs and saw that across my thighs were two thick black rubber marks where the bus's bumper had raked my legs. The bus driver had stopped his bus and gotten off to make sure I wasn't hurt, and one of the mothers crossed the street to lead me back to the other side. She was visibly shaken, and as soon as we crossed over and entered the swimming pool, she took me to the ladies' room to wash the black rubber off my thighs. Even with aggressive rubbing with a bar of soap and my swimming towel, the marks were still visible. They would come off when I got in the chlorinated water of the pool, she told me. They did not come off in the pool.

Despite the nearly disastrous start to our adventure, our day at the swimming pool was wonderful. For four hours, we swam, frolicked, and sunbathed, and by the time we packed up to leave, we were a waterlogged, sunburned, exhausted group of happy youngsters.

Before my mother could ask me why I had black marks across my thighs, I told her what had happened. I told her it had been my fault; I had been too excited to go swimming and had not looked both ways. I said I had learned my lesson and would never be so impulsive again. My mother just looked at my legs. As though in a trance, she ran her fingers across the black marks. Suddenly, she burst into tears; grabbed me to her; and kept saying, "Thank God. Thank God," over and over.

Later that night, the marks came off with a good scrubbing in a hot bath. As I lay in bed afterward, I relived the entire incident. When I closed my eyes, I could still feel the sensation of being lifted backward. I could still feel the strong hands under my arms, lifting me upward and backward and placing me feet-down in a standing position on the sidewalk. As I was drifting off to sleep, I thought, *Tomorrow I really should write a letter to Sister Philathea to ask her if it sounds to her like I was saved by my guardian angel.* The most perplexing part was that when I immediately had turned to see who had lifted me back onto the sidewalk, there had been no other human being in sight anywhere on my side of the pavement.

Twelve

HE FRENCH SUN WAS A DAZZLING, BLINDING ORB FROM morning to evening, and then, suddenly, the cool night air rushed in, bringing fireflies and stars that appeared so low they looked as though they could have been scooped out of the sky with a butterfly net.

I lay on my back, looking up at the inky night, counting stars and trying to identify the constellations. I was practicing my accent. We were going to England, and I anticipated I would see a lot of my old friends on Windsor Avenue. I wanted to impress Kenny Ainsworth with my new accent, which he would probably think made me sound like an American movie star.

"You'd be better off practicing your French," said Dad when he asked what I was doing. "We won't be living here forever, and you'll be sorry you missed the opportunity. When we get back to the States, you'll have to take a foreign language in high school, and the battle will be half won if you work a little harder while we're here."

He was right, of course. I was beginning to realize that Dad was always interested in my school progress. On the contrary, Mom didn't seem too bothered. She had left school at fourteen–I guessed that was normal in England–and started working in a factory at fifteen.

One day, when Daddy was scolding me for yet another poor math score, Mom came to my defense, saying, "Oh, Robert! Don't go on so. After all, as long as she can manage her household money ..."

I chimed in to agree with Mom, but Dad gave me such a look I decided I had better close my mouth. There were times with my dad when I could be outspoken and times when I knew I'd have been crossing a line by speaking out. It was funny, really, because I hardly ever talked back to Mom, at least not when she was in striking distance. She'd not hesitate to smack me a good one on my bottom if I was within arm's reach. Dad, though, never spanked Connie or me, and he was much more patient than Mom when I was being even a little challenging. *Challenging* was his word for the times when I was being argumentative.

I sighed and went into the house to work on my French.

My parents were confusing. My mother read poetry all the time. Her favorite poet was Rupert Brooke. She also liked Keats, and she had a set of very old matching books by someone named John Milton that were called *Paradise Lost* and *Paradise Found*. She could sit for hours reading Russian novels with funny names, such as *Anna Karenina* and *The Brothers Karamazov*. I had tried reading some of her books, but they were seriously boring! She also liked ballroom dancing, and she used to go to a place in Flixton called the Alker–and sometimes the Plaza or the Ritz in Manchester–with a boy from Urmston named Lawrence Noone. She said he was a fabulous dancer. She said she wished Daddy could dance like that. The only fast dancing she and my father did was something called the jitterbug. He was good at that, she said.

Last month, my parents had gone to the army base in Wiesbaden, Germany, where everyone stationed in France went if they needed to buy something important. For some reason, the army bases had much better exchanges than our air force bases. They had gone to the post exchange and had come home with a huge radio-record player combination called a Grundig. Now Mom played Mario Lanza LPs for hours. I liked most of the other music my mother played too, including Gogi Grant, Joanie Sommers, Frank Sinatra, and, of course, Nat King Cole, which always reminded me of Vivica's papa.

On the other hand, Dad liked country music; rock-and-roll dancing; comic strips in the *Stars and Stripes* (his favorite was Sad

Sack); and sports, sports, sports. So of my two parents, I wouldn't have thought he would be the one obsessed with my education. My parents were definitely funny–odd funny, not ha-ha funny.

So far that summer, I had read all the Little House on the Prairie books by Laura Ingalls Wilder. I'd discovered them in the library and thought they were amazing. I decided without a doubt that if I had a choice when I grew up, I would live in a log cabin in the woods, most likely in America since I didn't think England had log cabins. But maybe I would end up changing my mind, I thought, because I really wanted to live in a thatched-roof cottage too, and America didn't have any of those as far as I knew.

I finished the Little House books and found a new series of books I liked called Nancy Drew. I checked out two from the base library to take with me to England. I said I wasn't going to start reading them until I got to Nanna and Granddad's, but I couldn't help it–I started reading the first one, and soon I was nearly half finished. I knew I probably would run out of books to read before we got back.

We were lucky that France was near England. Most of my school friends who had two American parents probably never got to see any of their grandparents, aunts, uncles, and cousins for the whole time they lived in France. A few of the other kids also had British, French, or German grandparents they got to see, but only a few. Of course, sometimes relatives from the States came to France for a visit, but so far, none of ours had. Dad wrote to my American grandparents and reminded them that Grandpa's great-great-great somebody-or-other had been one of Napoleon's generals–an American relative had done a family history and found that out. He said if they came for a visit, we would go see the Arc de Triomphe in Paris, which supposedly had General Grilliot's name on it from some war. I hoped they did come to visit, even if they didn't much care about an ancient ancestor.

July 2 arrived. I had packed, unpacked, and repacked my small hand case–most of my clothes were in Mom's suitcase–with odds and ends I thought I would need and with a few toys for Connie. Dad insisted I take my French book with me to study in my spare time. I didn't think I would have any spare time, but I stuffed the book into my case at the last minute, and we all piled into the car.

Six and a half hours later, we arrived in Calais. Daddy drove our car right onto the ferry's lower parking deck, and then we all sat at a table on the upper deck of the boat, where the view was the best. Once the ferry left the dock, the snack bar opened, and we each got a sandwich and a drink. The English Channel was rough that day, and we were tossed about on the huge swells. I sipped my soda and refused to feel even a bit sick. I was going home to Nanna and Granddad. *Going home, going home, going home …*

When I woke up, we were pulling into the docks at Dover.

I would have known we had reached England even if someone had blindfolded me and I hadn't known my destination. Every cell in my body was awakened to the unique smells and sounds that were England, and six hours later, long after dusk, Daddy drove our car down Whitelake and turned left onto Windsor Avenue. At last, we were home!

By the end of our first week in England, we had seen aunts, uncles, cousins, friends, and neighbors. My mother and I had eaten every single food item we had dreamed of and longed for. Mom told Nanna she didn't think she would ever crave a pork pie again; she had had one for dinner almost every day. Dinner was what we called *lunch* in America, and tea was what we Americans called *dinner.*

For tea, in the course of one week, we'd had steak and kidney pie; fish and chips; Cornish pasties; a fry-up (Wall's sausages, chips, eggs, baked beans, and mushrooms); shepherd's pie; and fish and chips again—all the things we had missed the most. Plus, we'd had a dessert, which Nanna called *afters,* of some sort every night, which we had drenched in Bird's custard. And we'd had proper English bread; there was no equivalent in America or France. French bread was nice, but nothing compared to a breakfast of toasted English bread slathered in Welsh butter and topped with Robertson's marmalade.

Of course, the thing everyone missed the most when he or she moved to America from England was the tea. Nanna only used PG Tips. She swore there was not a better tea in the world, and my first cup when we arrived at number 7 made me realize how much I missed proper tea. I fancied myself quite a connoisseur of tea, even though I was only ten; after all, I used to drink it in my bottle before I was a year old. Nanna was a big believer in the benefits of tea, and when she had come to France last summer, she'd had no use for the American tea bags Mom had to get from the commissary. She'd said that had she known how terrible they were, she would have been mailing us proper tea all along—which she had started doing as soon as she returned to England. Even though we'd had PG Tips for almost a year now in France, it still didn't taste as good as when Nanna made it at number 7. Mom said it was because of the different water. English water, said my mother, was superior.

On our third Sunday at Nanna's, she fixed a leg of lamb with Yorkshire pudding.

"Why are we having Yorkshire pudding with lamb?" asked Granddad. "We've had it two weeks in a row with the Sunday roast."

"Why do you think, Jack? Vivienne told me that she almost died from starvation when we sent her off to America and that if she ever got to come back to Flixton, all she would ask for was Yorkshire pudding with every Sunday dinner. And, of course, Grimwood's ice cream with raspberry vinegar. Oh, and Cadbury Flakes."

I noticed Nanna said this with a straight face, but I knew she was kidding. Nanna's posh behavior was just a front, Granddad and I decided. Anyway, she was right—if she could have made Yorkshire pudding for me to eat with my fish and chips, she would have, but nobody wanted fishy-tasting Yorkshire pudding.

I walked to the top shops every day to buy Granddad's newspaper from the newsagent, as I had done when I turned five. Now I realized that every newsagent's shop in Britain smelled the same. Whether Nanna and I walked to the top of Whitelake, to the newsagent's in Flixton Village, or to the paper shop on Moorside Road on the way to Urmston, they all smelled exactly the same. I thought it odd that when I'd lived on Windsor Avenue, I never had noticed how amazing the newspaper shops smelled—or, for that matter, the greengrocer's and Mrs. Welsh's grocery. How could I not have noticed?

One day Nanna and I were shopping as we used to do all those years ago when I lived with her. Nanna asked Mrs. Welsh for a quarter pound of butter—she asked for four ounces, to be exact. How odd that it didn't come prewrapped in quarter-pound sticks bundled in the same package, I thought. For that matter, why wasn't it simply wrapped as a big square labeled as one pound? It was the same with sugar. At the commissary, my mother bought sugar in five-pound bags. I was not sure any grocery store employee in America would have understood—even in a small town like Freeport—if someone had asked for four ounces of butter and six ounces of sugar. Nanna told me the reason people in England still asked for small amounts was because even if they had a refrigerator (and most families didn't), for years after the war, many food items were still rationed. Did I not remember walking with her to the post office, where she had to pick up her monthly ration book? "Plus," she reminded me, "hardly anyone has a car in England—imagine having to carry a five-pound bag of sugar home with all the other groceries too!"

"Will that be it, Mrs. Dempster?" asked Mrs. Welsh as she cut a piece of butter off a big block and weighed it. "It's just a bit over, but that's all right then?"

"Oh yes, Mrs. Welsh. Not to worry; it won't go to waste! And besides the sugar, I'd like a tin of salmon. Red, mind you, not pink."

"Lovely, Mrs. Dempster. Anything else then?"

"No, that will do a treat. Ta very much," answered Nanna as she placed the items in her shopping bag.

"Goodbye now, Mrs. Dempster. See you next time. And my, Vivienne, you have grown so! You're such a big girl now, aren't you?"

Nanna and Mrs. Welsh had known each other my whole life and maybe longer. Mrs. Welsh knew Nanna never bought tins of pink salmon, and Nanna knew if she didn't specify red salmon, Mrs. Welsh would ask, "Is it a tin of red you're wanting, Mrs. Dempster?" It was as though assuming on either of their parts would have been rude, and that would have been unthinkable—as unthinkable as calling each other by their first names. Nanna even still called Mrs.

Murphy Mrs. Murphy, and they'd lived next door to each other for nearly twenty years!

Kenny Ainsworth had moved. That was a shock to my system. The whole time I'd been gone from Windsor Avenue, I'd imagined coming home and finding everything the same. It had never occurred to me that now that I was ten, Kenny was fifteen. Even if Mr. and Mrs. Ainsworth had still lived down the street—and they didn't—Kenny would have been out of school and working. Still, I was a little sad that he wouldn't get to see how American I'd become.

"Does Kenny know that I'm a real American, Nanna? I mean, did you tell him after I left? Because I didn't know I was, so I'm sure he didn't know I was."

"Oh, I'm sure he knew all along, love. Remember, he is older than you, so he probably understood more than you would have about your daddy being American and stationed at Burtonwood."

Of course, I should have realized that.

While some things had changed a bit, most things were just the same, and the other children—minus Kenny and a few other teenagers—still played in the street. With my allowance (spends, they were called in England) and the remainder of my birthday money (with which I had been frugal), I bought a whip and top, a game played by children in streets all over the British Isles. The whip was comprised of an eight- or nine-inch wooden handle with a long, thin strip of leather fixed at one end. The game required coiling the strip of leather around the grooves of a wooden top about the size of a small pear. Then, with a flick of your wrist, you flung the top so that it went spinning down the street. The object was to see who could keep the top spinning the longest and make it go the farthest by whipping it to keep it going. It required skill—not the least of which was to avoid lashing some other child's bare legs—and for the first day, I was at a disadvantage. I'd forgotten that sending it spinning faster so it was the farthest top down the street was not necessarily the smartest thing to do if you couldn't catch up to it before it wobbled and fell over. By the second day, though, I had gotten the technique down again, and I loved the competition of the game. I mentioned it to Dad.

"You know, maybe you should start thinking of your French lessons as a competition," he said. "I bet you'd find it to be fun!"

"Oh, Dad! French is a language, not a game!" I giggled and added, "*Mais oui*, Papa!" Not for the first time, I realized my father more than likely would challenge my intellect or, at the very least, promote the benefits of an education until I got married and left home. I figured I had better get used to it.

I spent every waking hour possible with my cousins, my aunts, my uncle, and my friends. I ate a Grimwood's ice cream with raspberry vinegar every time the ice cream van came round Windsor Avenue, and I ate so many Cadbury Flake bars that Granddad said that by all accounts, I should have turned into one. Cadbury chocolate was the best in the world, and Cadbury Flake bars were heavenly. As with proper English bread, there was nothing like them in America or France.

One miserably damp Saturday afternoon, Granddad, Daddy, and Uncle Jack, Mom's brother, had gone to the Garrick for a pint. My cousins and I were spread out on the carpet in front of the fire that Nanna had just lit–in August–in the lounge. I'd forgotten that English summer weather was nothing like French summer weather, even though the two countries were not that far apart. My mother and Auntie June were catching up on what had been going on in their lives since my mother moved away from Flixton. Auntie June was married to Uncle Jack, but she and my mother had been friends long before that; in fact, Mom had introduced the two. They had a lot of catching up to do. My cousin Matthew, the youngest of Auntie June and Uncle Jack's three children, was keeping Connie entertained, and Valarie, Jacqueline, and I were doing our best to be as quiet as mice–we knew the minute we drew attention to ourselves, Nanna would shoo us outside.

The three women had been alternately crying and blowing their noses between puffing on their cigarettes as Mom recounted Johnny's illness and death. It was hard for me to believe that it had been more than three years and that any talk of him still gave me a big lump in my throat–particularly since I now knew I had been silly to believe the Virgin Mary could arrange for me to be taken up to heaven for a visit with him. Nanna made us all a cup of tea, and the conversation turned to my mother's life after she moved to America.

To my mother, America was a vast, modernized, technologically advanced country where everyone had a car, all men and most women drove, and everyone seemed rich. It was a country without the colloquial familiarity that permeated the small towns and villages of Britain, and at first, she had been overwhelmed with homesickness.

"I'd been in Freeport about four days, and I was missing England so desperately. You know"–Mom nodded her head toward Auntie June–"I'd never been out of Lancashire before. Anyway, we were all sitting out on the veranda–I've told you what a big house Bob's parents have–and I'd just made a cup of tea. I was thinking of England, how late the sun sets here in the summertime, and how lovely the night sky is once it does, and as I was looking up at the Illinois sky, I realized I hadn't seen the moon or a single star since I'd arrived. And that's just what I said to Bob's mum. 'What do you mean?' said Helen. 'What's a–what did you call it? A moon? And a star?'

"I was stunned. I was in shock. Bob said to his mother, 'Oh, Mom, you should see the English sky at night. It's amazing: there's this big silver globe that comes out as soon as the sun goes down and the sky gets dark, and it's so bright that it lights up the entire sky. And then there are little twinkling dots that are called stars. The whole thing is magnificent!'

"'Oh,' said Bob's mum, 'I'd love to go to England someday and see them!'

"June, I just burst into tears. All I could say was 'I want to go home! I want to go back to England! I can't live without ever seeing the moon and stars again!'"

"Oh, Doreen, that's hysterical! A bit mean, mind you, but you must admit it is funny," said Auntie June.

"*Now* it's funny! But I was devastated at the time. Of course, as soon as I burst into tears, Helen felt terrible. 'Oh, honey,' she said,

'I'm sorry! Of course we have a moon and stars–it's just been overcast since you arrived!' I guess I'm what Americans would call a *country bumpkin*," said Mom.

I said, "Tell Auntie June about your English friend Jean, who thought popcorn sounded like a nice American vegetable, and she boiled it for Sunday dinner when her husband invited some of the single airmen who worked with him." That was my favorite of the British war bride stories, as we referred to them.

"Oh, that *was* funny. You know how we always have potatoes, plus two veg, with the Sunday roast? Well, Jean's husband had invited some young airmen to Sunday dinner, as Viv said, and along with the roast, potatoes, and peas, Jean was looking for another vegetable to cook. She found a container of something called popcorn that her husband had picked up at the commissary. She knew Americans ate corn and thought it would be nice if she fixed something American for the boys. So she poured the kernels into a pot of boiling water, and when they started popping, they filled up the pot until the lid was pushed off! She'd never seen anything like it–it just kept coming–and she had no idea what to do with it. She tasted it and thought it was the blandest vegetable she'd ever tasted and could not understand Americans' obsession with corn. Thinking she'd cooked it wrong and couldn't possibly serve guests anything that bland, she emptied the popcorn into a big bowl and poured roast beef gravy over it to give it some flavor."

By then, we were all laughing, and Mom added, "She called the boys to dinner, and her husband asked, 'What's this?'

"'American corn,' Jean answered, 'but it was dry and didn't have any flavor, so I poured gravy on it to see if that helped'

"And do you know what? She said every one of those young men took a serving and said it was very nice."

Val, Jackie, and I were laughing hysterically and rolling on the carpet.

When everyone finally stopped laughing, Nanna said, "It's stopped raining; you girls go outside and play until tea is ready."

"When did they lock up the air-raid shelter?" I asked my cousins as we walked toward the field across from our grandparents' house, and I noticed the heavy chain through the iron rings on the shelter door.

"Oh, ages ago. Dad said the council is going to pull it down or fill it in and build council houses there," answered Valarie.

"Council houses? On Windsor Avenue? Are you sure?"

I felt a bit sad at the thought that our air-raid shelter would be gone. I had noticed too that now there were cars parked here and there up and down the street. My beloved Windsor Avenue was changing.

That night, I begged my mother to let me stay up late while my aunt Barbara told me stories of all the ghosts that had haunted number 7. My mother let me make my bed on the little horsehair sofa Nanna called a divan, saying that as long as Aunt Barbara stayed there with me, I could spend the night waiting for a ghost.

Auntie Bar, as I called her, was my mother's younger sister, and she was exactly ten years younger than my mother and ten years my senior. I loved every minute I spent with her; it was like having a big sister. That night, as we sat by the fire, she painted my nails with nail polish, and when I said I wasn't allowed to polish my nails, she said, "Oh, shush," and dabbed pink gloss on my lips. I was thrilled and half-heartedly said, "I'm not allowed to wear lipstick either."

"So let me tell you about all the ghosts in this house!" said Auntie Bar. "Now, mind you, there are probably more than I know of, because it's a very old house—well over a hundred years old—and my mum and dad only just moved here four years before I was born, when your mum was five or six.

"The nicest ghost was a lady in Victorian dress with a cameo broach fastening the starched white collar at her neck. She visited your nanna, who had been dozing right in this chair by the fire late one evening, while your granddad was still working the two-ten shift at Turner's Asbestos. Then, another night, your granddad—who isn't scared of anything—saw something so horrible in the upstairs wardrobe that he walked to the nearest phone box as soon as it was light outside and called your nanna, who had gone on the bus to stay in Winton with her brother who had broken his leg and needed nursing. I wasn't born yet, and your mum and Jackie must have been with your nanna.

"Apparently, your granddad's ghost was quite unpleasant, and your granddad thought it prudent to call your grandmother home, given that she has quite a way with ghosts. She has the gift, you know."

I didn't doubt her for a minute. I'd heard lots of conversations about Nanna's so-called gift.

"On the other hand, your nanna's ghost was very nice," she said, explaining the apparition that had visited my grandmother in the living room. "She was giving her a message to give to her daughter—the ghost's daughter, that is—named Kathleen, who, at that time, was a friend of your grandmother's."

Just then, Nanna walked into the lounge with tea for everyone.

"Oh, Nan, I do hope we see your ghost! What shall I say if she shows up?" I asked.

"Ask her what horse Granddad should bet on next week," said my grandmother with a straight face.

"Mind," said my mother, who had followed Nanna into the room, "when the fire goes out, you're going to be cold!"

I argued, of course. "It's August, Mom! I have a blanket; I'll be fine."

My aunt and I stayed up until long past midnight, and she told me stories of the resident ghost who turned the light in the hallway by the stairs off and on for at least five minutes every time a Chapelle or Dempster relative died. Day or night—it made no difference. Well into the wee hours, she told me stories that made the hair on my neck prickle and gave me goose bumps on my arms; and on two occasions, I saw an apparition at the window, even though she drew the curtains after I saw the first one. While I couldn't wait to see an inside ghost, having one peer at us through the window was too much! I wished Vivica had been there to share the experience; she would have loved how scary it was.

The fire finally died. I had fallen asleep on the divan, and Auntie Bar was curled up with a blanket in Granddad's chair. My mother was right: I woke up freezing cold. I crawled into my bed upstairs in the wee hours of the morning, having met neither my grandparents' ghosts nor any others.

Our time in England was magical. Every day was filled with people I loved and memories I had cherished in the years I had been gone. Then, soon enough, it came to an end.

Thirteen

USING ONE OF MOM'S FAVORITE PHRASES—*FUNNILY ENOUGH*—I said to her, "Funnily enough, Mom, I'm excited to be home. I've missed France."

"Well, well," replied my mother. "Will wonders never cease? Do you realize that is the first time you've ever referred to anywhere but number 7 Windsor Avenue as home?"

It was our first day back in France, and Mom and I were unpacking suitcases and sorting through laundry. Connie was cranky, Daddy was mowing the lawn, and I was anxious to go over to Bob's house. Finally, Mom said that if I put Connie in her stroller and took her with me, I could go outside.

"It's me! I'm back!" I announced as I knocked on Bob's screen door. I had my Chinese checkers, and I was desperate for a game, since I had been gone for a month. I hoped Connie would fall asleep in her stroller.

When Bob wasn't playing football with the boys in the field beyond the playground or playing baseball with me in the field behind my house, we usually were playing checkers. Bob liked Monopoly too, but I couldn't seem to develop a liking for it, probably because the game took too long, and I didn't have the patience. There were no English-language television stations, and none of us had a television anyway, except for one boy whose mother was French. It stood to reason the family watched French programs; after all, they had a built-in interpreter. I tried to tell my father that if we had a television, it would help me with my French. He didn't even bother to answer.

"Do you want to play Chinese checkers, Bob? I've really missed playing. No one on Windsor Avenue had ever heard of them, and I didn't take mine with me, so I couldn't even teach them."

"Sure," answered Bob, "but there's a new girl called Linda, and she's been waiting for you to get back. We guys have been playing a lot of baseball, and Linda doesn't like baseball."

"Have the French kids been coming to the playground?"

"Yep, and we've been playing some soccer with them. It's hard for us to beat them at soccer. And one of the French guys wants to play baseball with us. He's been coming round, and he's pretty good. If we could get more of them interested, we might be able to come up with enough of us to make two teams."

In a flash of insight, I realized that as much as I loved England, loved Windsor Avenue, loved my cousins, and adored my grandparents, I was no longer the English girl. I still preferred English food, but in every other way, I was thoroughly American. While in England, I had been thrilled that everyone made a big deal over my American accent–it made up for my American friends asking why I sounded British. Although hardly anyone ever mentioned my accent anymore– maybe all the practicing had been worth it. I was delighted that one of the English kids had called me a Yank.

"Oy," someone had asked, "are you Canadian?"

"Naw," Trevor had said before I could answer, "she's a Yank."

The last remaining unfettered days of summer, replete with Chinese checkers, baseball, comic-book trading, and fireflies caught in jelly jars, were the epitome of an idyllic childhood. With long hours of August sunshine, tanned bodies and sunburned noses, and cool nights of inky skies filled with twinkling stars, how could we not have felt like the luckiest children on the planet? Soon our parents were taking us to the PX for our school supplies, assessing our wardrobes, and trimming our hair with the kitchen scissors.

On the Friday before Labor Day, Linda and I were so excited we couldn't sleep. I was spending the night at her house, and her mom had agreed to pick up two Toni Home Permanents at the base when she went shopping on Saturday. My mom was going to perm our hair. Toni Home Permanents were the best; we had read about them in one of my mom's magazines. Two twins had had their hair permed at the same time—one had gone to a beauty parlor, and one had used a Toni Home Permanent. Both of their pictures were in the advertisement, and we agreed: we couldn't tell the difference!

"I just hope our perms don't turn out frizzy," I said.

"Oh, don't even think that! I want my hair to look like Betty's. You have darker brown hair, though, so I think yours will look more like Veronica's. Not a pageboy—curlier."

Until we finally fell asleep, we discussed how stuck-up Veronica was, how Archie should have realized that Betty was the one true girl for him, and how sorry we felt for Jughead: we were pretty sure he had a crush on Betty, but she was too in love with Archie to even notice. Once asleep, I dreamed Linda and I were both redheads, and our permed hair looked just like Little Orphan Annie's.

Soon it was Labor Day, and the following week, Bob, Linda, and I would enter the fifth grade. This day, though, everyone in the base housing was either cooking out or picnicking. In our section, charcoal grills and coolers full of soft drinks and beer were visible around the perimeter of the baseball field. There were helium-filled balloons scattered around the neighbors' backyards, and bunting was draped across the fences of the few units that had been enclosed to keep pets and children from wandering off. Various types of music could be heard playing from the houses around the square, and from our open back door drifted the sound of my dad's favorite country singer, Hank Snow, singing "There Stands the Glass." After filling up on grilled hot dogs; baked beans; and cupcakes with red, white, and blue frosting, we children ran around to the front of the houses to catch fireflies in glass jars and to wait for the fireworks that our dads would be putting on after dark near the playground.

Suddenly, a wonderful thing happened: when the air force safety patrol came around, as they did every evening at dusk, a dog jumped out of the patrol truck and came running up to us.

One of the airmen in the truck shouted, "Magoo! Come on! Get back here!"

A few of us tried to urge the dog back toward the truck, but he was having none of it; he wanted to play with us, I guessed.

"His name is Mr. Magoo!" shouted one of the men. "He does this occasionally. Just take care of him until we patrol tomorrow!"

That was how I finally got a dog.

At the end of the Labor Day celebrations, Mr. Magoo followed me into the house and into my bedroom, where I had hidden my parents' latest copy of *Reader's Digest*. That morning, I had stumbled on an article that seemed written for me. I just knew my guardian angel had somehow influenced the author to write it, the magazine to publish it, and me to find it.

With something akin to glee, I read the entire article twice. I held my breath occasionally in case there was a *however* sentence, but there wasn't one. According to the author, in the United States of America, people could call themselves by whatever name they chose; moreover, they could change their name at will, and they didn't need to go to court or hire a lawyer to do it! There was, however, one very minor *however* (it was actually a *but*) that was so obvious even I got it: you couldn't break the law or become a criminal and then change your name to avoid getting caught or arrested. But I had no plan to ever break any laws–going to confession under those circumstances would have been excruciating, not just uncomfortable. *So what name should I choose?*

I reached my hand over the side of the bed and patted Mr. Magoo's head. What did Mr. Magoo think? Susie? Julie? Marie? Lynn? Lee? Leigh! That was it! It made sense, didn't it? I was named after Vivien Leigh, so I would just go with her last name instead of her first. I drifted off to sleep, dreaming that I had become a famous female baseball player and that the other players and coaches only ever called me Grilliot anyway, so my first name didn't matter. In my dream, Grilliot was a perfect name for an all-star, which solved the name quandary completely. My spectacularly talented dog, Magoo, fetched the balls whenever I hit line drives and home runs.

Just as I was dreaming that I was at Wrigley Field and the *Chicago Tribune* was getting ready to feature me in an article, I woke up. That was disappointing, because I must have been recruited by the Cubs—otherwise, why would the *Tribune* have wanted to interview me?—and I would have liked my dream to end there.

I announced my name change at breakfast the next morning, assuring my parents it was perfectly legal. I opened the *Reader's Digest* to the page the article was on.

"Uh-huh," said my father without looking up from his paper.

"If you don't stop this nonsense about changing your name, Vivienne, I will give you a good spanking. It is ridiculous, and we are not going to start calling you Leigh. There is nothing wrong with your name. I like it. In fact, it is my favorite name, which is why I named you that. You are named after Vivien Leigh, whom I saw in *Gone with the Wind* when I was pregnant with you. Now, eat your cornflakes, and stop mithering about your name."

I'd heard that a thousand times—maybe a million. I'd have said so, but my mother wasn't in a good mood that morning, and I didn't want to get smacked on my butt when I stood up to leave the table.

That evening, we kids were catching fireflies again at dusk, when Mr. Magoo suddenly went running toward the truck as the airmen drove down our housing area's main road on their evening patrol. He hopped into the back and rejoined his friends. I could hardly breathe. No sooner had I fallen in love with the dog of my dreams than he was off again, and my heart broke. I sat down on the front porch and pondered just how dismal the world could be sometimes.

Ever since first grade at Saint Mary's in Muncie, I had thought off and on about becoming a nun. The most appealing thing now was that I would have to choose the name of a saint whose good deeds and holy reputation would serve to guide me through all the challenges of my life. I wouldn't even need to go to court or be worried about whether it would upset my mother; after all, I was sure she'd be ecstatic that I had become a religious, as Grandma Grilliot called people in the faith. There was a nun in the family in Illinois or Minnesota—I couldn't remember which. She was the sister of my uncle Jack–my aunt Sally's husband, not my mom's brother–on the Mulcahey side. Her name was Sister Pat, and I think she'd be really flattered that I decided to become a nun because of her. I would be carrying on the family tradition, so it wouldn't just be about the whole name thing.

When the airmen completed their patrol, they would pass by our cul-de-sac again. At least I could catch a glimpse of Magoo every evening when they made their rounds, and occasionally, he might hop off the truck and visit us.

I was deep in the reverie of imagining myself a nun–holy and self-sacrificing, a blessing to mankind–when the airmen drove by our street at the end of their patrol. Suddenly, Mr. Magoo jumped out of the truck and ran back to our yard, and for the next two and a half years, the routine never varied.

"He's a boxer," said Daddy, who had taken him to the vet on base to make sure he got his shots. "And the vet thinks he's a full breed, but who knows? No one knows where he came from; he just showed up one day."

"Why did the airmen name him Mr. Magoo, Daddy?"

"They said he just looked sort of goofy–and lost. Just like the myopic Mr. Magoo in the Sunday funnies," said my father with a big grin on his face.

That's guys for you. I'd have named him something wonderful, like Rex or King. Or Archie if we were going with a comic book figure. Daddy said I couldn't change his name, though, because he was a dog and knew that his name was Magoo, and it wouldn't be fair to change it now that he'd learned to answer to it. So he was stuck with Mr. Magoo, like an old cartoon character, and I was stuck with Vivienne, like an old actress.

Worse even than my name was my hair. Neither Linda nor I looked anything like Betty or Veronica, which we sort of understood, but we held not a shred of likeness to the Toni Twins either. The perms my mother had given us made us look like mousy brown-haired Little Orphan Annies. I hoped our hair wasn't ruined forever. Of course, the solution, I reassured Linda, was simple: I had made my mind up to become a nun, and the head coverings they wore as part of their uniforms—I thought they were called veils—covered all their hair. That was because, said Grandma Grilliot, nuns couldn't show any part of their bodies, not even their hair. That would have been immodest, and they couldn't look attractive ever. Only their faces and their hands could show. "You should think about that line of work too," I told Linda.

Weeks turned into months, and the days that filled those months seemed to me, when I tried to commit everything to memory, to be like shards of glass in the kaleidoscope I had gotten in my Christmas stocking. Bright with promise, they briefly lit up my life with possibilities, but then they were gone before I was able to even grasp their potential. In January 1959, my mother had another baby, a girl, and she and my father named her Christine Jean—another cute American name, in my opinion. She was a happy baby. She hardly ever cried, had curly dark hair, and smiled constantly.

Except for a few newsworthy events, fifth grade was so unmemorable that by the following year, I couldn't even remember the teacher's name. She was plump and jolly—could have been Mrs. Santa—but failed to promote either a passion for learning anything or a yearning for school holidays. I didn't even remember if we had holiday parties attended by room mothers. In any case, my mother was pregnant for the first half of the year and too busy with a new baby during the last half to even think about being a room mother again.

French and arithmetic were still a challenge; Bob, Linda, and I were still best friends; and Linda and I were Girl Scouts. Our dreadful perms grew out in less time than either of us had imagined they would, and by Thanksgiving, our hair was back to normal. Discussion between us of joining a convent had fizzled and finally been dismissed completely. Linda had no desire to become Catholic, and I had developed a crush on Uri Sagget, which seemed, even to a fifth grader, to create an obstacle to becoming a nun. Beyond that, America had grown; we had two brand-new States. In January 1959, President Eisenhower announced that the Alaska Territory had become our forty-ninth state, and in August, the Hawaiian Islands became our fiftieth.

On a sunny day in September, with another summer of baseball and Chinese checkers behind us, shortly after Bob, Linda, and I started sixth grade, the principal held a school-wide special assembly in the auditorium. The purpose was to exchange our old flag for our new one. I thought it was amazing that Betsy Ross not only had been a talented seamstress but also had had such insight. To have anticipated that America would expand all the way from New England to the West Coast, from the Canadian border in the north, and south to the Mexican border might have been a common assumption by the founding fathers, but to have designed a flag that would be ever changing in recognition of each newly added state? Well, I thought that was simply brilliant!

When we stood and said the Pledge of Allegiance to our new flag, my heart was bursting, and I had tears in my eyes. I was so proud to be American! And just as we reached the end—"with liberty and justice for all"—a fighter jet flying over the base broke the sound barrier! It was a perfect ending. Nothing in the whole world was better than being an air force brat. Absolutely nothing.

That night, I rummaged through Dad's stack of *Stars and Stripes* newspapers until I found the recent one that had announced we would be getting a new flag since acquiring two new states. If I ever got married and had children—since I wasn't becoming a nun—I wanted my children to be able read about that amazing day.

Fourteen

THE FIRST DAY OF THE NEW SCHOOL YEAR SMELLED JUST LIKE every other first day of school I'd ever attended: blackboards, chalk, books, and freshly polished floors. Nothing else smelled quite like a school, and the next nine months would never smell quite like the first day of the new school year.

The sixth-grade class was made up of most of the same kids from last year's fifth grade, plus half a dozen new students. Our teacher was Mrs. Brookstone, and she was young and pretty. She would teach all our subjects except French and physical education. At 11:00 a.m., Mrs. Brookstone dismissed us to go to the gym, where we met our new PE teacher. Mr. Parker was a disappointment; we had assumed we would be getting Mr. Jones again.

Mr. Parker seemed old; he looked at least as old as my dad, who was thirty. Last year's PE teacher, Mr. Jones, had looked exactly like Ricky Nelson and had just graduated from college. All the girls had had a crush on him. It was third period, and we sixth graders sat on the bleachers as Ricky Nelson's replacement introduced himself. He began by telling us about his plans to teach us all tumbling and said there would be a change from the usual physical education curriculum at Phalsbourg Elementary: we would not be doing one sport per term but learning gymnastics throughout the school year.

"Think of basketball, baseball, volleyball, and bowling as occasional rewards—when we participate in them—for acquiring and perfecting your skills in gymnastics."

Linda and I looked at each other and rolled our eyes.

"You are perfectly designed machines, and other than perhaps swimming, no other sport uses every part of your body like gymnastics. You will be fine-tuning your small and large motor skills, exercising your brains, and developing physical precision as you never have before."

It sounded to me like it was going to be hard work—and not nearly as much fun as baseball or bowling. Still, if it meant we weren't going to have to play volleyball, I would keep an open mind—I was pretty sure not getting smashed in the face with a spiked ball would be a welcome relief to all of us short people.

Mr. Parker ended the class by putting us through a series of exercises and then dismissed us as the bell rang for lunch.

"What's gymnastics?" I asked Linda and Bob as we walked to the cafeteria after leaving the gym.

"I think it's like tumbling and stuff," answered Linda.

Cafeteria was a euphemism for a large room with folding chairs and long Formica tables. There was no real kitchen, just a back counter with a commercial-sized coffeepot for when the school had PTA meetings and such, and we students all had to bring our lunches from home. That year, I'd decided I was too old for my Dale Evans lunch box, and I had given it to Connie to play with. I'd picked out a red plaid one, which I thought was much more appropriate for someone who would be starting junior high next year. Bob always brought his lunch in a brown paper bag—he said unless he could find the kind of metal lunch box that construction workers used, he wouldn't be caught dead with a little square tin box, even if it didn't have cartoon characters on it. We three sat at one of the tables and took a few minutes to see what our mothers had packed. I had an egg salad sandwich, which was fine, but ugh, peanut butter cookies! Mom knew I hated peanut butter!

"I'll trade," said Linda. "I love peanut butter anything. Here—take my Moon Pie."

Bob never cared what his mom packed; he would eat almost anything.

"I'm pretty sure gymnastics is a lot like tumbling," said Bob. "If it is, I'll do my best, but I'm not that flexible. I'm a really good tackle, but that just means I'm fast and have good upper-body strength. I'll try anything, though, as long as he doesn't make me wear tights."

Bob was now six feet tall—he had grown even more during the summer—and he loved playing football. He usually played with the boys in the junior high because he was so much bigger than any of the fifth and sixth graders. Plus, the only football played in the grade school was flag football, and I thought that must have been to football what T-ball was to baseball. On the contrary, Linda and I were the two smallest girls in our class: we both weighed about seventy pounds and were barely five feet tall. I was pretty sure we made a funny-looking trio.

I was not sure how Mr. Parker managed it, but about two months into the school year—just before Halloween—I was on a mat in the gym and did two somersaults. Except for being a pretty good shortstop, I had no real athletic ability, the hula hoop notwithstanding. Really, my dad was right: the hula hoop could not be considered—at least at my level—a sport. But those two somersaults gave me the same sort of feeling I got when I caught a low fly ball and shot it to second base to make a double play.

Linda and I thought gymnastics turned out to be a lot more fun than what we thought of as *real sports*. Even Bob agreed. Just before Christmas break, Mr. Parker told us that we sixth graders were going to be training to make a human pyramid next semester, which would be the grand finale in the gymnastics exhibition he had planned for the end of the school year.

When I told my parents at dinner, my father said, "Hmm, you sound quite excited. Aren't you the girl who complained about how terrible you thought physical education was going to be this year?"

"Well, I didn't really know what gymnastics was then, did I? But obviously, I was wrong."

I noticed my mother give my father her "Now, Robert, don't start anything" look. Dad loved to challenge me about everything.

Soon enough, it was December 18, and my classmates and I were in high spirits as we rode the school bus home. That day began our Christmas vacation, and we wouldn't be returning to school until January 4. There would be no arithmetic and, if my prayers to the Virgin were answered, no French lessons for three whole weeks—as long as I made myself scarce and Dad didn't get it in his head that I should work on my worst subjects during the break. Even my father, though, wouldn't make me study that weekend, I knew, because we were going to do the most exciting thing I had ever done: we were going up on a mountain to cut down our own Christmas tree—just like Laura and Pa in *Little House on the Prairie*.

I was so excited that when I got up the next morning, I could hardly eat.

"Eat that Cream of Wheat, young lady!" said my mother. "It's below freezing out there, and you'll need something to stick to your ribs when you're up on that mountain."

"How will Cream of Wheat get outside my stomach in order to stick to my ribs? I think that's physically impossible!"

"Eat," she said, and I didn't challenge her this time, because I never knew with Mom. I feared she might punish me for having a smart mouth by making me stay home and dust.

The Martins lived next door to us. Tanya, the mom, and her husband, Terry, had two little kids: Mimi, who was three, and Joe-Joe, who was one. Sergeant Martin was going with us. The men figured it might take two of them to cut a tree down and strap it to the top of our Opel station wagon, and they were planning to get one each. I was in charge of picking the two best trees.

There was barely an inch of snow on the ground as we left the housing area. We drove toward Luxembourg, and the flatter cobbled streets of Sarrebourg soon gave way to gradual elevations. The snowdrifts got deeper the higher we climbed. Dad had the address of a farmer who charged a fee and allowed people to cut down their own Christmas trees in his forest. We arrived in less than an hour, and Dad and Sergeant Martin each paid fifty cents, which gave them permission to cut one tree each on the honor system. We parked the car close to the tree line and began walking around the evergreens. So deep was the snow and so frigid was the air that within ten minutes, we were chilled to the bone.

"How about this one, Viv?" asked my father.

"Mommy won't like that one: there's two bare spots right here and here, so there would be no good way to position it to hide them." Even though it was going in a corner of the living room, I could tell at least one bare spot would show somewhere.

"Oh," said Dad. "Well, here–this looks like a better one!"

"Daddy! Look how crooked the top is! The treetop ornament with the tassel that Mom loves will never fit over that!" I realized that was why I was there: apart from the fact that my mother knew I would love an outing, she also knew I would not let my father settle for a less-than-perfect tree.

Soon we couldn't feel our feet, and we hadn't found one tree that was acceptable, let alone two.

"Hey, Bob," said Sergeant Martin, "I think this one will do for me!"

I looked at the tree he was walking around and said, "Sergeant Martin, Tanya said she wanted a fir tree, just like Mom. Look how long those needles are, and they look kind of fluffy. I don't think it's a fir, and I don't think the lights or the ornaments will show very much. They'll kind of get hidden."

Sergeant Martin and Dad looked at each other and seemed to take a deep breath.

"OK, Viv, let's get serious here," said my father. "It is bloody freezing up here, and I now can't feel my fingers, let alone my toes. There may not be a perfect tree. Let's just do the best we can."

I could not believe what I was hearing. My father was telling me to settle for less than the best, something he had never suggested before. I was not sure how that would equate to French lessons, but I filed it away for possible future ammunition.

"Dad," I said, "I'm perfectly OK with a not-perfect tree. If you can explain that to Mom, just cut down the next tree you think will do."

He cut down the next tree he thought would do. He shook the snow off and tapped the trunk on the ground, and I was positive it was the most pathetic-looking Christmas tree on the mountain. I said nothing, but my father shook his head, shrugged, and clearly recognized it would never do.

"Daddy! You cannot stand a cut-down tree back up and pack it with snow so it looks like it hasn't been cut!"

"Well, Vivienne, I see now that this tree is the worst one in the whole forest, and your mother will be beside herself if I bring it home. She will think I did it on purpose. And," he said, leaning down and narrowing his eyes at me, "Mom will blame you for not doing your job! Did you think of that?"

Adopting my mother's mannerisms, because I thought that might be the perfect time to be British, I said, "Quite right, Father! However, there is no need to try to prop it up; just give the farmer another fifty cents when we leave, and it won't matter a whit!"

Finally, forty-five minutes later, we had two lovely Christmas trees. I thought Sergeant Martin might just buy his next year, though. He, like my father, would have taken any old tree toward the end of our search, and I was glad I had come along to make sure Mom and Tanya were not disappointed. As we drove down the hill, the old man was sitting by the gate–probably to check our bounty. He lifted a hand in a farewell wave, and I quickly leaned across the back of the front seat.

"Daddy! Don't forget to give him another fifty cents for the wasted tree!"

My father stopped the car, got out, and handed the man more money. The man looked confused, and I could tell he didn't understand what my father was saying. I rolled down my window and explained: *"Nous avons coupé un sapin de Noel,* um, *que nous n'aimions pas. Desole!"*

I wasn't sure I had explained correctly, but he nodded, smiled, and accepted the money my father was offering.

"Joyeux Noel!" I called as we pulled away.

I felt relieved that we had not stolen from the old man. I did think briefly that it might be a nice change to have a serious sin to confess next Saturday–thievery could not possibly have been considered venial–but as I was pretty sure Father Enright recognized my voice, and I knew I would end up feeling awkward the next time he came to breakfast at our house. He probably even knew I was the one who confessed about sneaking into the closet to read after my parents went to bed.

I was frozen to the bone. Daddy had the heater in the car turned all the way up, and as we drove down the mountain, he pulled the car into the first parking lot he saw that was attached to a pub. *Les Bistrot,* the sign said.

Inside, the warmth from a huge fireplace with crackling logs flowed over me like a wave. There were wooden tables and benches, and there were pots and pans hanging from the timbered ceiling. We sat down, and a pretty young woman in a frilly apron came over and took our order. The menu was simple enough that I was able to translate, and I told Dad and Sergeant Martin that there were two soups and a chicken casserole being served for lunch. We each ordered French onion soup. I was not sure why I did, because I had never had onion soup before. Neither my mother nor Nanna had ever made it. Daddy said he'd never had it either, but it sounded French enough that the best place to try it for the first time was a French pub, he thought. It was delicious, and the crusty bread that the pretty mademoiselle served us was hot from the oven. My toes and fingers were tingling from the fireplace heat, and just as I started to feel drowsy from the delicious food and the warmth of the fire, my father said we had better go before I fell asleep.

"Daddy," I asked when we were back in the car, "can we decorate the tree today?" Next to going to England to visit Nanna and

Granddad or moving to a new base, nothing was better than the beginning of the Christmas season.

"That," he answered, "is entirely up to your mother."

The tree was so perfect that Daddy rearranged the living room furniture so the tree could go in front of the picture window, and we decorated the tree that night. My father strung the lights–which were fat bulbs of different colors–on the branches, and Mom and I hung the ornaments, some of which were from my first Christmas in America. Mom's favorite tree-decorating thing every year was the silver tinsel. She called the strands icicles.

"Vivienne! One at a time! You're putting it on in clumps!" My mother could be fussy about details. "That's much better, love," she said as I painstakingly picked one long silver strand from another and looped them over the tips of the branches.

Nanna had read my tea leaves once. She'd said I had no patience. She'd shown me the pattern on the bottom of the saucer after she tipped over my cup to spill the dregs.

"See that short crescent pattern that leads the leaves to the dead-end edge of the saucer? It means you have no patience, my love. Not a whit."

I reminded Mom that it wasn't my fault. "Ask Nanna; she'll tell you."

We put on our coats and filed outside to judge the tree and to make sure it passed muster. I thought it was the most beautiful Christmas tree we had ever had.

"If we're here next year, can we go back and cut down our own Christmas tree again?" I asked.

"Sure," my father said, grinning, "as long as you can order a three-course lunch in fluent French using complex sentences."

He just never stopped.

Fifteen

Christmas Eve finally arrived. Throughout the day, Mom had been busy with last-minute preparations. She always started Christmas Day dinner early in the day on Christmas Eve because, she said, eighteen-pound turkeys stuffed with sage-seasoned bread and vegetables took a long time to cook. If the turkey didn't cook for hours, we might get sick, and as dire as she made it sound, I certainly did not want to die of undercooked turkey. Now I was waiting for my parents to finish getting ready for church.

We always went to Midnight Mass on Christmas Eve. Except for the Christmas on Fulton Street when Johnny had been sick, my parents had made this a Christmas tradition. This year, as in every other, the presents were wrapped; the tree, with all its lights and ornaments, was decorated and beautiful; and the turkey was being kept warm in the oven, because Daddy and I always had a turkey sandwich after Midnight Mass.

I thought of last Christmas Eve; I remembered it clearly. I had knelt right there at the picture window next to the Christmas tree and watched the first snow of the season fall in big, fluffy flakes.

"Mommy," I had asked, "wouldn't it be just magical if our new baby was born at midnight? Well, I mean just after we get home from Midnight Mass–I wouldn't want it born in the church, of course. But just think: a baby born on the same day as Jesus!"

"This baby is not due until the beginning of the second week of January. Christmas will be over and done with; you will be back in school; and with any luck, the runways will be clear, because all of us women who are expecting will be flown to Wiesbaden at the beginning of the week when our babies are due." I had forgotten that.

Had it been a whole year already? A year since what I thought of as the Christmas of the Midnight Mass with Connie. Mom had put Connie down for a nap after dinner last Christmas Eve and had wakened her at ten o'clock to get her dressed in her new dress and her little velvet coat and bonnet. She'd worn patent-leather shoes and white socks edged in frilly lace–she'd looked adorable–and we'd arrived at the church early to get a good seat. Connie had been fine for exactly four minutes and then had begun squirming.

"Sh," Mom had said. "Here–have an animal cracker, and sit still like a good girl."

That had lasted about three minutes.

Connie had stood down on the floor and tried to squeeze around me to get to the aisle. I'd lifted her back up onto the seat between Mom and me. She had turned around, backed down off the seat, and stood on the kneeler, accidentally pulling off the mantilla of the lady sitting in front of us. That had caused a little bustle of annoyed activity. Finally, she'd rested her chin on the back of the pew, which had made me nervous because with one wrong move, she'd pull the lady's mantilla off again. We should have found a seat behind a lady wearing a hat. Connie's view still had been limited, so she'd turned back around and climbed up onto the seat of our pew. Standing up, she'd looked all around, taking in the whole congregation.

The altar boys had gathered at the entrance doors, waiting for Father Enright to signal the start of the procession. I could smell the incense contained in the brass orb, called a censer, that hung from the chain Father held. Before he started Mass, Father would walk around the church perimeter, swinging the censer back and forth. It was called benediction, and I had wondered whether the incense was to rid the church of evil spirits or to make the church and all the parishioners holier somehow. I'd made a mental note to ask Father the next time he came to breakfast.

Midnight Mass was always High Mass–which took a lot longer than regular Mass–and I had been able to tell that my little sister was going to be a real problem. The organist had announced which Christmas hymns we would sing, and he'd said when Father gave the sign, we would start with "Silent Night." Until then, he had just been playing quiet music that sounded really holy.

Connie had remained standing up on the seat in the pew. While looking from left to right and front to back, she suddenly had said in a loud, clear, annoyed voice, "Hey! When is this darn movie going to start anyway?"

Because of that and because now we had another sister, Marie had come to spend Christmas Eve with us. Mom said she couldn't imagine coping with an infant and Connie at Midnight Mass. I felt relieved because recently, I couldn't stand to have any attention focused on us at church. I couldn't say when I first had noticed I felt that way, but of late, I'd been hurrying my father up on Sundays, saying, "Let's get there early, please, Daddy!" Since Chrissy had been born, Mom only came to church if Marie could come on a Sunday morning to babysit, which wasn't every Sunday.

In any case, I found I hated arriving just before Mass started, when the church was already full. If we didn't get there early, the only seats left were front and center, which meant having to walk up the middle aisle, looking to see where we could squeeze in. Christmas Eve was my favorite Mass of the entire year, although Father Enright said Easter was the holiest, and I was looking forward to it. It was the true beginning of Christmas, as I thought of it, and I always wondered exactly what time Jesus had been born.

Usually, I was allowed to open one gift on Christmas Eve–which was then Christmas morning–after we got home from Mass, and Dad was in his element, eating his turkey sandwich. He always said a hot turkey sandwich with stuffing and cranberry sauce on Christmas Eve was almost better than Christmas dinner the next day.

This night, though, as we were waiting for Dad to finish shaving, Mom told me to reach under the tree and find the little square box with my name on it.

"Go ahead," she said with a smile. "Open it."

Inside, I found a lovely silver bracelet with ten bells of different shapes and styles dangling from the links. The lettering on the box said *Sarah Coventry*, and it was the most beautiful bracelet I had ever seen.

"Oh, Mommy, thank you! I love it! Here–help me put it on! It's beautiful!"

I was bubbling over with excitement because other than a little cross and chain that Nanna had given me, I was never allowed to wear jewelry. I had gotten pop beads to make toy necklaces and bracelets the Christmas before last, but that didn't count. My mother always said, "Lipstick and jewelry are for big girls–you'll get there soon enough."

We arrived at church early enough to get a seat in a middle pew and just off the center aisle, and I gave a little wave to two classmates sitting nearby. Soon it was packed. We watched the preparations as the altar boys lit the candles and set up the table just next to the altar for the ritual hand washing that represented Caesar washing his hands of his guilt when the crowd kept calling for Barabbas to be freed instead of Jesus. Once, when we had been really early for Sunday Mass, Father Enright had motioned for me to come up to the altar. He had shown me how to prepare it for Mass and said, "There is no reason we can't have altar girls." I didn't think that would be a good fit for me: if Father had even more opportunity to be around me, I had no doubt he would definitely be able to identify me in confession, even if I tried to disguise my voice. I thought confession was already awkward enough–not exactly the bane of my existence but close enough.

Midnight Mass began. The altar boys walked ahead of Father up the aisle from the entrance of the church to the front, where the communion rail bordered the altar steps. The first boy carried the cross, and the next boy carried the Bible. Father carried the incense orb, swinging it gently back and forth on its chain. As he passed the pews, we congregants all stood and made the sign of the cross. Throughout the mass, when the altar boys rang the bells, we would kneel and strike our breasts in reverence. It was High Mass, so there would be lots of kneeling and breast striking.

Once Mass started, I had a hard time staying awake. Midnight Mass at Christmas was usually packed with people, and that night, within a short time, the church was uncomfortably hot. The ushers opened the doors to let in the frigid air, but that only helped a bit. I dozed, and then I woke to Mom shaking my shoulder. We stood for the gospel; it was Luke, of course. Then we sat for the sermon. I tried to concentrate, but I couldn't stop looking at my bracelet–it really was beautiful. Soon the most important part of the mass began: the preparation of the gifts, which was a reenactment of the Last Supper. The altar boys rang the bells, and we knelt. Then we were standing, but then the bells rang again, and half the people around us immediately knelt. We were up, we were down, and then we were down when we were supposed to be up, which I attributed to the late hour and people getting so sleepy they got confused. Again, the bells rang and people in the front rows knelt. I was pretty sure we should have been standing. Sensing something going on in the congregation, Father Enright turned to face us, took a quick glance around, and motioned for those who were kneeling to join those who were standing. People were looking around; they were confused. Congregants on the opposite side of the church and those in the back looked perplexed. We all stood, and the bells rang again–but now the altar boys looked confused too. One of them looked at Father and shrugged as though to say, "I'm not ringing the bell, Father."

Suddenly, Mom grabbed my arm, and I became fully awake. "Take the bracelet off!" she hissed. "Right now–be quick!"

I struggled with the latch on the bracelet. It finally opened, I slipped it off, and Mom put it in her purse.

Father Enright turned and looked at us. "Angels from on high, Mrs. Grilliot?" asked Father. "Heralding the birth of the Christ child? Most fitting for this mass, I'd say."

I realized what had happened, and I was mortified with embarrassment. I didn't want to go up for communion and kneel at the altar, but Mom gave me a gentle push, so I had no choice. This had become the longest mass of my life.

As soon as Mass was over, I tugged at Daddy's sleeve and pulled him toward the church's side door. He didn't resist. At least I would not have to face Father Enright that night.

Later, when Mom fixed Daddy and me turkey sandwiches, she told me I could open one more gift. I shook my head. I had no appetite and didn't want to open another gift.

"It was entirely my fault," said Mom. "I didn't even think when I had you open it before Mass. Now, stop worrying, and don't let it spoil your Christmas!"

On the next Sunday, which was between Christmas and New Year's, Father Enright came to breakfast after church, as occasionally was his custom with the Catholic families on the base. He always said breaking bread with his parishioners was the best way to tend his flock. Being the eldest sibling and, therefore, always feeling the burden of needing to step up to apologize, explain, or face the consequences of any mishap, I felt I had to clear the air.

"I'm sorry about Midnight Mass, Father," I said.

"And just what would you be apologizing for, Vivienne?"

"The bell-ringing that confused everyone, Father. It was my new bracelet I'd gotten as a Christmas present, which has bells on it. But I was so sleepy I didn't realize I was causing such confusion."

Father smiled. "Do you know, child, sometimes the most interesting things in life can be those in which a wrench has been thrown into the midst of an ordinary occurrence? Now, I'll tell you something: Midnight Mass is a quandary for some people. They like the pageantry, but they seldom prepare properly for the solemnity of the event. They have everything but the nativity of the Christ child on their mind. They wonder if they've chosen the right present for Aunt Matilda or whether they overlooked sending some special person a Christmas card. They worry about Christmas dinner being as perfect as it's portrayed in the ladies' magazines. And though the

ladies seldom doze off, I've noticed a growing trend among the men."
Did I imagine he took a quick look at my father? "I'll even go so far
as to say I've noticed more than a few people lately who only come
to church on Christmas and Easter, so clearly, they are missing the
point of regularly attending mass."

He shook his head and made a tsk-tsk sound. "But Christmas
Eve, when I looked out at my flock during the preparation of
the gifts–which is the holiest part of the mass, as you learned in
catechism–everyone was either wondering where the tinkling of bells
was coming from or, if sitting in the back of the church, wondering
why on earth the people in the front were up and down and very
obviously confused. But I did not see one person who was not fully
awake. God indeed works in mysterious ways, my dear." He gave me
a hug and said, "Now, go get that bracelet so I can see what all the
commotion was about!"

The days after Christmas, for me, were always a letdown. It
seemed as though the excitement generated by the anticipation of the
event was never able to be sustained beyond the event itself. I never felt
that way about any of the other holidays that merited a circling of the
date on the calendar Mom kept on the kitchen wall: Valentine's Day,
Saint Patrick's Day, Easter, July Fourth, Halloween, Thanksgiving.
They came, and they went. They fulfilled our expectations with no
disappointment, no morning-after feelings of regret, and no feelings
of wishing it hadn't ended so soon or differently. Christmas, though,
was the exception. So thoroughly did anticipation of the best holiday
of the year saturate every fiber of my friends' and my beings that it
was bound to leave a morning-after void: a hard-to-define, vague
dissatisfaction. I'd tried to explain the feeling to Mom last year.
She'd said it was called an anticlimax and told me to wait until I
was married with children–I'd be glad enough to see the end of
Christmas so I could put my feet up.

This year, though, I didn't have time for vague feelings of
anything; I couldn't wait to get back to school and find out what a
human pyramid was! The night before school started again, I packed
my lunch, wiped out my book bag, tidied up my spiral notebooks and

got rid of pages full of scribbling, and even polished my saddle shoes—and not just the white parts but the black parts too. That task usually prompted my military father to threaten to withhold my allowance if I didn't stop procrastinating. Finally, I fell into bed, too tired, for once, to stay awake so that I could sneak into my closet and read after everyone else was asleep. I dreamed I was a circus performer—one who specialized in somersaults.

Linda and Bob must have been as excited as I was, because when I got to the bus stop ten minutes early the next morning, they were already there. We chatted excitedly about Mr. Parker and gym class, about how much fun physical education was this year, about the grand finale, and about how excited we were that we were going to perform in front of our parents. I even thought my father might decide that math and French weren't really that important if I was going to be a gymnast.

"You are amazing!" Mr. Parker shouted as we assembled in the gym. "I have been teaching gymnastics for fifteen years, and I have never had a more talented, enthused, and brilliant group of students than Phalsbourg Elementary's sixth-grade class!"

For the next three and a half months, we would practice three days a week until every student was proficient in whichever tumbling or gymnastics role he or she had been assigned, however great or small the assignment. The school weeks revolved around gym class, at least for my friends and me, even as our weekends remained filled with homework assignments, as usual. Between those assignments, our comic book trading, baseball games, and Chinese checkers thrived. Valentine's Day, Saint Patrick's Day, and Easter were welcome interludes, as usual, in the tedium of academic life, but they held little of the enticement my friends and I had felt in previous years. Our minds were filled with visions of our awesome talents, our superhuman feats. I didn't realize then—I didn't think any of us did—that as amazing as Mr. Parker credited us with being, the self-confidence he instilled went far beyond our physical achievements and lasted years beyond the sixth grade.

We were bursting with pride. Bob and I thought the *Stars and Stripes* newspaper might even cover the event. Mostly, we were astonished that in less than eight months, our new physical education teacher had trained us to do things we'd had no idea our bodies could do.

We were going to do, as the grand finale to the Phalsbourg Elementary School gymnastics show, a tumbling act that would make our parents think we were good enough to join the Wallendas. Mr. Parker said so. There would be backflips and cartwheels, forward and backward rolls, handstands, kick-overs, and something called bridges. The maneuvers had been taught to all the students from first through sixth grade, according to each child's ability, but the pyramid–performed by the sixth-grade class–would be the grand finale. Twelve students would first form the base of three rows of four students each–for strength–and then fewer students would form subsequent levels. As the smallest girl–by a slight margin–I would run toward the pyramid at top speed from the far end of the stage, to be flipped first by Tommy in the front row upward to the next level and then the next, until I was standing on Bob's shoulders as the single gymnast on a pyramid four students high.

The auditorium was packed. I thought every parent of every student must have been there. We had all lived through the challenges of being children of parents who were in the military. We knew that because of work schedules, travel, and temporary duty to other parts of the world, parents were not always able to attend special events and school functions. But every one of the parents who could be there was there.

My mother was not there. She had not actually said whether she would or would not attend, and I honestly hadn't thought to ask, because I had talked of nothing else after school every day since March. But peeping from behind the curtain before the event started, I saw only my father. He was chatting with friends, and then he took a seat by himself.

The hour-long show finally started, and the performance of everyone from the first through the sixth grades was brilliant. I stood off to the side during certain parts of the show, in awe of what Mr. Parker had achieved during the school year. I pondered the fact that my mother had chosen not to attend. I knew if I asked, she would say she hadn't had a babysitter, and it would be easy for me to challenge her: "Marie is always available when you go to bingo or a floor show at the NCO club, and you've known about this since Easter or longer." But I forced myself to think beyond my disappointment.

That night, I realized, even if I didn't then know the word, that I judged everything by a certain perspective, and I also realized I had been doing so for a long time. I assessed everything that seemed to be a challenge and compared all disappointments, failures, and hurts to how significant they were compared to the death of my beloved brother. That, for me, was a reliable measure and one that served me well. It seemed to me to be a reasonable way to deal with the curveballs I had found to be inevitable in life.

In the end, I did not rail at my mother for not attending, nor did I placate her by telling her I knew she couldn't possibly have come, having two little ones at home. I simply accepted the fact that she had not made it a priority. Furthermore, I realized again that regardless of her attitude toward education–gymnastics included–my mother loved me unconditionally, but it was my father I wanted to shine for, and he had been there.

The *Stars and Stripes* did not cover the greatest gymnastics show ever performed at Phalsbourg Air Force Base Elementary School.

Bob and I agreed: they missed a brilliant performance.

Sixteen

T HE BEAUTY OF SUMMERTIME IN FRANCE NEVER CEASED TO amaze me. The days were brilliant with sunshine, and the inky nights were radiant with starlight. It rained but seldom like in England, where sometimes the damp and gloom, even in summertime, lasted for weeks on end. It was to be our last summer there, and I wanted to let everything about it soak into me, so I'd remember it forever. It was also to be the summer of our last trip to England to visit Nanna and Granddad–at least our last trip for a while. It was anyone's guess, said Dad, if we would ever get transferred overseas again. Some military personnel, he said, never got stationed out of the United States, and we'd been lucky, he pointed out, because this was his second tour of duty in Europe.

It was another summer of baseball, Chinese checkers, and comic books. Bob, Linda, and I gathered frequently with our French friends on the playground to play soccer and hide-and-seek. Now our parents felt we were old enough to catch the base bus that came daily to our housing area, and several times a week we went to the base and either bowled or saw an afternoon movie.

I spent most of the month of July in England, and I ate as much Cadbury chocolate, Grimwood's ice cream, and Yorkshire pudding as I could. I realized it might be a long time before I saw Nanna and Granddad again, so I spent countless hours with them: going to the top shops with my grandmother; playing draughts and dominos with my grandfather; and spending evenings gazing into the back garden at twilight, pretending that there really were such things as fairies and secretly hoping that number 7 really was haunted.

Also, during that visit to England, I reconnected with a friend of mine from infant school–that famous third year I later had had to start over at Saint Mary's in Muncie.

Ina Davenport and I had somehow discovered each other again on my final visit to Flixton for a while. Her father had a motorcycle with a sidecar, and nothing was more thrilling than riding in a sidecar while flying down narrow, winding English country roads where the hedges were so tall we couldn't see anything in front of us. My father had not accompanied us that summer, and I was sure if he had, the thrill of riding in that sidecar would have been an unrequited longing.

Almost as thrilling–but not quite–was the scheme Ina and I concocted to explore the ruins of an Anglican church that had been bombed in the war but never demolished. In Britain, as in France, the scars of war were still evident. My mother complained every time we went to Germany that the Allies had had no problem pumping money into that country to rebuild it.

Ina and I were sure there must have been artifacts of some sort under the existing rubble of the church. To enter what was left of the lower part of the building, we had to go down a set of steps that led to what must have been a basement at one time. If we stood at the top of those steps, we were eye level with the church's altar, which was now open to the elements. How it had not also crumbled into ruin we had no idea. In any case, we were sure we would uncover something of great interest–perhaps a relic that the BBC would want to interview us about.

We bought tiny flashlights, notepads, and magnifying glasses with our spends, hoping those items would enhance our abilities as investigative journalists. How my grandfather found out what we were scheming was perplexing; we had gone to great lengths to avoid any activity that would raise suspicion. However, in no uncertain terms, Granddad forbade us to go onto the church's property again, which was near his pub, the Garrick. Ina thought he had probably seen us while he was going for a pint. Still, we had spent hours both exploring the ruins and enjoying the anticipation of being involved in what we thought could be considered World War II espionage.

Like my previous years' visits to England, this one was over much too quickly—and I realized it would be a long time before I would again help Nanna in the kitchen or sit curled at Granddad's feet while we watched the telly together, if ever.

Despite my intention to savor every second of our last summer in France, it seemed as though it was over before it even had a chance to bloom. Like runaway film on our eight-millimeter projector, it sped by, leaving behind blurred glimpses of memories that settled into their own frames for eternity.

It was the beginning of the seventh grade and my last school year in France. I had finally, to a degree that satisfied my father, conquered math—multiplication and long division. French remained my single greatest challenge academically. Our cleaning lady and babysitter, Marguerite, had moved to another town to live with her daughter and take care of her grandchildren in the summer between my fifth- and sixth-grade years; since then, we'd had Marie, who was more German than French. Even though she spoke more fluent English than Marguerite did, her French was practically nonexistent. She was no help whatsoever with my lessons; in fact, my French, such as it was, was better than Marie's.

Interestingly, I found I could now communicate quite easily with the French children from the village, but alas, that did not translate to any level of academic fluency. Linda said she couldn't learn any of it, period. Her parents had told her it didn't matter. "We won't be in France forever," they had said. Bob took it all in stride—I thought his brain was better at learning a foreign language than mine was. Or maybe he was just a better test taker. In any case, French was an albatross around my neck.

I'd learned what an albatross was because Mom had read a long poem during the summer while we were in England called *The Rhyme of the Ancient Mariner*. She had found one of her old poetry

118

books from school on Nanna's bookshelf and told me she thought I'd like it, as it was quite exciting. She was right—it was. Now everything I found challenging or annoying became an albatross around my neck, and French was at the top of the list.

"If you use that term one more time," said Mom crossly, "I'll hang something around your neck, young lady! That will teach me to encourage you to read above your grade level!"

I loved to read. At night, I still read sometimes into the wee hours. I was amazed that my parents still didn't know I had a flashlight hidden in my closet! I had read everything I could find that interested me, including all the Nancy Drew, Hardy Boys, and Trixie Belden series. I also had read an interesting book called *Sue Barton, Student Nurse*. In the book, Sue was a student in nursing school, and not one time did the story mention that any of the nursing students needed to know French. Why would they have? They were going to be American nurses. But I found it most important that Sue never mentioned needing math. The students just had to learn how to measure medicines and give shots. I'd been learning to cook for years now, and I imagined measuring medicine wasn't much different from measuring flour, sugar, or anything else for a recipe. There were other books in the series, but they were all checked out on my class's library day. Mrs. Decker, our library teacher, said she would put aside the next one for me when it was returned. Maybe I would think about being a nurse when I grew up—I'd decide after I read at least one or two more Sue Barton books. Lately, though, I had been more interested in different kinds of books. Somehow, the series books seemed a bit juvenile. It was hard to explain, but right now, my favorite book was *Wuthering Heights*; it was just delicious.

"How can you read it?" asked Linda. "It's so awkward the way they talk and everything."

"I don't think it's awkward; I think it's exciting! Being far out on the desolate, cold, and rainy moor and knowing something is going on but not knowing exactly what! And," I said as I put a hand over my heart, "Cathy and Heathcliff are the epitome of star-crossed lovers!"

I found I was more than a little impressed with the three Brontë sisters. How was it possible they all had become famous authors? That was almost too coincidental. "In fact," I said to Mom, "I wouldn't be surprised if it was just one sister using different names—that's called using a pseudonym." But my mother rejected that premise.

"Indeed, there *were* three sisters. And it is not at all coincidental that they all became published writers," said my mother, who was ironing, "because *they* were not flighty at all."

She paused long enough to let the implication sink in and to wet her finger and touch it to the iron to make the spit sizzle. That told her it was hot enough—Nanna did the same thing. Then she continued. "They all did their homework without complaining, they did not contradict their mother at every turn, and they studied their French—even though it was difficult, and they struggled with it—until they got passing marks."

"Mother, I read in the 'About the Author' section at the back of the book that their mother died very young, and only Charlotte even vaguely remembered her. And how do you know they studied their French and struggled with it? How do you know they even took French?"

"Well, they would have, wouldn't they? They weren't titled, but I do believe they were gentry—like your Nanna Dempster—because their father was a minister, which means they would have been taught by tutors. And tutors always taught French in those days. Your nanna and her brothers had a tutor, and they all had to learn French. In any case, I'm happy you love to read, but you must try harder with the subjects you dislike. This is not England—you cannot leave school at fourteen. Now, set the table for dinner."

"Well," I said, having to get in the last word, "if I'm going to get married and have six children, I certainly won't need arithmetic or French! You told Dad as much!"

Seventh grade was much the same as sixth—and much different. The junior high school was in the same building as the elementary school, because our base was small, and so was the junior high school census. When the bells rang between classes in the junior high, we on the elementary side had always been able to hear them, but we never really had noticed them. I mentioned to my parents at dinner shortly after school started again that I had never really noticed the bells on the other side of the building being rung between classes—except for lunch and dismissal—when I was on the elementary school side of the building. Didn't they think it odd that now I clearly heard them?

My father said no, it wasn't odd at all. "That's how our brains work. We can passively absorb, subconsciously ignore, or actively process things going on around us simultaneously. That's because human brains are so highly developed, and it's such a shame we don't do more with what we've been given."

I sensed an imminent lecture about French lessons looming, and I quickly changed the subject.

"There's a new girl in school," I said, turning toward my mother. "She just started today, and she is so cute!"

"That's nice, love."

"No, really! She wears her hair like you used to wear yours all the time—in a pageboy. But she clips a barrette in the front, and she wears something she calls a twinset. It's two sweaters that match—one is a pullover, and the other is a cardigan."

While most of the seventh-grade boys still read and traded comic books and while I hadn't given up comics completely, we girls now pored over our mothers' ladies' magazines for hours, taking note of the latest fashion trends. My American grandmother had sent us the Montgomery Ward catalog every spring and autumn for the past three years, and between those, the Sears catalog, and the magazines, we girls had gleaned a substantial amount of fashion knowledge. The new girl had shown up at school wearing her cardigan draped over her shoulders. She looked so *tres* chic that we all said we were going to wear our sweaters just like that. It was October 1960 when Cissy arrived at our school.

"Mah real name is Cecelia, but ever'one has always called me Cissy," she said with her southern drawl. Suddenly, I knew. I had an epiphany: Cissy had exactly the accent I wanted to acquire! It was as though I'd been searching all those years for a perfect accent, and that was it.

We girls were immediately dazzled by her *je ne sais quoi*. (There were certain French phrases that just didn't sound as chic in English, so why bother?) We all agreed she had that indefinable quality. For instance, on the days when she wore a cardigan, she wore a little chain with two clips on each end that fastened to the two front edges near the neck.

"It stops it from slippin' off mah shoulders. Y'all know what I mean?"

We nodded. Yes, of course we knew.

One day she wore something she called a circle pin, and she told us that if you wore a circle pin on the right side of your blouse or sweater, it meant you were single. If you wore it on the left, over your heart, it meant you were going steady. We swooned at the thought. Not that any one of us would have been allowed to go steady–my girlfriends and I weren't even allowed to wear lipstick–but we decided that if our parents didn't allow us to go steady by the eighth grade, we would do so secretly.

We made a pact: none of us would tell our parents the significance of the circle pins we were going to buy. That, of course, was dependent upon the base exchange ever carrying such a thing at the jewelry counter. I made a vow: starting that day, I was going to be less of a tomboy and was going to spend a lot more time on my appearance. When my mother wanted to put Alberto VO5 in my hair to make it behave, I was not going to argue. And I was never going to complain about being a girl again.

"Ah've disahded," I said after Cissy had been in school with us for about two weeks, "that Ah'm givin' up baysball fo' a while." We were eating dinner, and I was pushing my salmon patty around my plate, trying to decide if I could swallow a bite or would rather go hungry.

Frowning, my father said, "What? You've done what about giving up what?"

"Ah said, Fatha Deah, that Ah'm givin' up baysball fo' a while."

"Vivienne has decided to try to speak southern," said my mother. "She thinks Cecelia, the new girl in school, has the most wonderful accent she's ever heard."

"Well, just imagine that. Who would ever have guessed that our southern states have a completely different language? I mean, here I've been thinking for three years now that you just do not have an ear for languages. And just like that," he said, snapping his fingers, "you're bilingual!" I could tell he was being sarcastic.

"Well, I might not have it down pat yet, but I've only just started learning it. Ah mean, Fatha Deah," I said, correcting myself, "Ah've only jes sta'ted learnin' it. An' Ah'm thinkin' it could take a while."

"Good grief." He looked at my mother. "Please tell me she's not afflicted. I mean, I honestly cannot believe that every family with a twelve-year-old girl goes through this. One minute she's quite normal—playing baseball, reading comic books—and the next minute she's speaking a made-up language."

"It isn't made up, Dad! It's traditional southern, and everyone in the southern United States of America speaks like this. Cecilia said so!"

One day at the end of October, we were in the gym. Thus far, physical education had been a complete bore. As a group, we were devoid of the energy and excitement that Mr. Parker had been able to generate among us last year when we were sixth graders. He wasn't there at all this year, and the grade school again had a new physical education teacher. Seventh and eighth graders, because of our low numbers, had physical education together three times a week, and Mr. Perry, the math teacher, doubled as our PE teacher. Bob, Linda, and I thought he was singularly disinterested in athletics, and I thought those of us who'd had Mr. Parker last year could probably have done a better job of teaching his class. I broached the suggestion of his just letting us play baseball all year.

"Ah think," I said, forgetting that I had given up baseball, "that we all would jes love to play baysball ever' day—weatha permittin', of co'se!" My comment drew blank stares from everyone. Even Bob suggested I interpret what I had just said.

"I said I think we should just play baseball every day, weather permitting."

"Great idea!" said Bob, and most of the boys agreed.

My suggestion was met with such gasps of horror from the girls–with the loudest one being from Cissy–that I had to pretend I was just kidding.

By the end of the month, I gave up my attempts at trying to speak southern–it was exhausting to have to translate everything I said.

It was going to be a long year.

Seventeen

I WAS TWELVE GOING ON TWENTY, AND I HAD BEEN CHECKING my sisters for bruises regularly, because even though Mom and Dad said aplastic anemia was not a hereditary disease, I wasn't convinced.

"If the doctors don't know what causes it or how to cure it, how can they be sure?" I asked Mom.

"Well, I'm not a doctor, but they assured us at Fitzsimons that it was not hereditary," Mom said, probably for the hundredth time, when I dragged Christine in from outside and told my mother to look at her legs. She had a bruise on each calf.

"I'm putting mercurochrome on them anyway," I said. "It can't hurt."

"Just don't give her anymore Vicks VapoRub," said my mother.

I rolled my eyes at my mother and shook my head.

We had gone over this before. Last year, my parents had left me to babysit my sisters on a Saturday night when they went to the NCO club for a floor show. Christine had had a cough and a runny nose, and my mother had instructed me to give her a spoonful of Vicks if she woke up coughing, which she had. The mouth of the jar had been too small for me to reach inside with a teaspoon, so I'd used a measuring spoon and meticulously measured out two half teaspoons. My sister had swallowed with gusto and jumped up and down in her crib, saying, "More, Vibi! More!"

I'd given her another half teaspoon and said, "No more, Chrissy! That's all you get."

"What? You gave her Vicks VapoRub to eat? You were supposed to give her Vicks cough syrup! I can't believe you gave her VapoRub! Was she sick? I can't believe she didn't choke or throw up!" my mother had said when my parents got home, clearly distressed at my report. She had rushed into the bedroom to check that my sister was still breathing. I'd followed her, suddenly panicking, fearing I'd killed my sister.

"I'm eleven, for Pete's sake! How was I supposed to know you didn't mean regular Vicks, the Vicks that you always rub all over us when we start coughing? And I can't believe you went to a floor show at the club, knowing Christine was sick!"

"Really, Vivienne, you can be so dramatic! Marie couldn't come, and it was a chance in a lifetime to see Gogi Grant! After all, she is the best torchlight singer in the world, in my opinion! Anyway, Chris seems to be breathing OK, so no harm done."

After that night, we never had a babysitter again. Apparently, my mother felt that if Chris had survived eating Vicks VapoRub and if she made a point of being more specific with her instructions to me going forward, I could probably handle anything.

We had now been in France for more than three years, as my father had extended his assignment for an extra year when given the opportunity. He had already told us that he would not extend again and that we would be going back to the States sometime in the spring. As usual, we looked forward to finding out where we would be going, and I loved the anticipation–even while knowing I would miss France and my friends.

The seasons came and went, and I was aware constantly that our final days in France were filled with lasts: our last Halloween, our last Thanksgiving, and our last Christmas, or Noel, as it was called there. Finally, on an overcast early March day, Dad got his next assignment.

Once again, the thrill of anticipation coursed through my veins as I looked forward to a new adventure and a new base: we would be moving to Keesler Air Force Base in Biloxi, Mississippi, at the end of the month.

"Oh, you'll love it!" said Linda. "That's where we came from before we came here. The beaches are great, and they are in walking distance. In the summer, my mom used to take my sister and me all the time!"

On March 27, 1961, I was sitting at the second-story window of a lovely old hotel in Sarrebourg. It was after dinner on our last day in France. There was an incredibly beautiful sunset, and the charm of the narrow cobbled street and the ancient brick, stone, and timber gabled houses thrilled me. How many families had lived on that street through the centuries? I wondered. How many soldiers had perhaps paraded down that street on VE Day, and how many pretty mademoiselles had run out to them with flowers and kisses, overjoyed that the war was over? I was torn about moving back to America: I both wanted to and didn't. My father said that was called feeling ambivalent. I sighed and rested my head on the casing of the open window.

The movers had come that morning and packed up our furniture in the big crates that seemed to be a constant presence in my friends' and my lives. Someone was always coming or going, moving in or moving out. Bob and Linda gave me the new comic books they had gotten a week ago with their allowances, so I would have something to read on the plane, and in turn, I gave them my whole comic book collection. My mother had insisted my sisters and I get rid of everything that didn't need to be shipped to the States.

The moving van left, and Bob, Linda, and I, along with several of our other friends, gathered on the playground so I could say my goodbyes. Four of our French friends were there too.

"Au revoir, Vivienne! Bon voyage! Goodbye, *ami. Ecrivez-nous une letter a l'Amerique!*"

"Goodbye! Goodbye! I'll write!"

Of course, I wouldn't, and neither would they. Where would we have sent the letters?

I was determined to try again to read *Alice in Wonderland*. Nanna had given it to me for my eleventh birthday nearly two years ago. I'd tried to read it three times now, and I was not sure why, but I never seemed to be able to finish it. But being on a plane for ten hours might be the perfect time to try, I thought.

I felt a bit sad, unlike when we'd left Lowry Air Force Base. As I thought back, I couldn't even remember all the names of my friends in Colorado. Now I was going to miss my two best friends. Still, Linda was sure I'd love Biloxi, so I was determined to keep an open mind.

The daylight gradually became dusk, and the streetlights came on up and down the avenue. Mom and Dad were reading the *Stars and Stripes*, and my little sisters were playing with their dolls. As I leaned my arms on the wide sill of the open hotel window, I suddenly saw an old gentleman in a beret walk out a door across the street, leading a dog on a leash. It was Mr. Magoo!

Leaning out the window, I shouted, "Magoo!" I felt tears welling up in my eyes. When Dad had taken him yesterday to his new home, I hadn't been allowed to go. Dad had gone by himself.

I saw Magoo's ears perk up, and his stance stiffened. His nose went up in the air, and some deep instinct catapulted his sinewy body across the cobbled street, dragging the poor man behind him. The man finally let go of the leash—to avoid being pulled off his feet, I thought—and I turned to run out of the hotel room.

"What have you done?" asked Dad in an angry voice as he glanced out the window. "Stay right here in this room, young lady!" He left the hotel room.

Mom came to the window and looked out. "Well, that was a silly thing to do! Did you not think, Vivienne? I hope the old man isn't hurt!"

No, I hadn't thought. I had just seen my dog after leaving my two best friends, and my joy at seeing him one more time had caused me to react impulsively.

In the end, no real harm was done. The old man assured my father that he was not hurt, and Mom gave me a hug and said she knew I hadn't meant it. Still, the sadness I felt, which was so raw and so unlike how I had felt during other moves, overwhelmed me, and I pulled the covers over my head when I got into bed, so my sisters wouldn't hear me crying.

The following morning, we left Alsace-Lorraine and drove to Germany. Tomorrow we would leave Rhein-Main Air Base and fly to Mississippi. I spent most of the time in the hotel room looking out the window to see if I could catch one more glimpse of Mr. Magoo, but I didn't see him. I hoped the old man who was now his master understood what an amazing dog he was. I tried my best to swallow the lump in my throat and not lose patience with my little sisters as we left France for good.

We arrived at the guest quarters on the base at Rhein-Main in the early afternoon, and there was time for Mom and me to go shopping in the base exchange one last time.

My mother decided she wanted me to have an Alpine hat, a traditional felt hat that Bavarian and Swiss people wore all the time. They adorned the crown with fishing lures, silver pins, and other collectables.

"Where would I wear it, Mom?" I asked, not caring one way or the other if I got a hat, when I couldn't have my dog.

"Well, wear it wherever you want or not at all. It's just a nice reminder of all the trips we took to Germany to shop and the historical places we went."

We had visited one or two holy shrines in France during our frequent Saturday drives, but I immediately thought of the concentration camp we had visited one weekend. I recalled the horror I'd felt in the main room that had been the camp's headquarters, where a shrine of pictures and memorabilia had been on display to properly illustrate the horrific cruelty of the Nazis.

"Besides," my mother said, "not many girls in America will have one."

We bought the hat and half a dozen Bavarian-looking pins to adorn it. My mother stocked up on her favorite perfumes and picked up a few other travel items.

When we returned to the guest quarters, my father was anxiously waiting for us. I could tell by his face that something was wrong–he was so pale all his freckles stood out, and his eyes looked sad. He took Mom's shopping bags from her and led her to a chair. He knelt by the side of the chair, and Mom and I knew by the look on his face he was not going to do or say anything funny.

He took a big breath and said, "We've had a telegram from England. Your father has died. He had a massive stroke."

Mom started to cry large, hacking sobs, and Dad boiled water in the tiny electric kettle on the dresser and fixed her a cup of tea. Then he boiled the kettle again and fixed me one. I felt as if I couldn't breathe. Nor could I cry or speak. I wanted to go home.

I wanted to fly across the English Channel and over the heaths and the moors, as I had in my dreams when I was little. I wanted to run up the entryway once more, run through the scullery into the lounge, and see Granddad filling out the betting form for the horse races.

"Why do you lick the pencil lead?" I would ask.

"Well," he would say, "it's a habit. In the old days, lead wasn't as soft as it is now, and the only way you could get it to make a proper mark was to put spit on it. And if there's anywhere you want the mark to be unequivicable, it's on your racing form."

"Nasty habit that, spitting on the pencil lead," Nanna would say. "And there is no such word as *unequivicable*, Jack. It is *unequivocal*."

I'd hug them both as tightly as I could and say, "You can't die, Granddad! I don't think I can live without you. Even though I don't live with you anymore, I know I can't live without you both!"

"Drink your tea, love," said my mother, who had blown her nose and stopped sobbing.

I found my voice, but when I spoke, it didn't sound like me. "Are we going to Flixton? Are we going to see Nanna? To make sure this isn't a mistake or something? Maybe the telegram people got it wrong."

Dad said something about putting in for some special sort of leave–bereavement something, I thought he said.

Mom shook her head. "There is nothing I can do—we can do."

We were not going to England.

On our last night in Europe, I pulled the covers over my head and cried myself to sleep as Granddad whispered in my ear, "There once was a man who lived in a can down in the bottom of the garden …"

Biloxi

Eighteen

E FLEW DIRECTLY FROM RHEIN-MAIN AIR BASE TO Keesler Air Force Base in Biloxi, Mississippi. I did not read *Alice in Wonderland* on the plane. Overcome with grief, I couldn't even concentrate on the new comics Bob and Linda had given me. We landed after what seemed like the longest flight in the world, and we exited the plane. We were escorted into a hangar made of steel, where a semicircle of folding chairs several rows deep were arranged around a podium.

"Why do we have to wait in here, Dad?" I asked. "We've never had to do this before."

"There is always a debriefing of some sort; it just depends on the base's protocol and whether the base commander wants to include the families. You don't remember, but in France, we got a welcome packet with the information the family would need, and we airmen attended an additional debriefing in the headquarters building later."

I tried to keep Chris from squirming all over the place and get comfortable in the metal folding chair while wishing someone would hurry up and do something so we could get to where we were supposed to be. Finally, a tall man in uniform approached the podium, adjusted the microphone, and introduced himself.

"Welcome to Keesler Air Force Base. As most of you know, we are the largest base in the United States Air Force personnel-wise, and as such, we make every attempt to be as thorough and precise as possible in the distribution of information. When you exit the hangar, you will be given a manila envelope. Inside, you will find details familiarizing you with the base and surrounding community. It will include base services and housing information. Most of you will be housed in temporary quarters until either base accommodations or housing on the economy is secured for you.

"I am sure most of the adults in this room are, to a large degree, aware of the social unrest that is currently occurring throughout the South, which is predominantly targeting Mississippi and Alabama. There are, at latest count, no fewer than four organizations assembling groups of Freedom Riders from northern states. These groups consist largely of racially integrated college students who are bused south on Trailways and Greyhound buses for the purpose of peaceful demonstration. However, recently, these demonstrations have triggered some violence, so let me be perfectly clear: this is a military base. As such, neither our personnel nor their dependents will participate at any level, at any time, in any demonstrations, peaceful or otherwise. Should there be any incidents—or risk of incidents—in the adjacent civilian areas, the base will be put on alert, and travel off the base will be restricted. All military personnel are encouraged to emphasize the seriousness of this protocol to their dependents. Thank you."

We were transported by buses to temporary quarters, and Mom immediately busied herself in getting us settled in. My sisters had been amazing, all things considered: Connie was only six, and Chris was only three. Daddy said our car would be ready to be picked up tomorrow. As soon as we were cleaned up, we went to the lobby to take the available transportation to the base snack bar or the NCO club so we could eat. Mom had been feeding us snacks, and we'd had a meal on the plane, but we were all starving.

Later that night, after we were back in our quarters, as Mom was getting my sisters ready for bed, my father sat me down at the small table off to the side of the kitchenette.

"Now," he said, "I want you to listen to me and to take what I'm going to say very seriously. This is not me trying to challenge your reasoning or give you anything to stretch your imagination. I am deadly serious, and you need to pay attention."

This was a parental speech I had not heard before. To me, it was—to use a favorite word of my Granddad's—flummoxing. Dad was not trying to plant a seed so that I'd question something, as was his usual tactic.

"What you heard today during the debriefing is of grave concern. We are now in Mississippi, and although we are technically on neutral ground in the integrated environment of a military base, you will not—let me emphasize this: you will not—challenge anyone or anything that you think is unfair, unjust, or prejudicial. Mississippi is a segregated state, meaning people of different races are not treated equally, and whether you think that is fair or not is of absolutely no concern to the locals in this community. You cannot change the minds of people who have been raised in a segregated world. At best, you might cause someone harm if you try to right what you think is a wrong, and at worst, you yourself might be harmed. Do you understand me?"

"Well, if you are saying I can't stand up for someone or act upon my principles, which you are usually so determined that I act on, then what am I supposed to do? Am I supposed to just let things happen? Even if I know they're wrong?"

"Yes. That is exactly what I'm saying. You are a little girl—I know, I know," he said, holding up a hand. "You have developed an amazing sense of fairness, and Mom and I are very proud of you for that. But listen to me: you cannot do anything at all to change the mind of anyone who is or might be involved in local conflict, either verbal or physical. And I am forbidding you to have an opinion on segregation outside our family."

I could not believe what my father was saying—my father, who had taught me always to be truthful, stand on my principles, and fight for the underdog. He was now telling me to have no opinion and to let obvious injustices go without my bringing attention to them. I knew I was just a kid and couldn't change anything, but he'd never before told me not to try.

"I'll try." I sighed.

"No, you will not try; you will absolutely do as I say! I don't want to have to put you on restriction for however many years we live in Biloxi, Mississippi."

There might have been a beach within walking distance of the new base, but I wanted to go back to France.

I was immediately enrolled in a school on the east side of the town of Biloxi. My parents had rented a bland house in a lovely old neighborhood that had massive oak trees with moss hanging down so low I could jump up and catch handfuls of it. Just down the street from us was a family who had a daughter my age who attended the school I had been enrolled in. She took me under her wing and was patient as she tried to decipher my strange life.

"You mean y'all are from a foreign country?"

"Well, not really. My dad is in the air force, and we are American. We've just lived mostly outside of America."

"You sure do talk funny. But don't worry; last year, some boy from the base went to school here for a while. He had a weird accent too, but he got on OK."

I talk funny? I have a weird accent? I knew it!

Her name was Kathy, and she was allowed to have a boyfriend. His name was Kenny. She told me Kenny was in the eighth grade and when he graduated from the ninth grade next year, he was not going to finish high school. He would be sixteen. None of his brothers had finished high school, and they all were doing just fine; they had various jobs, but the one who was doing the best worked on an oil rig off the coast of Louisiana. As soon as Kenny finished ninth grade, he and Kathy would get married–with their parents' permission, of course–and they probably would move to New Orleans. I pondered that. Why it sounded so outlandish I couldn't decide; after all, in my beloved England, students usually finished school at fifteen and sometimes fourteen. It was common. I didn't know any who were getting married, though, so maybe that was the difference.

I liked Biloxi Junior High School but found it odd that every student in the whole school was Caucasian. That was a first for me, at least a first since I'd started going to American schools. However, the subjects at Biloxi Junior High were comparable to what I had been studying in France, and except for the history of Mississippi, I was up to speed in all my classes, so I was happy. Hopefully, even though I wasn't taking French, my father would be too.

"Now, Miss Viveen," said the history teacher, "I don't spect you know too much 'bout our history here in Mis'sippi. But that is OK. You will get to know it soon enough; and, class, your homework assignment is to teach Miss Viveen ever'thing you know about our wonderful state!"

I didn't consider correcting him on his incorrect pronunciation of my name. Some things were just not important when starting a new school, particularly one I wouldn't be attending next year. I contemplated telling him that everyone called me Leigh–I thought a new school would be a perfect place to implement the change–but I doubted I'd be there long enough for it to matter. What I noticed most about his speech, though, was the lax pronunciation coupled with the emphasis placed on each word. He did not say, "That's OK." Each word and syllable was articulated separately–some words were given extra syllables; some words lost a few–and given equal stress. With his heavy southern accent, it was not so much distracting as mesmerizing. "Our wonderful state" sounded like "Ow-ah wundah-ful state." It was pleasant, and I realized my attempts at acquiring a southern accent à la Cissy had been closer to the mark than I had thought.

Life in Biloxi settled into a comfortable rhythm. It was April now, and Dad started umpiring baseball games again as soon as we moved into the rental house. Mom and I found ourselves curled up on the couch most nights, watching different programs. We realized how much we had missed having a television during the past four years. The evenings when *The Twilight Zone* and *The Alfred Hitchcock Hour* aired were our favorite. We watched reruns of old movies too. Inevitably, right at the climax of anything–like the thrilling moment in *Gaslight* when Ingrid Bergman descended the staircase, finally realizing she was not actually crazy–the television screen went fuzzy, and we had to take turns sliding the tinfoil up and down the antenna that sat on top of the console.

I was invited to spend the night with Kathy one Friday. As odd as it seemed, her house reminded me a bit of number 7–it was small, with tiny rooms that all had a door, something I did not remember seeing before in America. It seemed to me that in America, only bedrooms, bathrooms, and occasionally kitchens sported doors. Living rooms, dining rooms, foyers, and hallways all seemed to be open to one another and were usually flooded with light–so very American, I thought.

Kathy's mom fixed red beans and rice for dinner–it was a traditional Cajun dish, said Kathy, and although her family wasn't Catholic, they didn't eat meat on Fridays. Most Cajuns had Catholic roots, her mother said, and they just followed the old traditions. Red beans and rice, I decided, were delicious. I was going to tell my mother about this southern tradition–I'd emphasize its Catholicness–and maybe she would fix it on Fridays instead of tuna and noodles or salmon patties.

Soon it was late May, and seemingly overnight, the magnolia trees bloomed. They were everywhere. I had never lived anywhere that had magnolia trees, and I thought they were the most beautiful trees in the world. School had just let out for the day, and as I slowly walked under a canopy of the waxy green leaves and beautiful creamy white blossoms, I wondered how long the blooms would last. Suddenly, three girls came running up to me, giggling and breathless.

"Guess who wants to take you to the seventh-grade end-of-year dance! Only Philip, the cutest boy in the seventh grade!"

I wasn't sure I understood what they were saying. It was like listening to three Cissys speak over one another all at once. I wasn't allowed to date, and I couldn't believe any of them were either–except, of course, Kathy, who was practically married.

"What exactly do you mean? Like take me as in a date to a dance?"

"Well, of course, silly! You don't date girls, do you?" The comment created a melee of giggling among the girls. "Philip is very popular, and he only asks cute girls to our dances."

I had no point of reference for the conversation because, obviously, I had never dated at all. Of course, I'd had a crush on Uri Sagett for nearly two years, but there was no way my parents would have let me go out on a date with him or with any other of the boys I'd played baseball and Chinese checkers with.

Not wanting to seem in the least unsophisticated, I said, "Oh, of course not. I just wasn't sure if you meant a *date* date. I'll have to get permission, of course. My father insists on meeting all my dates." I was pretty sure any local boy would be so intimidated at the thought of meeting my father that it would solve the problem of my having to do something as excruciating as go to a dance with a boy.

I spent the whole walk home worrying about how I was going to tell the girls to tell Philip no, I wasn't going to the dance with him. I would sound like a baby if I said my parents had said no, I couldn't go out on a date because I was too young. On the other hand, I couldn't just say no, I didn't want to go to the dance with him.

"Oh, that's really nice, love," said my mother when I told her about Philip. "I assume you'll be going as a group, and as long as you stay with the others–because I don't want you walking home alone; we have no idea, really, about this neighborhood–I think it's lovely that you've been included."

What on earth was my mother saying? I had just told her that some boy named Philip wanted to take me as his date to the seventh-grade dance. This, I realized, was what happened when your mother was from a country where kids left school at fourteen to go to work. It was the English thing again. Had she no concern that I was three weeks short of being only thirteen and, by normal American standards, much too young to date?

"So," said Dad, "you have been asked to the seventh-grade dance by a boy named Philip?"

"Well, not exactly. I think I know which boy he is. He's really cute, and all the girls think he's a dreamboat. But he hasn't really asked me himself. The girls just said he wanted me to go with him."

Now that I was saying it out loud to my father, I felt a little flicker of excitement. Philip was really cute, and all the girls just loved him to death. Of course, I hardly knew the girls either, but based upon their squeals and eye-rolling when they'd rushed to tell me, I now thought I might like to be the girl Philip took to the dance.

"Well," said my father, "I think that as long as you go in a group, you should probably tell the girls to tell Philip that you can go to the dance."

Had I caught a note of amusement in my father's voice?

Three girls and two boys showed up at my house at six forty-five on the evening of the dance, and we walked the three blocks together. Mom and Dad stood on the porch and waved goodbye. As they turned to go in, I thought I heard Mom ask, "Which one do you think is Philip?"

"Probably the short one," Dad answered.

It turned out that Philip was a nice boy, the girls all adored him, and he taught me how to slow dance. Then he walked me home and gave me a chaste good-night kiss on the cheek. That was when I decided I might consider going steady with Philip. I also considered that the base exchange at Keesler, which was much bigger than the one at Phalsbourg, might have circle pins.

The school term ended on Friday, June 11. Philip walked me home by way of his house—a large, southern-style two-story brick mansion with ivy growing up and around the eight front windows, which were all flanked by shutters. The ground-floor windows had wrought-iron window boxes filled with blooms, and massive oak trees filled the front and side yards. The front door was painted pale blue. I commented on how many doors I'd noticed were painted that color in my new neighborhood.

"It's haint blue," Philip said. "To keep away malicious spirits."

I looked at him to see if he was kidding.

"Seriously," he said, "there are lots of superstitions here in the old South. Evil spirits are rebuffed by that certain color of blue–I don't know why–so people who believe in ghosts or just want to promote southern tradition often paint their doors and their porch ceilings haint blue."

I thought that people all over the world must have had odd traditions or superstitions. In England, every New Year's Eve, either my grandfather or my uncle Jack went out the back door and came in the front door, offering sixpence and a loaf of bread to the lady of the house to ensure the New Year would be filled with plenty. It always fell on one of them, because Nanna insisted it had to be done by a tall, dark, handsome man. Granddad said that it was all malarkey and that Nanna just threw in the *handsome* part to make sure one of them would do it, regardless of how bloody cold it was. Suddenly, I felt a lump in my throat: Granddad *used* to say it was all malarkey. Now it would only ever be my uncle Jackie who carried on the New Year tradition.

We entered the kitchen by way of the back door, which was also painted blue, and Philip introduced me to the housekeeper, Miss Shirley. She had hazel eyes, and her skin was the color of café au lait, the coffee Mom always ordered when we went to the bakery in Sarrebourg. When Miss Shirley smiled, I saw that her right eyetooth was crowned in gold, which matched the gold hoop earrings in her pierced ears. I decided right then and there that if I ever had to get a tooth crowned, I would beg my parents to let me get a gold one. Of course, that was if it was a tooth that showed. Otherwise, it would have been a big waste of money.

Miss Shirley was the most glamorous woman of color I had ever seen. I thought about Aunt Betty, our next-door neighbor in France.

In base housing, we had lived next door to a black family, which was nothing white families in the military even blinked an eye at; in fact, now living in a segregated neighborhood seemed odd to me. My mother was friends with Betty. All us kids called her Aunt Betty, because she was from Alabama, and in the South, just like in England, every adult who was a family friend was referred to as

Aunt or Uncle. Unlike Miss Shirley, I now realized, Aunt Betty was not glamorous.

Betty and her husband had four boys ranging from two to eight, and since I sometimes babysat for them, I could attest to the fact that there was probably no time left over for Aunt Betty to squeeze in glamour. She was plump, comfortable, and vehemently against something she called interracial marriage. I knew that beyond a doubt because I came home from school one day while she and Mom were having their usual cup of tea. Aunt Betty was sobbing into a hankie, and when I asked my mother what was wrong, my mother said, "Nothing. Go change your school clothes." Aunt Betty wiped her eyes with her hankie and put her arm around me. She said her family was disgraced. She said her youngest brother had eloped with a white girl, and everyone knew—in the state of Alabama at least—that could only mean trouble. All her relatives were devastated, and they all knew things could not possibly end well.

I told her I was sorry. "But, Aunt Betty, if they are really, really in love, maybe everything will turn out fine," I said. "Maybe when your family see how happy they are, they will be OK with it, and after a while, everyone will stop worrying."

She hugged me and said, "Oh, baby, you have no idea."

Now that I was older and living in Mississippi, going to an all-white school in an all-white neighborhood, and visiting the home of a white boy from an old Biloxi family, I had an inkling of the angst Aunt Betty's brother had caused the family.

Philip and I sat at the kitchen table, and Miss Shirley wanted to know all about me and my family and where we were from. She gave us both a glass of sweet tea. It was cold and had ice cubes in it, but I remembered my manners and sipped it slowly despite finding it dreadful. My American grandmother drank iced tea, but neither my mother nor I could acquire a taste for it. Miss Shirley fixed us peanut butter and jelly sandwiches, which I could not, under any circumstance, eat—even in the presence of the cutest boy in school. I mumbled something about still being full from lunch.

Eventually, we said our goodbyes to Miss Shirley, who made me promise to come back again, and Philip walked me part of the way home.

He pressed a piece of paper into my hand, saying, "Here's my phone number. As soon as you get a phone, call me!"

"I will," I promised.

I found my mother in the kitchen, cooking dinner.

"Do you think any of the movie theaters will ever show *Gone with the Wind* again?" I asked. I had never seen the movie, but my mother had talked about it enough that I had an idea of how grand Scarlett's house must have been.

"I don't know. Why?"

"I'm just wondering whether I'd like to marry someone and live in a house like that."

"I think you would find that it wouldn't be to your liking. The upkeep would be thoroughly exhausting–from dusk till dawn, you'd be scrubbing floors, cleaning windows, polishing furniture, and doing laundry. And even if you survived that, taking feather beds and carpets outside once a month to beat the dust out of them would do anyone in. Ask Nanna–she grew up in a house where there were servants, and then she had to go to work as a servant herself. You'd never have time to watch *American Bandstand, Alfred Hitchcock*, or *The Twilight Zone*."

I could always count on my mother to put things in perspective.

Two weeks later, we moved into base housing–and by the time we got a phone, I realized I had lost Philip's phone number.

Nineteen

CONTRARY TO WHAT I HAD IMAGINED, LIFE ON KEESLER AIR Force Base, located in the beachfront town of Biloxi, Mississippi, just blocks away from the Gulf of Mexico, was not anything at all like a Gidget movie. Granted, all the ingredients were there: lots of teenagers, lots of sunshine, and miles of pristine beach with waves lapping endlessly at the shore. There was a concession stand on the beach, and there were toilets with changing rooms. There was even an island that we could take a ferry to. Deer Island was a small island that was deliciously haunted: lots of people who had camped out there at night had seen a headless skeleton, and some even reported seeing mysterious blue lights that shot out across the water and then disappeared beyond the horizon. Since my friends and I only went during the day, when the ferry ran, we weren't likely to see either the headless skeleton or the blue lights.

On a clear day, when the ocean was like glass, we could put on our snorkels and watch the stingrays gliding along the ocean bottom. If we became bored with swimming and sunbathing, there was a small amusement park located just up the beach, at the western edge of town, and all the rides were either a nickel or ten cents.

However, despite the many splendid things about the town of Biloxi, Mississippi, there was also the ever-present dark, insidious thing that lay barely veiled just beneath its lovely veneer: segregation.

At the beginning of August 1961, we had been in base housing for about six weeks, when a new family moved in next door. Our new neighbors–"a family of color" was the term the more genteel locals used–had a daughter my age. Her name was Ginny, and as with all military children, we simply said "hey" and became friends. For the next few weeks, we went to the parks on base, to the swimming pool, and to the movies–typical summer activities for young people on the base. The teenagers from our housing area hung out with a group of teenagers who lived in another housing area that was a half mile or so from our section of housing. Another new friend of mine, Danny Cochran, lived there. Ginny and I were both thirteen, and our parents let us stay out until twilight as long as we stayed in areas surrounding family quarters; we were not allowed to roam the streets that bordered either the military barracks or any of the clubs–the airmen's, NCOs', or officers' clubs–located in other sections of the base.

One evening near the end of August, a group of us were sitting on the low brick wall that bordered the movie theater, waiting to meet some of our friends who had gone to the early show. School would be starting soon, and we were talking about how wonderful the summer had been.

Danny suddenly said, "Hey, I have an idea! Let's all go to the beach tomorrow!"

"Yeh! Let's do that!" was the resounding reply.

"And we can walk down to the amusement park if we feel like it," said Patsy, who lived across the street from Ginny and me.

"Or take the ferry to Deer Island," said someone else.

We agreed to meet by the base's front gate at ten o'clock the next morning.

As we walked home, Ginny said, "You know I can't go with you all to the beach, right?"

"Why? Let's talk to your mom–if she knows there are a bunch of us going, I bet she'll let you! Why wouldn't she?"

"I'm not allowed because colored people aren't allowed on the public beaches in Mississippi."

147

"I know we won't be going to the same school in September, but I didn't know you weren't allowed on the beach!" As I said it, I realized it should have been obvious. To Ginny's point, I had never seen any part of the beach that was integrated.

"Just what did you think segregation meant? Have you ever seen any colored people on the beach?" Her voice had grown tight, and her mouth was a straight, grim line.

"It isn't right!" I ranted when I got home. "Her dad is in the air force, and I bet there are more air force people living in Biloxi than civilians! Why doesn't the base commander do something about this? The air force should threaten to move the base if the stupid state doesn't change its stupid laws!"

My mother rolled her eyes. My father looked at me with a glint in his eyes that I thought meant he was going to lose his temper with me.

Instead, he said, "Remember what I said? You do remember, don't you, what you and I discussed when we first got here? This is serious, Vivienne. Very serious. There are riots taking place all over the South regarding segregation. Someday things will change for the better, but before they do, there will be a lot of grief. You are one person—and a child at that—and you cannot, no matter how passionately you feel, change what hundreds of years of precedents have created. Do not, under any circumstances, take your views outside this house. Give me your word!"

"Well, I think it's wrong. Very wrong. And if my friend can't go to the beach tomorrow, I'm not going either."

It was rare that my father ever hugged me—he just wasn't the hugging type. But he leaned down, gathered me into his arms, and said, "Never, ever, ever change. You are a great kid, and you make me proud."

It gave me a happy feeling to know that even if I was terrible at math and not much better at French, he still thought I was a great kid. Nevertheless, I was not happy about segregation.

On the first day of school, Ginny and I waved at each other as she got in her parents' car to be driven by her father to the school for children of color, and I walked the several blocks to the all-white Mary L. Michel Junior High and entered the eighth grade.

Although the junior high was segregated—and, in my mind, flawed because of that—I liked my teachers, my classes, and most of the other kids; some were from the base, and some were from the town of Biloxi. A few weeks into the school year, though, an ugly situation reared its head, and it was, I supposed, inevitable.

It was lunch period, and I was sitting with a group of students at one of the long tables in the cafeteria. A couple of the boys were talking about northerners who were coming to the South to protest segregation. The general attitude of those at the table was that northerners should mind their own business and stay away from Mississippi.

"If they want to go to school with niggers, well, that is their business," said one boy.

The coarseness of the word—I had heard the term before but never in a conversation of which I had been a part—shocked me. I could not understand how otherwise ordinary young people from ordinary families could be so ignorant. I started to speak, and I remembered what my father had warned: "I am forbidding you to have an opinion on segregation outside this home."

"So," I said, ignoring my father's voice in my head, "you have been to school with people of color? Or have you lived next door to them? I mean, to have formed such a strong opinion?"

The boy who had made the statement looked at me as if I had just eaten a roach and then followed it up with a second. Most of the other students looked equally stunned that I might seriously think either of those situations had ever occurred there in Mississippi. Before any of them found their voices, I picked up my tray.

"Because I live next door to a family of color, and I'm friends with their daughter. And when I lived in France, my best friend's father was a man of color, which made her half colored, I guess. But those are people and families who have traveled and lived all over the world, and they recognize this is a planet full of different cultures and people of different races. I now realize they have learned to make allowances for small-minded people like you all, who have never had an opportunity to leave their small town and broaden their ignorant minds."

As I walked away, my heart was thumping. I had never in my life so thoroughly disobeyed my father. I wasn't sure what would happen now. If the group of students I'd been sitting with reported me to the principal and the principal called my father, I was in big trouble. On the other hand, how could I have just sat there and said nothing? That would have been as bad as agreeing with them. And it would have made me a coward.

I felt sick for the rest of the afternoon. By the time the bell rang, word had gotten around the school that Vivienne Grilliot was a *nigger lover*. That didn't bother me; I was enough like my mother and father to realize that the opinions and prejudices of other people would never influence my personal beliefs. What did, however, cause me grave concern was whether the principal, Mr. Johnson—who was bound to have heard what I had said by now—had already called my father, who would be angry that I had been so flagrantly disobedient. I was left with little choice: I was going to have to tell my father as soon as I saw him. I supposed I could hope the principal had written my father a letter, which wouldn't have arrived yet—it might have been easier than trying to reach Dad at work. Or maybe he had called our house—that would have been the best scenario. I knew I could count on my mother to give him an earful. Of course, I could count on my mother to give me an earful too.

That night, my mother said, "Vivienne, stop pushing that food around on your plate, and eat your dinner. There are starving African children who would be grateful for meat loaf and would eat it every day if they could."

I looked hard at my mother. Had she heard what I'd said at school? Why would she have brought up children in Africa that night, of all nights?

"I'm not hungry, Mom. What time will Dad be home?"

"As soon as the football game he's refereeing is over. What on earth is wrong with you?"

"I might as well tell you. If I'm in bed when Dad gets home, he'll probably make me get up so he can punish me. I mean, he gets me up to redo my math homework when I get my fractions wrong, and this is much worse."

My mother raised her eyebrows and looked at me.

"I got in an argument at lunch–well, not an argument, really, because no one said anything back to me. But I disobeyed Daddy."

I relayed the conversation to my mother.

She said, "You know what the problem is, don't you? You are just like me. You let your temper get the better of you, and when it does, you speak without thinking. It's the Chapelle curse. Nanna is exactly the same. Well, there's no use in worrying about it now. In a week, it will be water under the bridge. Go take your bath."

I felt like Anne Boleyn marching to the guillotine when Mom came to my bedroom door two hours later, asked if I was still awake, and told me my father was home. I loved Ann Boleyn to death–well, that was a poor choice of words, but she was my favorite of Henry's wives and the prettiest, and I could imagine she'd felt just like this as she walked to the guillotine to get her head chopped off.

"So how about you tell me in your own words what happened at lunch today?" said my father.

"Well, I just got mad. People are just so stupid sometimes," I said, and with as much bravado as I could muster, I relayed the conversation to my father.

"So you disobeyed me." It was a statement, not a question. The subtlety was not in my favor. Historically, when Dad asked a question, he was seeking a truthful, and potentially exoncrating, answer. This, though, required either a yes or a no.

"Yes, sir."

"You know," he said, "there are times in life when things are best left unsaid. And then there are times in life when to leave things unsaid would be to seriously compromise your personal values. Compromise them in a way that diminishes your own self-esteem. Do you understand what I mean? I'm not sure if you will face ramifications for what happened at lunch today–I certainly hope not.

I think those students you challenged will probably have forgotten the incident by next week. If not, you will likely be labeled with that derogatory term for the rest of the year, but I have no doubt you will hold your head high and deal with it. Here's the important thing: you need to decide whether you will suffer the most from standing up for your principles or whether alienating other students will be worse. I think I know the answer."

I nodded in understanding and asked, "Am I on restriction?"

"You disobeyed me, did you not? However, I might have expected that you would always find it a challenge to ignore your principles, so no, you will not be punished for doing the right thing," said my father. "And I doubt the principal will call me. I think he probably knows that even in Mississippi, it isn't a crime to be nonracist."

Sometimes my parents flat-out astonished me.

Twenty

I WAS IN HIGH SCHOOL WHEN I READ *A TALE OF TWO CITIES* by Charles Dickens. Forever afterward, the opening sentence, "It was the best of times, it was the worst of times," was one of those phrases that came to my mind at various moments when life in general was being her capricious self. It perfectly described my feelings about the two years we spent in Biloxi.

After the lunchroom incident, I was ostracized by some of the students, and I understood with a level of maturity that I had never experienced the breadth and depth of their convictions or, more accurately, their indoctrination.

Except for racism, which I hated and which was impossible to avoid in Mississippi, there were a lot of things I loved about the state. I loved the massive oak trees draped in moss. I loved the old mansions that faced the gulf and the wrought-iron railings that enclosed their front lawns. One such house that I passed on my way to school every day was Beauvoir. It had a plaque fastened to its rails that said, "Former Home of Jefferson Davis, President of the Confederate States of America." I wasn't sure I knew what that meant. I knew, of course, about the Civil War, and I knew that Abraham Lincoln had been the US president during that war, but I knew little about the history, except that it had been fought to end slavery. Still, one of my subjects in school was history of the South, and I was sure I'd be learning all about it. Mostly, though, I loved the antebellum feeling of this town that was directly on the Gulf of Mexico.

One Friday, we were let out of school early because the teachers had a conference, and I decided to go two blocks out of the way to visit Louisiana. She had a business named Louisiana's Pralines, and she made the most heavenly pralines in the world. Louisiana looked a lot like the picture of Aunt Jemima on bottles of pancake syrup, and when I had first met her, she must have noticed me squinting as I studied her. I mean, with her being in the cooking business and all, her appearance on the bottle would have made sense.

"No, baby," she had said without asking what I was looking at, "that ain't me on that bottle of syrup in yo' mama's kitchen cupboard!"

Louisiana had a rickety wooden stand with a corrugated metal roof, and she cooked the sugary treats in a pan on a wood-burning grill. The first time I had ever tasted them during the summer, I had ridden the bus to town with three of my girlfriends, and on the way home, they had insisted we ride one stop beyond the base just so they could introduce me to pralines–which I had never heard of. Mostly, though, I preferred to go by myself. When I was by myself, Louisiana always told me to take a load off and sit for a spell.

When I first asked her about her name, she said, "Umm-umm. My mama and daddy moved from Louisiana befo' I was born. They's from a county called Concord, up 'long the Mis'sippi River. My brothers was named Ferriday, Parchum, and Monterey–all towns from around where all our kinfolk was born and raised. So when they move to Bay Saint Louis and had me–finally got them a girl– they intended to call me Louisa. You know"–she nodded–"after the bay. But the preacher misunderstood, 'cause he knew they was from Louisiana, so Louisiana was exactly what got put on the baptism certificate. Now, they coulda just shortened it and called me Louisa anyways, but my Daddy said, 'Now that I think 'bout it, I'm right proud of that name!' So I've always been called Louisiana! You know," she added, "that state was named after a famous king!"

I decided I liked her father's attitude, but more, I liked Louisiana's attitude, and I made up my mind right then and there to stop complaining about my name.

When Louisiana first asked what my full name was and I told her–including my middle name, which I usually never breathed a word of to anyone–she said, "Umm-umm. That's quite a mouthful fo' a little thing like you. Here–have another praline. You need to grow into that; yes, you do." It was not lost on me that even someone named Louisiana recognized the burden of my name.

As I walked the five blocks home, munching as slowly as I could on my second praline to make it last, I thought of the first quarter of the school year, which had ended last week. My first nine weeks of eighth grade at the public Mary L. Michel Junior High School had been much easier than any grading period at Phalsbourg Elementary School. For one thing, this year, I didn't have to take French, because foreign languages were not required in junior high school in Mississippi. I was holding my own in math, and I was light-years ahead in English. But the real surprise was that I was enjoying science. The teacher had taken us on weekly field trips: we had collected crawfish to dissect; gathered leaves and moss to look at under microscopes; and mixed chemicals in test tubes to make bubbling, smoking concoctions that were supposed to teach us what went on inside a volcano. Mostly, though, I was thrilled to be taking a class called home economics, in which we were learning to sew. I loved all of it, and before I knew it, the first term was over.

Unlike school in France, where report cards had been mailed, we were given our report cards in sealed manila envelopes to be taken home to our parents. I was pretty sure I had done OK, but years of report card anxiety weighed heavily on me as I walked home. I had slipped the envelope into my book bag, and within a short time, it felt as if I had put bricks in there. So this was what a real albatross felt like! Finally, I dropped the bag onto a patch of grass and pulled out the envelope. I held it up toward the sun, hoping it might become transparent. It didn't. I picked at the sealed flap with my fingernail and soon realized that any attempt to open it and reseal it would be evident, so maybe I should just open it and act as if it had never been sealed shut. I could imagine my father's reaction to that–not because he would care that I'd seen my grades, as I'd be seeing them anyway, but because that would be a violation of trust in his mind. With a sigh, I picked up my bag and continued home.

I decided the best time to give my father the report card was at the dinner table. I couldn't imagine it was going to be terrible, but it might not be great. If, for some reason, it was really bad–worse than French or math–he would eat his dinner before sitting me down and reprimanding me, by which time he would have reevaluated his response. My dad was always reasonable.

When I got home, I tried to concentrate on *American Bandstand*, but it was hopeless.

"Do you want to see my report card, Mom?"

"No, love, I'm not at all bothered about it. I'm sure you did fine, and if you didn't, you'll do better next time."

"I thought you were bothered. You were going on about the Brontë sisters and their tutor and stuff in France. Remember?"

"Was I? Well, I'm sure it was because you constantly moaned about arithmetic and French classes. Anyway, if you're not watching Dick Clark, you can set the table for dinner."

At five thirty, we sat down to dinner, and I could barely stand the stress as my father slowly opened the envelope to avoid tearing the sealed flap. As he slid the report card out, I closed my eyes and took a deep breath. An eternity passed while he scanned the report.

Suddenly, he waved it in the air. "I knew you could do it! You did it! You finally did it!"

At long last, I had made his dreams come true, and I slowly let out my breath: I had made the honor roll!

Immediately, I almost ruined it. I opened my mouth to say that compared to school in France, my first weeks in Mississippi had been pretty easy, but I caught myself and simply said thank you. After all, with one slip of the tongue, he might have realized that my achievement wasn't because I was smart, let alone brilliant; he would have known that the subjects weren't as demanding, and it would have been just like him to find more things for me to study. He would have reminded me that in high school, I'd have to take a foreign language, and he'd probably have made me start with the French lessons again, so I'd be up to par. So far, I was enjoying school, and I liked how making the honor roll now made me feel.

Now that I'd resolved, at least for another nine weeks, the biggest problem in my life—my father's expectations related to my academic performance—my biggest problem was my mother: she was still intractable about allowing me to wear lipstick.

"Mom, all the other girls in eighth grade are allowed to wear lipstick! Their favorite is Tangee, and they buy it at Woolworth's! And if I'm spending my own money on it, why can't I start wearing lipstick?"

"If all the other girls jumped off a cliff—"

I clapped my hands over my ears and flounced out of the room. My mother was so annoyingly British!

As my mother predicted, the furor over my anti-segregation remarks in the lunchroom was soon forgotten, and for the rest of the school year, eighth grade ran the risk of being unremarkable in all ways. Except for the fact that I consistently made the honor roll, it well could have fallen into oblivion, but the same could not be said for the rest of our time in Biloxi.

June finally arrived, and I—along with several other teenagers who lived on base—was hired for my first real job: part-time playground counselor. There was something eminently satisfying, I thought, about having been hired for a job that was important enough to be abbreviated: we were PPCs. Along with the illustrious title and name badges that announced who we were and what our role was, we were given ten dollars a week, plus an ample supply of craft paraphernalia. The moniker, I soon realized, was a euphemism for what could have been considered a babysitting job four hours a day, five days a week. Armed with finger paints, crayons, craft paper, glue, and plastic scissors, half a dozen of us teenagers spent from 9:00 a.m. to 1:00 p.m. daily entertaining children on the various playgrounds scattered around Keesler Air Force Base. My friend Patsy and I were assigned playgrounds near each other, and at least twice a month, we obtained permission from some of the children's parents to take them to the beach for a picnic lunch. It was a short walk, and for some reason I could not in later years fathom, those parents who gave their permission obviously thought two fourteen-year-olds were perfectly capable of managing more than a dozen five- and six-year-olds as we walked the four blocks to the beach. The route required crossing both the main highway that ran along the base and into the town of Biloxi and another main road that bordered the beach. It did not occur to us—or, apparently, any of the parents—that we were also breaking the law by gathering our integrated little group together and walking them to the public whites-only beach like ducklings following a mama duck. Either we escaped notice by the beach patrol due to our going during the low-utilization hours in the middle of a weekday, or they simply decided not to impose what we air force brats thought was a ridiculous rule to begin with.

In the evenings, I often babysat for the children of my parents' friends and made twenty-five cents an hour. On any given weekend, if I was frugal with my earnings, I might have as much as twelve dollars to spend. If I saved for two weeks, I could double that, and that was a small fortune, at least it seemed so to me.

While my friends and I bowled and went to movies on the base, shopping—of the type my girlfriends and I liked to do—required a trip to downtown Biloxi. The base had neither dress shops nor a Woolworth's, and those were the places we girls were most fond of.

One Saturday morning, I was catching the bus to downtown Biloxi by myself. It was not quite ten o'clock, and it promised to be a lovely early August day. The air was redolent with the fragrance of tropical flowers, new-mown grass, and the ever-present salt air carried inland by the gulf breezes. For some reason, none of my friends were going to town that day, which was unusual for a Saturday, but I was on a mission: last week, I had seen a dress in the window of the Three Sisters' Dress Shop, and with my babysitting money, the wages from my last two paychecks, and my one-dollar-a-week allowance, I had more than enough money to purchase it. It was pale yellow, with white piping around the neck. Down the bodice were white pearl buttons, and the skirt flared out beneath a shiny white patent-leather belt. It was beautiful, and I prayed the dress shop hadn't sold the one I'd tried on last week, because it had been the only one they had in my size.

The assistant in the dress shop showed me to a dressing room, told me the dress looked perfect on me when I stepped out to look at it in the three-way mirror, and wrapped it in tissue paper when I said I would take it. She put the purchase in a paper bag embossed with the shop's logo, and I felt very grown up as I strolled down the sidewalk toward Woolworth's. When I got to the dime store, I spent thirty minutes browsing through the various departments, trying to get up enough courage to buy Tangee lipstick despite my mother forbidding me to "paint my lips." Suddenly, I realized I was famished.

It was Saturday, and lots of people were eating at the Woolworth's luncheonette. The counter was completely full. I waited patiently, and as soon as a seat was vacated, I sat down, but I realized almost immediately I was sitting between two women of color.

Now I was in a quandary. I didn't want to jump up and say, "Oh, sorry. I didn't realize I took a seat in the colored section." How rude would that have been? I wasn't even sure whether Woolworth's had an actual policy about who could sit where. Most of the restaurants in town were either white only or colored only, and the people of color knew they couldn't go in the strictly white places. Once, though, my friends and I had gone into a colored barbecue by mistake, and everyone had been really nice. They hadn't kicked us out, and it made me feel sad to know that if a person of color went into a white restaurant, he or she would be made to leave. Though I hadn't had much eating-out experience, I hadn't encountered any sandwich or hamburger places except Woolworth's that were integrated. I was finally put out of my misery of wondering if I should have sat where I was sitting when the waitress put a menu in front of me and said she'd be right back to take my order.

I was pretty sure then that there was no segregation at the Woolworth's lunch counter, and when the waitress came back, I ordered a hamburger and a Coca-Cola and leaned forward to get a better view of the seating arrangement around the counter. I counted twenty-two swiveling stools placed kind of close together. Starting from the distant end of the bar, which was L-shaped, I counted sixteen seats in which were seated white customers. It appeared to me that seats seventeen through twenty-two might have been reserved for people of color, although there were no signs anywhere indicating that. Maybe that was just how things had happened today, with it being a busy Saturday and all.

"Honey, you want peanuts for your Co'Cola?"

The waitress was talking to me.

"Oh. No, thank you."

"OK, sweetie. Your hamburger will be right up."

I looked at the lady sitting to my left. As she glanced at me, I smiled. She turned her head in the other direction and swiveled in her seat. She did it so obviously that her right shoulder blocked my view. I felt as if I had somehow offended her, and now I was back to worrying about whether I had, regardless of the waitress saying nothing, sat in the colored-only section by mistake.

The lady on my right was older, and as I turned a little in my seat, she smiled and said in a voice so low I almost couldn't hear her, "Don't you worry none, chile; she jes' don't wanna do nothin' that will cause a scene."

Just as I was getting ready to question her about what she meant, the waitress came over, holding a plate with my hamburger on it.

"Honey, I got your burger here, but a place down at the end there just opened up, so you'd best move on down and free this here seat up." She turned and walked toward the other end of the counter, calling over her shoulder, "Bring your Co'Cola, baby."

People looked in my direction as I walked with my drink to the empty seat in the whites-only section, and I realized that attention was just as bad as walking into Mass at the last minute and having to walk up the main aisle and sit front and center while everyone watched. Actually, this was much worse. As I glanced down the row of seats to where I had been sitting, I saw an elderly man of color with a cane hobble over to the seat I had vacated, and I realized he had been patiently waiting for a place at the counter that should never have been taken by a thoughtless white girl.

I was learning that there were times when one uncomfortable situation after another could squeeze up inside you until you had to wonder how they didn't make you burst into a million pieces for lack of any more available space. It turned out that day was one of those times.

I paid for my lunch and left Woolworth's without summoning the courage to disobey my mother and buy a tube of lipstick.

I waited at the bus stop for the city bus that would take me back to the base and drop me almost exactly at the front gate. Maybe, I thought, I'd ride one stop farther to buy a praline from Miss Louisiana and have a chat, as it was Saturday. I could talk to her about my indiscretion of sitting in the colored section by mistake, and I was sure she'd soothe my guilt. Then I'd just walk back to the main gate. While I was musing about the possibility of treating myself to a praline, the bus arrived. It was packed full all the way to the rear. I managed to find a seat toward the back, carefully noting that it was in the whites-only section, although just barely. A large gray-haired lady moved her shopping bags in a little closer, giving me room to edge in next to her.

At the next bus stop, even though people got off, more people got on, and it was even more crowded. A few people now stood in the aisle, holding on to the straps hanging from the ceiling of the bus. The front door of the bus closed, and I heard the familiar *whoosh* sound that meant the bus driver had pulled the lever, but we didn't inch out into traffic right away. I knew that meant a person of color was walking to the back door of the bus after having to pay his or her fare at the front. An elderly woman with two large shopping bags got on, put the bags on the floor, and then reached up next to me to grab a strap. As the back door closed and the bus gave a lurch forward into traffic, the woman lost her grip on the strap and grabbed the back of the seat nearest to her as her shopping scattered across the aisle.

Quickly, I stood up to help her gather the items before they rolled forward and backward.

"Would you care to sit down?" I asked. "I'm fine standing. Really."

"Thank you, sugar. These old legs are sure tired today," she made an *umm-umm* sound just like Louisiana made as she sat down and tucked her bags under the seat in front of her.

Suddenly, the bus stopped so quickly that all the shopping bags that had been placed on the floor by people's feet slid forward, scattering everyone's purchases everywhere. At first, people in my immediate vicinity looked around and shrugged, not understanding why we had stopped so abruptly. As people in the aisle squeezed to one side, we noticed the bus driver pushing his way toward the back. A man on a mission, he kicked packages aside with his feet and soon stood before me with his fists on his hips. The scowl on his face pushed his sweaty red cheeks upward and made his eyes look like ominous dark slits buried in folds of flesh. He raised his right arm and pointed a finger at me, almost touching my nose. He scared me, but something deep inside me refused to cringe.

"You!" he bellowed. "You sit down!" Then, turning to the elderly lady I had given my seat to, he said in a low, threatening voice, "And you will stand until there is a vacant seat in the nigger section of this here bus!"

In my ear–so clearly that I turned to see where he was–my father's voice said, "Do not, under any circumstances, challenge this man. You will endanger yourself and every person of color on the bus." This time, I listened to him.

I could feel the heat as it crawled up my neck, and my face blazed with anger. My heart was pounding so hard my ears were ringing. The elderly woman stood up, and I sat down. The white lady in the window seat turned her head and looked out the window. People collected their shopping that had scattered due to the sudden stop. As the bus pulled forward again and inched into traffic, a young man in the very back of the bus got up, gathered the elderly woman's shopping, put it back in the bags, and led her to his seat.

My anticipation of going for a chat with Louisiana and buying a praline had evaporated, and as we neared the base, I pulled the cord that let the bus driver know a passenger wanted to get off at the next stop. I stood up and decided in defiance that I would exit through the back door, which white people never did. I would walk right under the posted Colored Exit sign. Several of the older men of color touched their hats as I turned and walked to the back of the bus, and one lady smiled and gave a little nod, although none of them looked directly at me. Their gestures brought tears to my eyes. As I stepped down from the bus, I realized there was a possibility the bus driver would get out of the bus to shout at me again for breaking yet another unspoken rule, and I was prepared to scream in his face what I thought of him. If that occurred, I hoped the airmen guarding the base's main gate would hear the commotion and come get me. If he managed to lay one finger on me, my father would kill him—or at least report him. I stood for several minutes after the bus pulled back out into traffic, still shaking with anger.

I burst into tears as soon as I walked in our front door, which caused my mother not a little concern until she could understand what I was saying. She calmed me down, wiped my face, and told me I had handled everything perfectly. She said that the lunch counter confusion was not my fault—she would have my father write to Mr. Woolworth about clarifying the seating situation—and that I had been correct in offering my seat to an elderly lady. During dinner, she relayed my day in detail to my father, who listened intently and said he was proud of me, both for showing my manners by giving my seat to an elderly lady and for recognizing what might have ensued if I had challenged the bus driver. My mother, though, surprised me: she wished she'd been there, she said, to put that ignorant bus driver in his place! He'd never shout at her daughter or anyone else's again!

That night, lying in bed, I had an epiphany: not one Caucasian man on the bus had challenged the bus driver or come to the defense of the elderly lady. How alien that was to me. I didn't know anyone—at least among my parents' male friends—who would have stood by while the driver bullied both of us. My father would certainly have stepped in–I was pretty sure he would have been embarrassed not to.

The following Saturday, my mother went shopping, and when she returned, she had a surprise for me.

"I've decided–even though I think you are perfectly lovely without all the makeup I see young girls wearing nowadays–that I don't want you to be the only girl in your class who isn't allowed to wear lipstick," she said, and she handed me a little brown paper bag. Inside was a tube of Tangee lipstick.

I threw my arms around her, and why it made me cry I had no idea.

I would no longer be the only girl starting the ninth grade at Mary L. Michel Junior High School who was not allowed to wear lipstick.

Twenty-one

ANOTHER SUMMER CAME TO AN END, LABOR DAY CAME and went, and school started again. I was in the ninth grade at Mary L. Michel—my last year of junior high school. I liked school, and although segregation was still a topic of conversation at our house occasionally, I learned to avoid challenging my school friends about their deep-seated views, however much I disagreed with them.

Segregation was as much a part of our daily lives as was oxygen. Even amongst my closest friends, it was seldom discussed—who went around talking about the air they breathed?—but ever present. From time to time, we read reports or heard on the news about a physician of color who was actively organizing peaceful demonstrations. Dad told me that Dr. Gilbert Mason had led two groups of men, on two different occasions, on what were being called wade-ins on Biloxi Beach. Of all the things I found hard to believe, depriving anyone of the beach or the ocean was the most confounding. How could anyone believe in God and, at the same time, think he or she had a right to deprive someone else of the things God had created?

For the most part, Mississippi had been quiet in the year and a half we had lived there, but on October 1, 1962, that changed. James Meredith, an air force veteran, had enrolled at the University of Mississippi. He was the first person of color to attend Ole Miss, and Walter Cronkite had been on the news, covering the disruption that his enrollment had caused in Oxford. Even though my father said the Supreme Court had abolished segregation in the 1950s, Mississippi had never integrated their schools and colleges. It was hard for me to understand how a man who had served in our military and who would have died to defend his country and its citizens could be denied admission to any college in any state in America. Walter Cronkite said that three thousand American troops and hundreds of United States Marshals had been sent to protect him twenty-four hours a day. I tried to grasp that number, and I tried to imagine how filled with hate people would have to have been to riot because an American citizen–one who had served his country honorably–just wanted to go to college.

"I don't think it's quite that simple, Viv," said my father. "Your life has been amazingly cosmopolitan. Do you know what that means? No?"

I shook my head.

"It means you are a citizen of the world. You have lived in three countries–actually, two continents and one island–in your fourteen years and have encountered many people of different cultures and different ethnicities. Your life, I think you will one day recognize, has been enriched and broadened beyond anything you would have been exposed to if you had been born in Mississippi and lived all your life here. These current developments are not requiring you to change your entire value system or change the things you think define you, as they are now forcing people who have lived here their whole lives to do. This is a very complex issue–too broad for you to grasp now."

I sighed. "OK, Dad, I'll do my best to try to understand people who have not lived in three countries and, therefore, think people whose skin color is different from theirs are not equal to them intellectually, socially, or–whatever else they think is importantly unequal."

My father frowned and said, "I'm not sure you can use that adverb to modify that direct object, which, by the way, needs an *i-t-y* at its end to actually make it the direct object of that sentence."

While I was trying mentally to diagram the sentence, he smiled.

"Try to think of it this way: during the time we are here, you will not in any measure change this culture, which is more than two centuries old and is distressing to you. Just recognize the fact that it will one day be obsolete–hopefully in your lifetime. Let it broaden your horizon so you will grow from the experience. And most importantly, try to be a kid, OK?"

"I'll try, but I can't guarantee it will work."

James Meredith was the headline news on all the channels, at both six o'clock and ten o'clock, and then, suddenly, he was not. The rioting, Ole Miss, and the Ku Klux Klan became yesterday's news so fast that it made our heads spin.

We were glued once again to the television, and this time, we would not be shrouded in the safety mantle that living on the base provided. In fact, Keesler Air Force Base would likely be one of the least-safe places in America within a short time. At school, my friends–particularly those who, like me, were children of military parents and lived on the base–spent recess, lunch, and study period talking about the rockets that Cuba was threatening to launch against America.

"Why is Cuba aiming its missiles at us?" asked one girl while we ate lunch.

"I'm not sure," I replied. "My dad tried to explain it to me, but it was really confusing. He said it was in retaliation for something called the Bay of Pigs. And he said Fidel Castro has made a deal with the Russians, and they are the ones supplying Cuba with missiles. One of our spy planes got pictures of the missiles, and they're aimed at America."

"They could wipe out the whole Southeast, which means most of the southern states," said one of the boys. "Of course, America would then wipe Cuba off the map."

"Fat lot of good that would do Mississippi–we'd all be dead," said another boy.

"Well, my dad said not to worry yet. President Kennedy is smarter than Khrushchev, and America has better resources, so he thinks we'd win."

I looked at the girl who had said that. It made sense, but my dad–who was always very logical in his reasoning–was concerned about the daily developments. "My dad said if it gets any worse, he's driving us to Illinois to stay with my grandparents. I really don't want to go, because that means my father would be down here, and if Cuba does bomb us, he might get killed," I said.

The rest of the kids at the lunch table nodded. The bell rang, and a somber group of ninth graders returned to class.

On October 25, 1962, my father loaded us into the Opel station wagon and drove us to Freeport, Illinois.

I would have been looking forward to going to school with my cousins again, but any pleasant anticipation was overshadowed by worry about my father and all my friends in the event Cuba launched its missiles at the United States. I had overheard my dad tell my mother that considering the saturation of air force bases within our coastal states–Keesler, Eglin, MacDill, and Patrick Air Force Bases were four of the biggest–the Southeast would be a compelling target for Cuba.

We would have arrived in Freeport on October 27, but in the tiny piece of Kentucky we drove through in the early morning of that day, a cement truck passed us going south on the two-lane highway, threw a rock, and shattered our car's windscreen. My father found a repair shop, but they had to send someone to Atlanta to get a replacement–no one in Kentucky had even heard of an Opel–so we spent the night at a motel in Calloway County.

Motels on the back roads of Kentucky in 1962 left a lot to be desired, in my opinion. I'd only ever stayed in French hotels prior to moving to Mississippi, so they were the only comparison I had. We were in a double-bed, non-air-conditioned room with a rust-stained toilet and shabby carpet. At the sight of the second roach, my father pulled the beds away from the wall at my mother's insistence. She reasoned that away from the walls and moved to the middle of the room, the beds would be like island oases: cockroaches would have to work too hard to get on the beds. Daddy went to the office to complain and was handed a can of roach spray.

"What are these boxes attached to the headboards? They say they take twenty-five cents," I said when I got into bed.

"Well, they say *Magic Massage*," answered my mother. "Let's put a quarter in and find out."

Mom and I could not believe how amazing the beds were. For twenty-five cents, the beds vibrated for fifteen minutes. Connie and Chris got tired of lying still, but after using every quarter my parents could come up with between them, my mother made my father go back to the office to get two more dollars' worth of quarters. Mom was sure the vibration kept the roaches away, which would have been nice had that been true, and it might have been, but I felt as if I were on a ride at the amusement park on the beach. I fell asleep dreaming I was on the roller coaster, and it was faster than the rockets that Cuba was launching at us.

The new windscreen arrived from Atlanta, as promised, and was installed in less than an hour. We were on the road again before noon the next morning. When we reached Freeport, Illinois, late in the day on October 28, my grandfather announced that the Cuban Missile Crisis was history. Khrushchev had given Cuba orders to stand down. That was my first experience of fear that had been so deep inside me I hadn't realized how crippling it had been. At the news, relief surged through my body and left me weak. My father would not have to return to Mississippi alone.

I was not sure anyone understood the sensation of an anticlimax like a military child.

On October 29, we turned around, left Freeport, and began the trek home. If not for the fact that nowhere was October 31 more viscerally exciting than in the Deep South, with all its moss-draped trees, haint-blue porch ceilings, and voodoo-laden, ghoulish customs, the end of the Cuban Missile Crisis might have been painfully anticlimactic. Instead, we were back in Biloxi just in time for Halloween.

Twenty-two

WE SURVIVED THE RIOTS, THE CUBAN MISSILE CRISIS, and the desegregation of Ole Miss. I learned to temper my temper, curb my tongue, and respect–or at least not react to–the mores of a society that was alien to me. I entered puberty finally recognizing that I could not change centuries of cultural and societal prejudice. I could enjoy activities with my African American friends on the base but not off the base, and for the most part, I learned to live with it. Ninth grade was unremarkable. In January, the Department of Health, Education, and Welfare announced that schools segregated based on race were not appropriate under law for children of military families, and as a result, the Department of Justice announced it was suing the Biloxi Municipal School District. It took almost three years for Mississippi to fully implement desegregation of its schools, and my family and I were long gone, but it was cause for celebration.

In the July before my sophomore year, I fell in love with a boy named Charlie and went on my first car date. Just before the new school year started in September, I was invited to pledge a sorority at the high school, something I'd learned was southern tradition. I had no idea what a sorority did, stood for, or accomplished, but if that was what southern girls did, then I thought I should throw myself into it. I could imagine Cissy cheering me on.

Just as I started feeling like a real southerner and looking forward to my cotillion–whatever that was–we were on our way to Dad's next assignment: Alconbury Air Force Base in England. We first spent three weeks in Freeport, as usual, before flying to RAF Mildenhall in Suffolk.

Housing on the base was scarce, and there was a long wait list. So on a glorious, breathtakingly beautiful, sunny September day, I found myself once again living at number 7 Windsor Avenue. Mom was thrilled that we could live with Nanna again, even if it was just temporary. I was enrolled at Flixton Secondary School for Girls–the school my cousins Valarie and Jacqueline attended. It was also the school my mother and her sister, my aunt Barbara, had gone to as teenagers. Once there, I found myself musing about their school days. *Did Mom ever sit at this desk or at this lunch table?* At morning assembly, I thought of my mother singing "God Save the Queen" and "All Things Bright and Beautiful." I found I liked the feeling of tradition, of familial continuity, which I had never before experienced.

It was 1963, and the rock-and-roll era was in full swing in England. My girl cousins were in love with a new group who had an odd name.

"What's a beatle?" I asked Jackie. "Shouldn't it be spelled *b-e-e-t-l-e?*"

"No," she answered, "don't you get it? It's a play on words! My dad said the name is a clever twist. Some bloke named Buddy Holly had a group named the Crickets."

Of course, I knew who Buddy Holly and the Crickets were, so it made sense. As I learned, even though Buddy Holly was dead, the Beatles were huge fans of his music.

Aunt Barbara said, "Wait until you meet the bread man. They have bread trucks now that come round just like the milkman, and my bread man in Woodsend is brilliant! He has us all in stitches: he dances around, juggling loaves of bread and sings silly songs. He's lead singer of a new group called Freddie and the Dreamers. They're still local, but by all accounts, everyone says they're going to be big! And, Do, do you remember Lol Noone?"

It sounded strange to hear my mother's name abbreviated; none of her friends in America called her anything but Doreen. Only Nanna and our English relatives shortened it to Do, and now, for the first time, I noticed how the British abbreviated every possible word that could be abbreviated.

"Of course! The boy I used to go dancing with!"

"That's him. His nephew is making a name for himself, at least locally. His name is Peter Noone, and he was on Coronation Street for a while. Well, he was with a group called the Heartbeats, but now he and his mates have formed a group called Herman and His Hermits. Nobody knows why they chose that name, but anyway, they play in and around Manchester, and they're quite good. I saw them play recently. I think they're really going to make a name for themselves too."

"Lawrence Noone," said my mother in a dreamy voice, "was–or is–a fantastic ballroom dancer. What I would give if Bob could dance like Lol. Did he ever get married, do you know?"

"Oh yes, I'm pretty sure he did," answered Nanna. "And have you ever heard of the Bee Gees? Well, they're from round here–the Gibbs–but have lived in Australia for eons. I worked at Park Hospital with their grandmother for years. Anyway, they've made it really big too."

Suddenly, I felt the need to defend Elvis.

"You know," I said, "I'm sure they are all quite good, but I doubt any of them will ever be as good as Elvis Presley. Or as handsome."

"Well, you might want to reserve judgment about that until you see Paul McCartney. He's dead handsome!" said my aunt Barbara.

It was hard to avoid seeing all the groups mentioned; every time we turned on the television, one or the other of them was on a program, and I had to admit my aunt was right: Paul was really cute. Freddie not so much, but he was a lot of fun to watch–in the bread van or on the telly.

No sooner was I enrolled in the Flixton Secondary School for Girls than I was included in the extracurricular activities of the other girls, which mostly consisted of going to dances at various teen clubs on Friday and Saturday nights to listen to local up-and-coming bands. I wasn't sure why, but unlike my mother's generation of dancing partners, modern-day English boys didn't dance. The girls danced with one another—something I had never seen in America.

Most of the local groups were made up of unknown youths who were trying to break into the thriving record industry and become the next Fab Four. Although Elvis had a British following as ardent and loyal as his American fans, the Beach Boys, Ricky Nelson, and Pat Boone were largely unknown in that corner of Britain, which was saturated with more rock-and-roll talent than anywhere else on the globe.

"Want to go to the Urmston Baths with us on Saturday night, Anne?" asked Sheila, one of my new school friends. I was testing my luck one more time at changing my name: I had decided that Vivienne, which most people spelled as Vivian anyway, could logically be shortened to Anne.

The Baths was an indoor swimming pool in the neighboring town of Urmston that became a nightclub of sorts in the winter. The pool was covered with a hard surface—just like in the Jimmy Stewart movie *It's a Wonderful Life*—and a variety of entertainment was scheduled throughout the fall and winter months. An added bonus was that the entire venue was relatively small, and the locals and the entertainers were likely to mingle during the evening. It wasn't unusual to hear one or more of the girls name-drop, saying, "I told Freddie I would definitely go see him in Manchester," or "Did you hear what Peter was saying about who'd they'd been practicing with? I'd be dead chuffed if I got to meet someone that famous!"

"Who's going to be at the Baths?" I asked now.

"The Rolling Stones are coming to town."

"What's a rolling stone?" I asked.

"A groovy new group. They're as good as the Beatles," answered one of the girls. With her broad Lancashire accent, it sounded as if she'd said, "A gruvy nuw grupe. They're as gudus the Be'uls."

"Oh. Well, OK. How much does it cost?"

"Foive bob," she answered.

I thought for less than a minute. I got an allowance–spends, it was called in England–of seven shillings a week, the equivalent of an American dollar. Five shillings would leave me with only two shillings for the entire next week–not enough to go horseback riding with Jackie on Saturday. The most it usually cost to see a local group, if anything, was two shillings. Somehow, I just could not bring myself to spend the larger part of a whole week's allowance on a group with a name as silly as the Rolling Stones.

"I think I'll pass," I said. "I really need to study this weekend–Pitman shorthand is killing me–but thank you for inviting me." If I heard on Monday that they were fab, I'd consider seeing them the next time they were in the area.

Until we returned to Windsor Avenue that autumn, my grandmother had housed several young policemen at number 7. Nanna explained that young, unmarried policemen were not allowed to rent accommodations independently. The policemen had two choices: they could live in a barracks-like setting at the police compound, or they could rent a room with a family who had been deemed acceptable. They could not, under any circumstances, live independently in an unmonitored apartment. I supposed the concept was much like the housing for young people who entered the military.

Now, since they'd all had to find other digs so Nanna would have room for us, the policemen all stopped by at various times during the week for cups of tea, and Nanna always put the kettle on for them. It seemed Bill came by more than the others and usually in the afternoons after I came home from school. He said that was because he worked the two-ten shift.

"He's chatting you up," said Auntie Bar.

"No, he is not!" I said indignantly. "He's too old for me!"

"Said no man ever," was my aunt's response.

"My father would never allow me to date a twenty-year-old. Besides, I'm not interested in him!"

"Well, tell that to him."

"Oh, honestly, Bar, you are too ridiculous."

My aunt dropped the conversation but not before I remembered the teeny bit of fluttering feeling I got when Bill walked into the room in his police uniform. The hat alone–or, rather, helmet–was so very attractive. There was, after all, something about a man in uniform.

"Vivienne! Are you listening to me?" My mother's voice broke through my musings.

"Yes! What?" I answered, jarred from my thoughts.

"Go get your school uniform while I've got the ironing board up. I need to run the iron over your skirt," she said, shaking her head. "I don't know what on earth is wrong with you lately. You're off in a world of your own! Now, hurry up! I want to get in the kitchen to help Nanna with dinner!"

Nothing could put a damper on a daydream like having to trudge upstairs to retrieve a school uniform. There was nothing romantic about a blue shirt, a navy-blue-striped tie, and a plaid skirt, which had to be worn day in and day out. I missed wearing cute clothes to school. Still, it didn't matter much since the upper schools in England were either all girls or all boys. Gosh, was I missing school as I used to know it.

"You can set the table," my mother said as I came back with my skirt.

Vivienne, do this! Vivienne, do that! I couldn't wait until I was old enough to live in my own apartment. Between my little sisters, who could be annoying, and my mother, who was bossy, I wished I were eighteen. At least *Top of the Pops* was going to be on the telly that night, and my aunt would be over to watch it with us. She was the only one who understood me and understood how difficult it was to live with all those women.

England

Twenty-three

T WAS AS THOUGH I HAD NEVER LEFT NUMBER 7 WINDSOR Avenue. Mrs. Murphy still lived next door in number 9, the top shops were unchanged, and the apple tree was alive and well in the corner house with the stone wall just before the passage leading to Moorside Road. Mrs. Murphy said the lady with the icebox had moved years ago, and now, across the street and diagonal from number 7, the air-raid shelter was gone. In its place were four new semidetached houses that were managed by the council. Attractive bungalows with tidy front gardens, they were not the eyesore I had imagined they would be. I thought Nanna should put her name down for one; she wasn't getting any younger, and I had noticed Granddad's garden out back was getting a bit dodgy.

Now that I was fifteen, I was no longer restricted to the geographic boundaries set by my grandparents all those years ago. Back then, my limits to the east had been the shops at the top of Whitelake Avenue, where I had been allowed to go get Granddad's paper for him when I turned five, and down the bottom of the avenue to the passage just before Moorside Road. To the west, I had been allowed to go as far as the Ainsworth house on Windsor Avenue. Now, though, besides walking to school and back, I could ride the bus to the city of Manchester with my friends or go horseback riding and ice-skating with my cousin Jacqueline in Altrincham, a town beyond the city. My cousin Valarie, who was my age, was leaving school at the end of the term. Val and I went to the teen clubs together on Saturday nights, and occasionally, we went to the Curzon when a film caught our interest.

There was some discussion upon my being enrolled in the girls' school about my taking French, which I learned was the usual foreign language course in English schools. Fortunately, my mother, not my father, enrolled me in Flixton Secondary School for Girls, and Mom pointedly said that she would prefer I take typing and shorthand, which she believed would be far more useful. *Merci, Mama!* Soon I was learning British history, baking a proper Christmas cake in cookery class, struggling with Pitman shorthand, and relishing my new name. Everyone called me Anne, and I did not consider it a lie, let alone something to be questioned. At most, it was a little fib. I was Anne with an *e*, just like Anne Boleyn, and if my mother didn't find out or my cousin Jacqueline didn't hear about it at school, it should work out just fine, I thought.

Britain never celebrated Halloween, a fact I had forgotten. However, on November 5, Guy Fawkes Night was celebrated all over England. In school, we were reminded that the celebration was to remember the failure of the plot that would have blown up the Houses of Parliament in 1605; killed the Protestant king, James I; and restored Catholic rule. Judging by the expressions on the faces of the other students in my history class, that would have been a fate worse even than being Irish Catholic. Could we imagine a Catholic England? Indeed, we could not! As Guy Fawkes had been the traitor caught guarding the stockpile of gunpowder intended to complete the dastardly deed, his demise had been cause for celebration for centuries. Not that anyone asked, but I was prepared to say I was Anglican and leave it at that rather than admit I was Catholic in that environment. Still, I wasn't sure I could stretch the truth that far, and I was vaguely conscious that my little fibs were going to add up quickly if I wasn't careful.

In any case, Parliament had wasted no time in creating a day of national celebration after thwarting the plot: the first Bonfire Night had been celebrated in 1606. It was hard to fathom something that far back still being relevant in the modern day; I remembered, though, that Britain had been around for eons. In fact, our little town of Flixton, my grandfather had told me years ago, had been settled by Vikings on the banks of the river Mersey long before the tenth century and long before the city of Manchester had emerged. He'd said it was named for the Viking Eric the Flik, who had led the expedition. Of course, Granddad also had had me convinced there was a tiny man living in a tin can in the back garden. Still, Flixton's local church, Saint Michael's, had a sign at the gated entrance announcing to one and all that it had been established in AD 1166, and there were tombstones on the floor of the church that supported the antiquity claims of the parish. I had a hard time fathoming anything that ancient.

Regardless of my lack of interest in the bomb plot, Bonfire Night was a lot of fun. Fires were lit–large and small–all over town for the purpose of burning Guy Fawkes effigies after local youth made the rounds asking for "a penny for the Guy." When groups had collected a satisfying amount of cash for their efforts, their Guys got burned at the stake. A burning effigy was a bit macabre, I thought, but probably no worse than some of our Halloween paraphernalia and the resurrection of sorcerers and haints in the coastal South. Just as I used to think of Halloween, the November 5 Guy Fawkes celebrations signaled the beginning of the holiday season there in Britain. For our family, in three weeks, it would be Thanksgiving: the beginning of my favorite time of year.

Auntie Bar said she was excited about celebrating an American holiday at number 7, and she said she couldn't wait to learn to cook a turkey. Mom told Bar that was fine, but she'd better not drink while we were cooking. Thanksgiving turkeys had to be started early in the morning, said Mom, if not the night before. "Last week," she said, chastising my aunt, "you were drinking before dinner on Sunday while the roast was in the oven, and when you stirred the gravy, you splashed it all down my best skirt. I'd just had that skirt dry-cleaned too."

Nanna looked at me and rolled her eyes. "Some things never change," she warned, "no matter how old your children get."

On Friday, November 22, 1963, just a week before Thanksgiving, I hurried home from school. There was an Elvis Presley film showing that night at the Curzon, and Valarie and I were going. I loved the Curzon and, for that matter, all British movie theaters. Although most theaters now had a concession stand in the foyer, they also still had pretty concierge girls who walked around with trays of sweets, ice cream, and drinks before the movie started and during the intermission. They also sold cigarettes, so Val and I always tried to find a seat away from groups of adults who most likely would smoke throughout the whole movie. I wasn't sure why I cared: Nanna smoked, Barbara smoked, Mom smoked, and Dad smoked cigars; and they all smoked in the house, in the pub, in the car, and even in the shops. Still, I preferred not to be enveloped in smoke while watching Elvis–that would have seemed almost sacrilegious since every American girl knew Elvis did not drink or smoke.

"What are you watching?" I asked as I walked into the cozy room Nanna called the lounge, where the family always gathered. The clock on the mantel read 4:30. I had plenty of time to get ready for the movie–Valarie was coming round at six.

My mother and grandmother were sitting with cups of tea in front of the tiny television, which was an unusual thing to find them both doing at that hour.

"President Kennedy's been shot," blurted out my mother. "He and Jackie and the Johnsons are in Dallas. The Kennedys were in a convertible with the Texas governor and his wife, and someone–they don't know who–shot the president. He's been taken to a hospital, but there's no update yet, and the Texas governor was shot too."

I was stunned. I sat down, and Nanna poured me a cup of tea.

"Here you are, my love. Drink this," she said.

So this was why the entire world thought the British believed a cup of tea could solve anything. I sipped my tea, but it wasn't hot enough. My tea had to be almost scalding for me to drink it. Still, in the big picture of things, as Dad would have pointed out if he had been there, was the temperature of my tea all that important in the face of an international disaster?

"I don't think I'll go to the pictures with Valarie," I said.

"Oh yes, you will, young lady," said Nanna. "There is nothing you can possibly do, and it will take your mind off things. Now, go tidy up, and I'll fix your tea. And"–she held up a hand–"I don't want to hear that you aren't hungry."

Valarie and I purchased our tickets and found seats away from larger groups of people as the concierge girls wove their way up, down, and around the seats. Shortly, "God Save the Queen" began to play, and we stood with the others. We sat through the news reels and clips of upcoming films, and finally, the movie began.

Follow That Dream was probably not a riveting movie. I really didn't know, because I couldn't concentrate. Elvis was as handsome as ever, but even a fifteen-year-old girl had the ability to recognize that Elvis had never actually made a riveting movie–it was all about just getting to sit and absorb two hours of Elvis.

At intermission, I decided I needed to walk off my nervous energy–a recurring feeling that something was welling up inside me and trying to squeeze out of my pores. I went to the concession in the lobby for my Cadbury Flake bar.

As he was ringing it up, the man behind the counter said, "Oy, are you a Yank?" He pointed over his shoulder to a tiny black-and-white television on the back counter. "Your president, that Kennedy bloke, died. They just announced it. Got himself shot he did, this mornin' in a place called Dallas. I hope they catch the bugger who bloody did it."

I paid for the chocolate and went back to my seat.

On the screen was a picture of President Kennedy, and "The Star-Spangled Banner" was playing. Everyone in the theater was standing with a hand over his or her heart. Some older men were saluting. It brought tears to my eyes.

When the American national anthem ended, I said, "Let's go home, Val. I don't want to watch the rest of the film."

Every newspaper and every televised news program over the next several weeks were filled with images, reports, and speculations about the assassination. There were pictures of Jackie in her bloodstained suit, standing next to Vice President Lyndon Johnson as he took the oath of office on *Air Force One*. There were pictures of Lee Harvey Oswald, who had already been arrested for the murders of both the president and a police officer named J. D. Tippit. Then, days after the assassination, a man named Jack Ruby somehow finagled his way into the basement of the Dallas police station, where he shot and killed Oswald, who was in the process of being transferred to a more secure facility. That led to speculation that Jack Ruby was somehow complicit in the assassination and wanted to silence Oswald. Why else would an ordinary citizen have elbowed his way into the Dallas police station and shot the suspect? The world was in flux.

It was the following weekend before my father next came to Windsor Avenue, and I found his presence even more comforting than usual, although I couldn't explain why. Maybe because he was the only American in my life just now or perhaps because he made our family feel safe. Nevertheless, when he walked into number 7 on the Friday following President Kennedy's death, I felt all was right with our little world, regardless of what was going on elsewhere.

"Gracie," asked Dad after we had eaten, "how's school coming along?" He had taken to calling me Gracie in the past year or so because he said I was anything but graceful, and on top of that, he said my personality reminded him of Gracie Allen. When I commented about the complex that could give me, he told me he seriously doubted I could possibly have a complex about anything—if my dismal grades in math and French hadn't caused one, then nothing could, he said.

"It's OK," I answered.

"Just OK? Aren't you ecstatic that you don't have to take French or math?"

"I'm really happy that I don't have to take French or math. But," I added, "I know why Valarie is leaving at Christmas. It's sort of boring going to an all-girls school. And even though there is no language barrier, the subjects are strange."

"Strange how?"

"Well, wouldn't you know? History this first term is about the English colonies in America—as well as English colonies elsewhere, of course—but the British think the American colonists should have been grateful to be able to live under the protection of the British Empire. Instead, the colonists revolted, and a lot of blood was shed."

"I see. Sounds like you don't agree."

"Well, the thing is, I do sort of see both points of view. But I also think the British should not have put outrageous taxes on goods that were needed in the colonies."

For the next thirty minutes, my father and I discussed the American colonies, Britain, taxation without representation in the Parliament, and the broad differences between British rule and American independence.

I hoped we got base housing soon—I loved Flixton, Windsor Avenue, and my grandmother, but I really missed Dad.

Twenty-four

THE CHRISTMAS LIGHTS FESTIVAL IN BLACKPOOL ALWAYS started in November and illuminated the city until January. Dad promised us that we would go to see the lights the Saturday after Thanksgiving, since he'd have a four-day weekend. I only remembered going once as a child with my grandparents, and we had gone on a tour bus. By the time the bus had inched its way through the traffic and finally reached the city, I had been sound asleep and missed the whole thing. But we all agreed it was a smashing way to start the holiday season.

Christmas on Windsor Avenue was better even than Christmas in France, where I had thought chopping down our own Christmas tree in knee-deep snow was thrilling. In England, there was an air of anticipation that permeated the house: friends, relatives, and the bobbies stopped by more frequently for cups of tea, and Nanna was busier than usual, scrubbing, polishing, and cleaning. Long lists of specialty items needed from the top shops were revised daily, and I was given the task of stopping on my way home from school to collect the items on Nanna's lists. The front steps got soap-bricked more than just on a Monday, and the fragrance of lavender-paste furniture polish lingered throughout the house. Although there was always a chance it would snow in the north of England in December, it seldom did until January. Auntie Bar and I agreed that frostbitten fingers and toes and runny red noses would have to suffice, and we couldn't wait until the Christmas season arrived in all its glory.

Nanna and Mom were excited when I came home from school the week after Guy Fawkes Night and announced that we would be making Christmas cakes in cookery class. We had been given a list of ingredients that each girl who wished to make a cake had to bring to class by Monday, November 11.

According to my grandmother, a proper Christmas cake should be made a minimum of twelve weeks prior to Christmas in order to be liberally sprinkled with adequate amounts of brandy every week, wrapped in cheesecloth, and stored in a biscuit tin in the larder to keep it nice and moist. Nevertheless, she and Mom were thrilled that I would be making one at school, regardless of the late date. Having made Betty Crocker cakes since I was ten, when we'd lived in France, I felt pretty confident regarding my cake-making talent.

Our Christmas cakes were started in class on Wednesday, November 13, and would be ready to bring home on December 18. "Seriously?" I complained to my mother. Four weeks? A whole month? I felt that told us everything we needed to know in a nutshell about American exceptionalism: I could whip up a chocolate cake with fudge icing in barely an hour, and this was going to take a whole month? Mom and Nanna promised me it would be worth it.

I almost failed to make it through the first lesson in the cookery class, which I doubted had changed since my grandmother had taken lessons.

"Stir, ladies! Stir! No lagging behind! Do you want a heavy fruit cake? No, you do not! It is all in the wrist motion!" shouted the teacher, who proceeded to demonstrate with gusto how thoroughly we had to aerate the sugar, eggs, and butter with our wooden spoons in order to ensure an edible fruitcake. I once had seen a cooking show on television with someone named Julia Child, and I thought this home economics teacher must have been her twin sister.

As it turned out, electric mixers in British school cookery classes were nonexistent, and I had been stirring the batter—as had all the other girls—for nearly thirty minutes. Just as I was about to chuck it in and tell my mother and Nanna I just couldn't manage it, Miss Tippett came over to my side of the wooden table I was sharing with another girl–"Only two to a table, ladies! Give yourselves plenty of elbow room!" she'd said–and loudly announced to everyone in her English-accented Julia Child voice, "Now *this* is how it should begin to look!"

She picked up my bowl and marched around the room with it so each girl could see how her batter should look.

Returning the bowl to me, she said, "Next, add the flour, and keep stirring. In a few more minutes, Anne, it will have reached perfection, and you can add your fruit that has been soaking! And if any of you notice that your batter looks as though it is beginning to separate or curdle, cease beating immediately! It means you have beaten too long!"

Then, to my mortification, she announced that because I was using real butter and not margarine, there was little risk of separation. She felt compelled at that point to add–I presumed she thought there were some girls who didn't know the difference between the two– that I was the only girl using real butter. I noticed eye rolls ripple through the classroom: something was definitely wrong when the American girl was using real butter and all the English girls were using flora, as it was called in England. After we finished the batter, a marker pen was circulated, and we wrote our names on the odd little tins, which had latches. After the cakes had baked and cooled, we would release the latches so the cakes could be lifted out. Those, I thought, were clever.

The class ended with our cakes being put in ovens to bake. "Not to worry, ladies!" shouted Miss Tippett. "Your cakes are in good hands!"

Nanna was in the kitchen, putting the kettle on to boil, when I came home from school that afternoon. My mother was at the table, making a grocery list for what she wanted Dad to get on his visit to the commissary before he next came to Flixton for the weekend. The two had been discussing the quandary, as they thought of it, of the Christmas cake.

"Well," said Nanna, "we were trying to sort out how we could get your cake home so it can be properly soaked in brandy before it's iced. We thought the best thing would be if you simply tell your cookery class teacher that you must bring it home in the interim. The thing is, it cannot be iced—or even wrapped in marzipan—before it's properly soaked. After all, it is a Christmas cake."

I was appalled. Clearly, they had no clue that the cooking teacher bore no resemblance to Betty Crocker—not in any stretch of anyone's imagination.

"I'm not telling Miss Tippett that I'm not to ice the cake! She has already said we're doing the marzipan the second week in December and the snow icing the third, right before we bring them home. And here's the list of ingredients she says we need for those things."

"Well," answered my mother, "as I am the one paying for the ingredients, I do believe I should have a say in the more traditional aspects of making a Christmas cake! It should always be steeped in either brandy or whiskey weeks before the marzipan goes on. And to be fair, we've already lost almost all that time!"

"Vivienne is quite right, Do. It is a bit awkward. Ne'er mind, love," said Nanna. "We will carefully peel the marzipan off and wrap it in cheesecloth to save it so that we can put it back on after the cake has been soaked. It won't be as good as a good soaking for a full eight to twelve weeks, but we'll manage."

"Well," said my mother, "I suppose we can do that. But honestly, the whole point of a proper Christmas cake is to soak it liberally in spirits, then wrap it in marzipan, and then ice it! The teacher must know that. This isn't an American cooking class, for Pete's sake."

"Mom, I really don't think the headmistress would allow anyone to bring a bottle of brandy or whiskey into the school to soak anyone's Christmas cake. And we can't bring them home, soak them, and then bring them back Christmas week to finish off. Is soaking it that important? Because it won't be just a matter of peeling off the marzipan; it will have icing covering the marzipan, and icing won't peel!"

Mom and Nanna looked at each other.

"Viv's right," said Mom.

"We'll think of something," said my grandmother.

Thanksgiving arrived on the coldest day of autumn. I didn't have the day off school, because it wasn't a holiday in Britain. As Mr. Aldershot pointed out, England had had no way of knowing how things would turn out, and it was probably a jolly good thing that the British never had gotten into the habit of celebrating the first Thanksgiving feast that the Pilgrims shared with the Native Americans. He added that although Anglo-American traditions were intertwined, most of the common holidays were such because the English settlers had been used to celebrating them before they emigrated. I thought he almost said "before they became traitors" but stopped short. He said the British eating turkey, corn, and sweet potatoes to celebrate the emigration of British subjects from England to the New World would have seemed more than a little odd.

Mr. Peck was the typing and shorthand teacher. He was very old and not very big. I thought he must have been at least sixty. He tried his best to keep us all in line, but given his squeaky voice and less-than-authoritative presence, I figured he must have found it hard work most days. Still, he was kind and never attempted control by humiliation, which I'd noticed often was the case with certain teachers. And unlike Mr. Aldershot, he was never sarcastic.

"Now, class, I'd like you to pay attention," he said five minutes before the bell rang to end the period. "Today it is Thanksgiving in America, which commemorates, I believe, the first shared feast between the American colonists and the indigenous people of the New World. Anne, would you be so kind as to tell us what American families will be doing today? How they will be celebrating?"

"Um, well, mostly, they will be eating turkey, which is the traditional Thanksgiving dinner. That's because turkeys are nice and fat and plentiful in the autumn in America. So that's what the colonists and the Indians cooked, along with things like corn, which the Indians called maize, and potatoes and pumpkin pie. And nowadays, after the big family dinner, almost everyone will gather in the family room to watch football games on the TV. Football is always played on Thanksgiving Day. Our football is nothing like your soccer—but it is a bit like English rugby. And most of the people will just fall asleep while watching it, because they've eaten too much."

"Now, doesn't that sound lovely, class? How many of you have ever eaten turkey? Raise your hands."

No one raised her hand. I was shocked, although why should I have been? I'd never had turkey until I went to America, and Nanna and Auntie Barbara were looking forward to our dinner that night because they'd never had turkey.

"Well," said Mr. Peck, "I shall look forward to one day having the pleasure of eating turkey while I'm still sharp enough to know what I'm eating! Class dismissed!" The bell rang.

Nanna and Mom were in the kitchen when I got home from school, roasting the turkey with all the usual trimmings. Auntie Barbara was reading to Connie and Christine, and she didn't look or sound as if she'd been into the gin. Daddy, said Mom, was on his way from Alconbury and had been able to get tomorrow off. He had rung Mrs. Murphy a few hours ago to let us know. I told them about Mr. Peck never having eaten turkey and about his interest in our American traditions.

"You must take him a turkey sandwich tomorrow," said Mom.

"Oh yes, love, you must," said Nanna.

"I remember Mr. Peck," said Auntie Bar as she walked in from the lounge. "He was my typing teacher. Very nice he was."

Barbara put the leaf in the dining table, which didn't much change the size, and Nanna built up the fire. Nobody was as good at building up a fire as my grandmother. Dad arrived at five o'clock.

There were seven of us gathered around the feast, and after we said grace, my father carved the turkey, which he had brought from the base commissary last weekend and which Mom had been cooking all day. Besides turkey, we had sage stuffing, mashed potatoes and gravy, sweet potatoes, brussels sprouts, and corn. We all looked at Nanna and Auntie Bar, waiting for them to take their first bites.

"It's beautiful," said Auntie Bar. "I've never had anything so good."

"Lovely it is," said Nanna. "Just lovely. Do, you've outdone yourself!"

I looked around the table and thought, *Here I am, sitting in the warmth of Nanna's living room in the house in which I was born and lived for so many years, eating this wonderful meal with my favorite people, in my favorite place in the world.* I felt a lump in my throat but managed to take a sip of water and swallow it away. I looked at Granddad's chair, and I imagined him sitting there, holding Johnny on his knee, telling him the rhyme about the little man who lived in the can down in the bottom of the garden.

Later, we sat around the fire, too full to move and too satisfied to want to. There was no football or rugby on, because in England, it was not a national holiday. Nanna started telling us about the estate she'd lived on as a child and about accompanying her father in their farm wagon to deliver food and Christmas boxes to the tenants who lived in the cottages and worked the fields. The stories made me think of Louisiana and her brothers, and I thought about Louisiana's pralines. *Tomorrow I must tell Nanna about how wonderful they are and see if we can find a recipe in Mom's American cookbook.*

The fire died, the BBC radio signed off the air for the night, and my father drove my aunt home. As I drifted off to sleep, my last thought was *It is officially the Christmas season, and this year, I'll be spending it in my favorite place in the world.*

Twenty-five

ANNA AND MOM WERE IN THE KITCHEN—THE SCULLERY, Nanna called it—when I got home from school the next day. "How did Mr. Peck like the turkey?" asked Mom.

"He took just a little bite, said it was the nicest thing he'd eaten in a long time, and said he was taking the sandwiches home for his tea tonight."

"Aw," said Nanna. "I'm glad you made him two, Do. He probably has to look after himself and doubtless doesn't eat properly." Nanna was always concerned that single men—like the policemen—didn't eat properly.

"He said to thank you both very much for thinking of him, and he said he's dead chuffed that he'll be able to say he's had American turkey sandwiches from an American Thanksgiving," I said.

"Have you noticed, Doreen, how very English our Vivienne is sounding again now that she's been going to an English school and living here in the house she was born in?" Nanna was always proud of the fact that she'd helped to deliver me.

"I have indeed," answered my mother. "And she always did have a lovely British accent, very proper and not common at all." My mother looked at my grandmother and added, "That's because of you, Mum. You were a great influence on her when she was little."

What was I hearing? After all my hard work in learning to sound American, now they were saying matter-of-factly that in less than three months, it had all been undone!

"What's the matter, love?" asked Nanna. "Don't you feel well? Sit down, pet, and have a cup of tea."

"I don't really sound English, do I?"

"Now, stop it, Vivienne! I've told you before: you have a very nice accent, and you need to stop trying to sound different all the time!" said my mother sharply. "You won't believe this, Mum, but she used to stand in front of the mirror—as though how she looked would influence her accent—and practice sounding more American! Some girl in France apparently had a southern accent, and Viv got it in her head to try to sound just like her. Honestly, it's so silly! In Biloxi, she actually picked up the habit of saying *yawl*, which definitely sounded a bit odd with her mostly English accent."

I couldn't help but giggle at my mother's pronunciation of *y'all*.

"But, Mom," I said, "it isn't as if I don't like your and Nanna's accents. I do! But when I get to Alconbury, I don't want all the other American kids to think I talk funny. That's all. I'm American, and I want to sound American!"

I turned to set my teacup on the table, and out of the corner of my eye, I caught an odd look that Nanna gave Mom. I turned back around and looked right at Nanna and studied her face, but it looked as it always did, so I figured I must have imagined the funny look.

Saturday arrived, and my sisters were bouncing off the walls in their excitement to see the holiday lights. Every five minutes, they asked how many lights were there. Did they look like the lights on our Christmas tree last year, would we be able to get out of the car and see them up close, and would Santa Claus be there? At four o'clock, we all finally piled into the car and headed west. Blackpool, said Dad, was a good hour and a half away—maybe more if traffic was heavy.

The traffic into Blackpool was backed up for miles. *At this rate,* I thought, *it might be Christmas before we get to the lights.* Connie and Chris were in the back of the Opel station wagon, wrapped up in blankets; I was sitting between Barbara and my grandmother in the backseat; and Mom and Dad were in the front.

"If you girls don't stop that fighting back there, we're turning around!" shouted Mom to Connie and Chris.

"Don't make me stop this car, girls," said Dad.

I knew he wouldn't stop the car, and I knew Mom wouldn't insist that we turn around. She loved Christmas and everything about the yuletide: the lights, the music, the shopping, the decorating, and the socializing. To Mom, too much of it was still not enough. Not that I minded, because I loved Christmas too.

Slowly, as we inched along, the first of the lights came into view on our horizon, and for the next hour and a half, we oohed and aahed at the spectacular displays and the amount of work and effort–let alone cost–that had gone into them.

"Brilliant! Bloody brilliant!" said Auntie Barbara as we left Blackpool behind and headed back to Flixton.

"Barbara! Language!" said Nanna as I leaned against my aunt and drifted off to sleep.

The week before the school term ended for Christmas break, we girls brought our fruitcakes home from cookery class. Two days later, as promised, my mother and grandmother devised a brilliant–if somewhat questionable–way to infuse brandy into the cake, which was wrapped in marzipan and completely iced: Mom held the cake out over the crystal cake stand it would rest on, while Nanna shot the underside of the cake with a brandy-filled syringe. Next to the cake stand was a whiskey glass filled with brandy, and my grandmother expertly drew up and administered multiple injections of liquor into the bottom of the cake. I walked in from school as they were executing the procedure.

"No different, love, than what my nurse does monthly when she comes round and gives me my vitamin B12 jabs!"

"Nanna, you aren't using the needle that went in your–"

"Don't be silly, Vivienne! It just came to me when my nurse was here yesterday to give me my injection that this seemed a perfect way to get brandy into the cake. I asked the nurse if she happened to have an extra, as it looked like it would do a treat basting the Christmas duck!"

"You lied to your nurse, Nanna?"

"Of course not! We'll rinse this and use it on the duck or the roast or whatever at Christmas! But in the meantime, is that enough, do you think, Do?"

"Yes, that will do fine, Mum. I'll set the cake down on the plate, and the bottom will soak up the brandy that got dripped. Good job, Mum!"

The term finally ended, school was out for the Christmas break, and my aunt and I went shopping in Manchester. We had a list of what to buy, whom to buy for, and how much to spend. We stopped at the Plaza and the Ritz for a look around, so my aunt could show me where the Dave Clark Five and the Hollies played sometimes. We'd go see them after the holidays, she said. We went to Lewis's department store to see the Christmas decorations and have a cup of tea. We checked out Father Christmas, who was the equivalent of the Santa Claus at Macy's in New York. This Father Christmas was a big improvement over the one I'd had a picture taken with when I was four years old. In the photo, I was sitting on his knee with a look of terror on my face. He was the least-jolly Santa I had ever, in my young life, seen—in person or in pictures. We left Lewis's and went to Marks and Spencer and Woolworth's to do our Christmas shopping.

"Now, I have the list your mum gave me of what you need to buy your grandmother and your sisters. Do you have the quid she gave you?"

"I do."

"Right," said Bar, "she wants you to buy wooly knickers and a vest for your nan and then whatever you think your little sisters will like. She thinks maybe those puzzle books or Weebles coloring books. They love to watch them wobble every day on the tele, eh?"

"Let me see that list! I don't believe it!" I said, snatching the list from her hand.

Sure enough, the list said, "Warm knickers and vest from Marks if they're still on sale or, otherwise, from Woolworth's—offer said both for 14s."

"I'm not buying my grandmother woolen underwear for Christmas!" I said incredulously.

"Well," said my aunt, "I understand how you feel, but your nan could use some nice warm knickers. Number 7 does get bloody cold in January."

"I will save my spends and buy her warm knickers in January. But now it's Christmas, and I'm buying her something nice."

Something nice turned out to be the most beautiful, lavish set of Yardley's English Lavender products I had ever seen: soap, bath salts, lotion, bubble bath, and talcum powder all nestled in lavender tissue paper in one huge—at least twenty-four by twenty-four inches—box with a big purple bow on it. I was smitten, and nothing my aunt could say would deter me from buying it.

"You'll have to explain to your mum," said my aunt, "and let me remind you: her temper is legendary."

"I will. She isn't the boss of me, by the way. She is only my mother." I had a little bit of a prickly feeling as I said that. "Besides, I'll save my allowance and buy Nan warm underwear for her birthday. I told you."

"Like I said, you'll have to explain to your mum. By the way, you were supposed to get your sisters something with that money also."

To that, I had no response.

Bar turned back and said, "Come on. We can't go home without at least buying Weebles crayon books and new crayons for their stockings."

Lunch in the afternoon was the highlight of our day. It was called high tea, and because it was the holiday season, we had to wait quite a while for a table in the tearoom in the Midland Hotel. The Christmas decorations were magnificent, and when we were finally seated, a waitress in an old-fashioned black dress with a frilly apron took our order.

"That's how the maids would have dressed in the big house your nanna grew up in," said my aunt. "At least until she was eleven years old and was put out to service. Then your nan would have had to dress like that herself."

"Why would her parents have made her go into service if they were rich?"

"Well," said Auntie Bar, "they were gentry, but I guarantee they weren't rich—at least not after your great-granddad got hold of his inheritance. When his father, my great-granddad, was alive and managing things, they were quite comfortably off. There's a street just down the way here named Chapel Street, and your grandma says it was named for her grandfather Nathan Chapelle—at some point, the family anglicized the name. Supposedly, he built a soup kitchen for homeless men on that street, somewhere between Manchester and Salford. That would have been in the early or mid-1800s. A real philanthropist he was. Heart of gold he had. But he died, and his son—your grandmother's father—was not a philanthropist. In fact, he was quite a philanderer.

"Eventually, your great-grandfather left your great-grandmother with four children and no way to feed them. They lost the manor house—or farm, or whatever you'd call it—which was in Nantwich, your grandmother says. Her two brothers were taken in by an aunt or uncle down south somewhere who could afford to send them to school—because in those days, it was thought that only boys needed a proper education. A relative in Cheshire took in her mother, my grandmother, and your nan's little sister, our auntie Dot, out of charity. Your grandmother was sent to work as a lady's maid at one of the other big houses nearby. She was eleven or twelve. That was old enough in those days, and since she'd lived a privileged life, as they say, she knew how to be a lady's maid. Well, she would, wouldn't she?"

"I never knew any of this! Still, it makes sense now why Nanna is always so proper and can talk in a posh accent when it suits her."

I had to wonder, though, how you went from having a lady's maid and tutors and learning to speak French to serving some other young woman whom you might have been friends with before your philandering father abandoned you. It sounded dreadful to me.

After our tea, we walked through the foyer of the hotel, admiring the architecture and opulence of the magnificent building. The concierge was kind enough to tell us a bit about the history. "Years ago," he said, "the hotel had an underground railroad operated by the Midland Railway Company, and which was connected to the train station here in Manchester. It was for the safety and security of important people, who often came to Manchester just to stay in the hotel. In fact, your President Roosevelt even stayed here during World War Two!"

"You know," said Barbara as we rode the bus home, "I thought the most interesting thing we learned was about Hitler. I never knew that German planes were ordered not to bomb this part of Manchester and that the reason was because the Führer wanted the Midland Hotel for his headquarters when he conquered Britain!"

We were sitting in the upper deck of the bus—my favorite place to ride—and as I looked out at the city of Manchester, I couldn't help but wonder what our lives would have been like if Hitler had won.

"You bought what?" my mother said when I got home. "You bought perfumed soap and talcum powder for a pound? Is that what I'm hearing? After I made it clear to both you and Barbara that you were to buy your nan warm knickers? Have you not noticed how cold this house is? How dare you be this disobedient!" Mom wasn't shouting, but the tone of her voice was one that I knew from experience meant there would be ramifications.

I had no response. How could I have? My mother was 100 percent right: it was her money, my nan needed warm underwear, and I had been willfully disobedient. I hoped she would punish me accordingly now so that by Christmas Eve, my guilt would be assuaged, and I could enjoy sipping the brandy-laced hot cocoa I'd be allowed to have that year. My cousin Valarie and I were fifteen, and that was the age at which Auntie June said we could have a touch of brandy in our hot chocolate. Auntie June was good about things like that, particularly since Val had now left school. If Mom didn't punish me, I would be so burdened with guilt about the Yardley's that I wouldn't enjoy being allowed to have brandy in my hot chocolate—and it was Cadbury's hot chocolate, not the old Nestlé kind we'd had in America.

"You are getting no spends this week, Vivienne. You are being punished for being willfully disobedient!"

I breathed a sigh of relief and looked forward to Christmas Eve.

Christmas Eve at Nanna's house was wonderful. It included our whole family, my uncle Jackie, my aunts, my cousins, and several of the bobbies who stopped by on their beat, or whatever they called it in Britain. We exchanged gifts, drank hot chocolate (mine and Val's were spiked, as Auntie June had promised), and ate Christmas cake. My grandmother proudly presented the cake after tea, and I had to agree with her and my mother: properly iced, it was a work of art and certainly more elegant than any Betty Crocker cake I had ever made.

Nanna said she loved Yardley's English Lavender—and the set was so lavish, she said, that she was sure it would last all year. She added that wooly knickers, while sensible, would never have measured up.

Just as we were finishing our cake, we heard carols and the ringing of bells, and as the singing got louder, we opened the front door. Carolers walked up our path and began singing "Good King Wenceslas." Of course, Nanna invited them in for a Christmas drink, and Daddy put a tip in the basket one of the ladies was carrying.

Just before eleven o'clock, as everyone was saying his or her goodbyes, Bill the policeman caught me standing under the mistletoe in the kitchen and kissed me.

"Merry Christmas," he said, and he put on his helmet and left through the back door.

I was standing at the sink, washing cups and saucers, when Nanna carried a tray of glasses in and put them on the table.

"Are you all right, love?" she asked.

"Um, yes. Why?"

"Well, you've been washing that cup for nearly two whole minutes, and I think it's clean. You look a bit flushed—are you sure you feel all right? It's been a bit of a busy night, eh?"

"Oh. Yes. I'm fine. And yes, it's been a busy night and a lovely Christmas Eve."

Mom put my sisters to bed, telling them they must try to go right to sleep because Father Christmas would soon be arriving. This house had a chimney, she reminded them, and Daddy had to hurry to put out the fire. Mom had given me the candy and odds and ends that were to go in my sisters' stockings, and Nanna and I filled them.

"Nanna, hasn't this been the most wonderful holiday season ever? I mean, with the Blackpool lights trip and just everything. I wish Granddad were here with us–then it would have been just perfect."

"No worries, love. He is right here with us, and he said to tell you that he is with you always, and so is Johnny."

I looked at my grandmother. She was looking at Granddad's chair. Did she really see him sitting there? I wondered. After all, she did have the gift.

"Now then," she said, "up to bed with you! I have an idea that those sisters of yours are going to be up at the crack of dawn."

"Merry Christmas, Nanna."

"Merry Christmas, my love."

Chelveston

Twenty-six

I was nearly summertime, and we finally, after almost a year, received notice that there was a unit available in one of the housing areas affiliated with the base at Alconbury. Since we'd left Flixton in February, we had been living in Peterborough, in a rented house. My mother had announced she was pregnant again and said it was time we were back to living as a normal family. The house was nice, and Peterborough was a lovely town with lots of ancient history. Katharine of Aragon was entombed in the city's cathedral.

Anne Boleyn was my favorite of Henry's six wives, but Katharine was the one I most admired. She had had such strong convictions, and even though Henry had locked her away for the rest of her life after he divorced her for Anne, she never once had abandoned her religion or her principles. She had been married to Henry's brother, who had died and left her a widow, and it certainly hadn't been her fault that Henry—who had become king upon his brother's death—had decided to marry her. *What was she supposed to say?* I wondered. *No? To the king of England?* Then Anne Boleyn had come along, and Henry had decided she was younger and cuter and had requested permission from the Holy See to divorce Katharine. After all, he probably had thought, the pope should never have given him permission to marry his brother's widow to begin with.

The pope had said no, it was against the church's teachings for a man to divorce his wife, so Henry had said, "Fine. I'll just start my own church, and I'll be the pope of it." And he had. I had to agree at least he had been smart enough to get rid of the whole confessional thing, though I thought his motives for doing so were glaringly obvious.

"Isn't that just like a man?" My mother and I had been shopping and had stopped in the cathedral to pay our respects at Queen Katharine's tomb one last time before we moved to Chelveston. "You were too good for him, Kathy, dear," Mom said as we peered through the ornate railing that enclosed the granite tomb.

The top of Katharine's tomb was embellished with an engraved slab of black marble. Before our first visit some months ago, I had hoped to find that her preserved body was visible under a glass dome, like the bodies of some saints I'd heard of. If she didn't qualify for sainthood, I couldn't imagine who did! I had been a bit disappointed to find it wasn't. Still, I was impressed that a queen was buried in a church where ordinary people attended Mass daily. Mom and I lit a candle and said our final goodbyes to Katharine of Aragon.

Chelveston was no longer an active base, but RAF Alconbury utilized the housing area to house the overflow of military personnel and their families. Since moving to Peterborough, I had been attending school at RAF Molesworth. There, the secondary school only went up to the tenth grade, after which students were required to attend Lakenheath American High School on RAF Lakenheath. LHS was a boarding school, and neither my new friend Janet Hutson nor I relished the thought of going to boarding school.

"I heard that all the girls are stuck up," said Janet, "and they are really, really cliquish."

"We probably don't have a choice," I said, "unless we want to go to an English school, and I can tell you they aren't nearly as much fun as American schools. You must wear a uniform, they don't have long summer vacations like we have, and they are all girls–or all boys. There are lots of differences."

"No, I don't mean I would go to a British school; I don't think that would suit me at all. Nope–I'm going to ask my parents if I can take correspondence courses until we go back to the States."

Correspondence courses. Brilliant. I made a mental note to ask my father if I could do the same. I decided to wait until I was challenged with having to go to boarding school to mention that to my father; after all, anything could happen between June and September. It was the beginning of summer vacation, and last Friday, May 31, we had moved to Chelveston. It was some miles from Alconbury, but a base bus ran frequently between the two, so we weren't completely cut off from the services at the main base.

I knew one girl in our new neighborhood. Her name was Rose Fortner, and I only knew her because my new friend at Alconbury, Janet Hutson, was friends with her. Rose introduced me to Lani Weidner, who had just graduated from Lakenheath also. However, both Rose's and Lani's fathers were being transferred back to the States: Rose was scheduled to leave next Saturday, and Lani was leaving in three weeks. A boy named Jack Kirk had just graduated with them also, but he wouldn't be leaving until the end of August. Besides Rose, Lani, and Jack, there were two teenagers who were going to be seniors at Lakenheath in the new school year: Alan Davila and Mary Lee Brantley. There might have been others, but I hadn't yet met them. Still, the ones I had met were friendly. It was obvious, though, social activities were scarce at Chelveston. I mentioned that to Alan.

"Oh, don't judge us so quickly," he said. "Wait until the Cow-Cow Club has a meeting."

"What kind of club is that? What is its purpose?" To me, it sounded a bit odd.

"Can't tell you until you're initiated. We do initiations on Friday nights," he said.

"How many members are there?"

"Everyone in the housing area between the ages of sixteen and eighteen," he told me.

"Oh, I won't be sixteen for three weeks," I said.

"We'll make an exception," he replied.

On Friday night, Alan, Jack, Lani, Rose, Mary Lee, and I gathered on the playground. We were the sum of everyone between the ages of sixteen and eighteen who lived in the housing area. It was dusk, and we had to wait for dark to do the initiation. Alan, who apparently was the head of the club, read an elaborate mission statement. It was comprised of jargon that left me wondering what I had just heard, but I was reluctant to admit to my new friends that I had no clue what Alan had just read. It sounded very formal, and there were lots of *yes* and *thou*s scattered throughout. The other four club members were murmuring among themselves and nodding.

Soon it was completely dark. Rose approached me and said she had to put a blindfold on me to lead me to the initiation site. Once I was initiated, she said, I'd be allowed to know where the secret meeting place was. Two of the girls had me by my elbows, and we began our walk into, it seemed to me, the wooded area adjacent to the playground. It could instead have been the barren area between the housing and the old RAF flight tower, but I thought I felt bushes brushing my arms and legs. I suddenly realized I really didn't know any of these people. My friend Janet was friends with Rose, but what did that mean? Janet didn't live at Chelveston. If there was some secret cult or some witchcraft society hidden deep in the bowels of this hamlet in East Anglia, who would have known? We were in, after all, the section of England most steeped in druid lore.

After what seemed like about fifteen minutes, we stopped. I was directed to stand still and make no sound at all.

"Give me you right hand," said a female voice. I thought it was Mary Lee, but I had only met her that night; for all I knew, we might have joined a group of other people.

If I had been brave, which I wasn't, I would have ripped the blindfold off and run for my life. My father would not hesitate to put me on restriction for the rest of my life if he were to find out I had been inducted into some witchy society that meant I had to meet in the woods every week and pledge allegiance to the devil.

Alan began speaking again, and the words still made little sense. Against my better judgment, I extended my right hand when ordered to do so, and the person I thought was Mary Lee plunged it into a soft, warm substance. Did it have an odor? I didn't think so, but I wasn't sure. My brain was befuddled, and I was trying to organize my thoughts.

"Now give me your left," said the voice, and my left hand was plunged into the soft, warm substance.

Yes, it did smell. It had a distinct odor of cow manure. They had stuck my hands into cow dung! Oh…

"With the power vested in me," said a voice I thought belonged to the boy named Jack, "I now pronounce you a full-fledged member of the Chelveston Cow-Cow Club." Someone removed the blindfold.

The five of them stood in front of me with big grins on their faces. Mary Lee held a Tupperware bowl of something white. Jack shone a flashlight onto it.

"Crisco." She giggled.

Someone had had the foresight to bring a dish towel for me to wipe my hands on.

We were on the playground, which we must have walked circles around, and Alan told me that now and forever, I was to be known as a Chelveston Cowgirl. I broke out into laughter, delighted that I had not been inducted into a society of witches and warlocks and even happier that it was Crisco I was wiping off my hands.

We walked to the swings, and Mary Lee and I each sat on one. Alan and Jack pushed us so high I thought I could have reached up and grabbed a star. I loved my new friends.

It turned out that Chelveston was a rather quiet, secluded, low-key place. Perhaps even that was an exaggeration—*low-key* implied that it had a modicum of socially redeeming qualities. It had none. To be fair, though, it was bucolic.

Even by British small-village standards, Chelveston was tiny: it had a pub, a church, a post office, and a railway station that had ceased to carry passengers last year—not enough business, I guessed. To get to the village, we had to cross a small stone bridge that went over a stream-sized river. Nearby was another village, Rushden, which was slightly larger, and Jack Kirk said that between the two villages, Queen Elizabeth owned a farm. I was not sure that was accurate, but if it was, I decided I'd like to visit it someday. Maybe there would be a tearoom on the property, and I could write to my cousins to tell them I'd had tea at the queen's farm.

It was a lovely walk from our housing area to the village, but of course, once we were there, there was nothing to do. The boys went to the pub occasionally because the drinking age in England was sixteen. Alan was seventeen, and Jack was almost eighteen. But my dad would have put me on restriction and locked me in my room for the whole summer if he'd found out I went to a pub with the boys, even if I only ordered a shandy. Still, it was a nice walk across the bridge to the hamlet on a sunny day.

At the end of our road and within the housing area, there was a school that was no longer used as such now that the base was nonoperational. Our base commander was Major Kirk, Jack's dad, and he let us use the school for various activities. From somewhere, he had procured a pool table; on the wall was a dart board; and in the corner was a portable record player that someone had donated. The record player's turntable wobbled, which made the voices on the records sound a bit wonky, but we didn't mind too much. Those items were in the largest room in the school building: the former cafeteria. The cafeteria's serving bar was still in place, and we were able to stock the little freezer with ice cream and Popsicles. On a shelf behind the counter were chips and candy bars, and everyone simply paid on the honor system for what he or she took. A cookie jar had been set up for us to deposit our money in when taking an item, and when supplies dwindled, I assumed the task that Lani had previously been responsible for: I made a list for Mrs. Kirk and carried the jarful of nickels and dimes that had accumulated over to Jack's house. His mom then replenished our stock when she next went to the commissary on Alconbury. It was a grand system.

On Sundays, Father Pica, one of the priests from Alconbury, came and performed Mass for us in one of the empty school rooms.

The base still hired a custodian to manage the building, and that person had found an old faculty desk in storage and moved it into one of the empty classrooms. The room, the desk, and folding chairs set up in rows served as a chapel.

Father Pica was an American priest, but he lived in a damp and drafty gatehouse on the grounds of nearby Kimbolton Castle, the castle where Henry had kept Katharine imprisoned for all the years she refused to divorce him. After Mass on our second Sunday at Chelveston, Mom invited Father Pica to breakfast. As with Father Enright in France, it was an invitation that became a tradition during the years we lived there. I soon realized that nothing tempers a teenager's temptations like having the family priest at the house every couple of weeks or so for Sunday breakfast. "And how was your week, Vivienne?" he'd ask. "Anything interesting going on at that boarding school you go to?" I was sure it had been my father's idea.

One Sunday, Father bemoaned the cold and damp at the castle gatehouse as he ate his full English breakfast: eggs, Wall's sausages, mushrooms fried in butter, grilled tomatoes, Heinz baked beans, and English bread. That was the best thing about having our parish priest come to breakfast: nothing was too much trouble for Mom, so we all benefited. I thought she probably knew he could recognize her English voice in confession, and I had to believe her culinary skills bought her not a little leeway.

"I know it's technically summer, if England has such a thing, but I can't think of another place on God's green earth that is as cold as my bedroom," Father said. "It's cold enough to freeze—anyway, I'm dreading another winter. If Saint Paul himself were to compare it to being kept in that dungeon where he suffered without a cloak, I'm not sure the gatehouse would compare favorably!"

"Oh, but, Father, isn't that exciting?" I asked. "To be surrounded by centuries of history! Katharine of Aragon—just think! Have you ever heard her footsteps in the dead of night? Or perhaps seen her apparition floating around? I read that she used to like to take walks in the castle gardens in the evening. Thank goodness Henry didn't chop *her* head off–that would be terrible to see poor Katharine's headless ghost. Don't you think?"

"No, I haven't seen Katharine with or without a head, and I'm not likely to since I don't actually live in the castle. But if I did, you can be sure I would perform an exorcism!"

His remark made me think of Biloxi and the haint-blue doors and porch ceilings–a sort of pre-exorcism, I supposed, or, in any case, a deterrent. However, for grisly, macabre, torturous inflictions by ghosts or humans, this scepter'd isle was hard to match.

Daily in the summer, the teenagers and preteens hung out in the old cafeteria, which was now the Teen Club. We played darts, listened to 45s, and played pool. Rather, we attempted to play pool. Alan was the only one of us who was good at pool. In fact, he frequently went into one of the pubs that had a pool table in the nearby town of Huntingdon and always came back flush. *Flush* apparently was the term one used when he or she won at pool or cards.

"It's called billiards," he said. "In England, the common name is billiards, and although it's a bit different from pool, with some different rules, the object is basically the same."

The Monday evening of my birthday week arrived. Rose had left two weeks ago, and Lani had left on Saturday. I hadn't seen Mary Lee since last Friday, when the Cow-Cow Club had gathered at the playground late in the day. This night, Alan, Jack, and I were on the playground, not doing much of anything.

"Hey," said Alan, "let's go to the tower. We haven't been for a couple weeks!"

The air tower on the runway was kept manned twenty-four hours a day; after all, it was a military airstrip, and even though it was no longer used as such, it required guarding.

"Not me," I said. "If my dad found out, I'd be in big trouble, and he'd put me on restriction."

The boys rolled their eyes, and Alan said, "No, you won't get in trouble, because no one will know. Who's going to tell? Don't be a baby." Name-calling generally had no effect on me, but in that case, it rankled.

"OK," I said, "just this once." I spent the entire walk over to the tower wondering if trespassing was a misdemeanor or a felony.

"Hey, Joe-Joe," called Jack as we stood at the bottom of the tower, "it's just us."

"C'mon up," replied a voice from the top of the tower.

Jack went first, I followed, and Alan brought up the rear. It was a straight-up, long, scary climb on a metal ladder. We finally reached the top.

The boys introduced me to Joe-Joe. He was wearing a flight suit, and he was cute.

"Well, hello," he said. "Nice surprise, guys. I bet you're interested in learning what all these switches and knobs are for," he added, looking at me.

"Oh yes. Of course," I answered, feeling flattered that he would take the time to explain the obviously important gadgets to me. Once he started, I realized it was like listening to Alan's gobbledygook about the Cow-Cow Club, but he had a nice American accent and amazing blue eyes, so I just smiled and nodded.

Five minutes into the lesson, Alan suddenly said, "Hey, Joe, I think we gotta go. But thanks for letting us come up. See ya next time."

"Anytime, guys. And what was your name? Veronica? It was very nice to meet you, and if you're with these guys, you're welcome anytime. Just don't come by yourself, OK?"

As if I would have.

On the way home, Jack and Alan swore me to secrecy. Jack said we were not allowed to go on the airfield, because the military strictly forbade dependents to cross the fence line.

"So we shouldn't have climbed the fence?" *I knew it! Strictly forbade—most definitely a felony!*

He said that his dad, as the highest-ranking officer in the housing area, oversaw everything on the base, and he would probably lock Jack in his room until he left for college in August if he found out Jack had taken me to the tower.

"Serious infraction, this," Jack added.

"I knew it. I knew I should never have let you guys talk me into climbing up the tower. I just knew it!"

"Don't worry, Victoria," said Alan with a grin. "Jack just wants to make sure you don't start feeling guilty and blurt out to your dad what you've done."

"It's Veronica. And I am never letting you guys talk me into doing anything I suspect is wrong ever again!"

I stood firm. When they wanted me to go to the pub in the village with them the following week, I said absolutely not. I told them that if they wanted to come to my house, I would fix a pitcher of Kool-Aid–they could choose grape or cherry.

They chose grape.

Twenty-seven

It was Saturday, June 20, and I hadn't seen any of the Chelveston teenagers since the middle of the week. Usually, when I walked over to the school, Mary Lee would be there, playing records, or Alan would be playing pool. Although it was my sixteenth birthday, there was no point in having a proper birthday party, because there was no one to invite. Nanna had come to spend June with us, and Mom had invited ladies from the neighborhood over for an afternoon tea: little sandwiches with the crusts cut off, tarts with lemon curd, and trifle with crumbled Flake bars sprinkled over the thick layer of cream topping. We were sipping our tea, when there was a knock on the door.

"Hey!" said Alan.

"Well, hi! Where have you been since Wednesday?"

"Here and there. Come outside for a minute."

"Why don't you come in and have some cake and tea? It's my birthday!"

"I know, but just come out here for a minute."

I stepped outside, and he handed me a box. "Happy birthday," he said.

"What is this? You didn't need to buy me anything, Alan!"

"Yes, I did—sixteen is a big deal."

I opened the box and found a silver bracelet: tiny filigree hearts linked together like paper chains on a Christmas tree. He fastened it on my wrist.

"Alan, it's beautiful! But you shouldn't have. Really. And where *have* you been all week? I haven't seen you since Monday!"

"Oh, here and there. Playing billiards in town mainly."

"All week? Really? You never play pool all week!"

"And my friend doesn't have a sweet sixteenth every week either!"

"You played pool all week to win enough money to buy me this bracelet? Alan, are you serious?"

"Actually, I'm not as good as I thought–I didn't win enough in the end, so I hocked my pool stick too." He laughed. "No problem. I'll get it out next week. Happy birthday, princess."

I stood on my porch for long minutes after Alan left, looking at the silver heart bracelet and thinking about the heart of the boy who had spent a whole week and his most valuable possession to buy it for me.

June melted into July. Alan got his pool cue back, and the Cow-Cow Club became defunct. Since only Mary Lee, Alan, Jack, and I remained–and Jack would soon be gone–diminishing membership would have become a problem anyway. In truth, the only time the club was really a club was during initiation. Jack said that was the biggest problem with the club–unless there was someone to initiate, it fell short of living up to its name.

July became August, and the first week of August rolled into the second. Jack Kirk would be leaving next week to go to college. He had been accepted at Johns Hopkins University, and he was going to be a lawyer. My mother loved Jack: he had nice hair; he wore nice shirts with button-down collars; and he always said, "Hello, Mrs. Grilliot. How are you today?" She thought he would make a nice boyfriend. He reminded my father of Eddie Haskell on *Leave It to Beaver*.

"He is nothing at all like Eddie Haskell," my mother would argue. "He's much handsomer and obviously smarter!"

Dad was a huge fan of Eddie Lucky, which Mom and I were sure was the reason he pretended not to like any of the boys I was friends with. He said he wouldn't mind if Eddie were my boyfriend, and neither my mother nor I could believe he said that. Personally, we both thought my father was hoping I would become a nun. Whenever Eddie could get a ride from his housing area to ours, he dropped by. Eddie was passionate about baseball, and my dad said he was one of the best players he had ever seen in his division, or whatever it was called. I had no idea where Dad had seen Eddie play baseball, but my father was never wrong about sports talent. I pointed out to my father that Eddie and I were just friends.

"Besides," I reminded him, "you don't like any of the boys I've ever managed to have a date with! Remember Charlie Barlow in Biloxi? Remember Bob Anglim from here? You hardly even knew him, and you put me on restriction after our second date! And by the time I was off restriction, he had another girlfriend! So what makes you think you'd still like Eddie if he asked me out?"

He raised an eyebrow.

"See? That is exactly what I mean."

One week, we ran into Jim McBride at the NCO club, and my mother remarked that he looked just like a famous and very handsome movie star. She wondered aloud why he wasn't my boyfriend–Jim, not the movie star.

"And that other boy who came to the house once with Jim–what was his name? I think it was Greg. Greg was very cute too, and tall," said my mother. "I do like tall, handsome men!"

"Greg has a crush on Janet," I said. "I can tell because he's always teasing her. Come to think of it, I think Jim does too–he said the other day that Jan has the smallest waist and cutest figure he's ever seen." I had to admit, that rankled a bit.

I spent most of my time explaining to my parents that Alan and I were just friends, as were Jack and I, Eddie and I, Jim and I, Greg and I ...

On the last Saturday night in August, there was a dance at one of the youth clubs on a neighboring base. I wasn't sure I wanted to go, but it was the last time I would see some of my friends. Warren was leaving soon, and some of last year's high school graduates–Marie Ingram, Eileen Martell, Bill Small, and Bob Anglim, whom I at least wanted to apologize to about my father–were all going off to various colleges. It was typical military life, but I wanted to say goodbye.

I should have stayed home.

Alan and I had never had a disagreement–of course, we'd only been friends since the beginning of summer–but how he could go from being my best friend and pawning his pool stick to buy me a lovely birthday present to causing me the greatest humiliation I had ever experienced, at least since the bell-ringing incident at Midnight Mass, I could not fathom.

Three and a half months later, on the bus ride home from boarding school on December 19, 1964, which was the beginning of the Christmas break, Alan finally said to me, "Are you really never going to speak to me again?"

I was sitting in a window seat, gazing at the passing scenery, and the aisle seat was vacant. He slid in next to me.

"I might consider talking to you next August. I thought I'd give it year, because I won't know until then if my humiliation is resolved or not. As of right now, it is still a searing sword stabbing my soul and ripping open my very heart."

"Nice alliteration," said Alan. "A bit dramatic for the actual incident, though, don't you think?"

"You caused me profound embarrassment, Alan! Just because a group of us girls showed interest in a cute guy, you singled me out and humiliated me. Did you promise the boy a week of your billiard winnings if he'd ask me to dance? My girlfriends obviously heard what you did and were giggling about it. And I have had to spend all semester scanning all the common areas at school in order to avoid him. I have no idea what I would say. He's a senior, he's handsome, he's an athlete, and he's in with the in crowd. How much more humiliated could I be?"

"Really? You really think he remembers the dance, let alone you? You have a serious ego problem. And you keep saying *he*. You don't even remember his name, do you?"

"Leave me alone! Go away. Remove yourself from this seat, and do not ever speak to me again in this life! Not ever!"

Except for the first week, my first semester at Lakenheath American High School, located on RAF Lakenheath, was not bad, despite some ups and downs.

The first week was dreadful. Jan and I thought the girls in our dorm were stuck up, and no one made any attempt to befriend us—it was exactly as her friend Rose had said, Jan reminded me. We pleaded with our parents to unenroll us immediately. To make matters worse, our third roommate, Diane Bagdasarian, requested a room change on Thursday of that first week: she was a returning dorm student, and all her friends from the previous year had been grouped together at one end of the hall. She told us not to take it personally, which was little consolation. We explained to our parents—we had practiced on the bus ride home on Friday—how truly dreadful Lakenheath was, and we said that in order to preserve our health and prevent our wasting away from the stress of it all, they must consider letting us stay home and take correspondence courses. Our pleas fell on deaf ears.

The second week started out worse. We learned there was a mandatory dinner dance once a month on a Thursday night, and there was no use in trying to get out of going. If you weren't ill enough to go to the infirmary, there was no chance you could get excused. We also could forget trying to hide in the top storage unit above our clothes closets, where we stored our suitcases, because the house mothers would look there first.

Janet and I were not the only students from the tenth-grade class at Molesworth; there were eight or nine of us. Our best friends were Greg Sederberg, Bob Holiday, Jim McBride, Eddie Lucky, and a new boy who had moved to Alconbury in the summer—Frank Kelley. During the evening they bolstered our courage and provided a haven for us, much like the circling of the wagons in a television western.

"I don't know why we have to stay for the dance," Janet complained at dinner. "I understand why they made the dinner mandatory. Tablecloths, tea lights, silverware in dinner napkins–I get it: teaching us proper protocols and all. But making us go to the dance part? Why should they care if we'd rather go back to the dorm?"

I had to admit Janet had a point. Why did they care if we danced? I'd rather have been back in the dorm, reading.

Dinner ended, and we moved to the dayroom, which was a large area on the other side of the cafeteria. It had seating, tables, and a juke box, and it was where students spent most of their leisure time. It had been decorated for the dance, furniture had been moved to create a dance floor, the lights had been dimmed, and there was a DJ.

Janet and I, along with our friends, stayed on the periphery of the dayroom's dance floor and danced with the Molesworth boys. Jim and Greg took turns asking Janet to dance, and I danced with Bob–when I wasn't hiding in the girls' restroom. We counted the minutes until we could go back to the dormitory and, beyond that, the hours until we could go home for the weekend and plead with our parents one more time. During the evening, I made sure I was nowhere near either Alan Davila or the boy he had somehow convinced to dance with me last summer. I didn't want to give Alan a chance to cause me more anguish; I could only imagine the havoc he could wreak in that setting. My nerves were a wreck.

At nine thirty, when our misery was almost at an end, two boys we didn't know suddenly walked over to our group. I wondered why, but they looked like athletes, so I assumed they had come over to talk to Greg or Jim, who were both on the football team. Instead, they singled Jan and me out.

"Would you like to dance?" asked the boy with dark hair.

I was caught off guard. I nodded and then immediately panicked. I looked around. If Alan had instigated this, I was really going to let him have it! Still, that would have made no sense. Why would Alan have done it again? He obviously regretted humiliating me at the youth club–I could tell by how quiet he had been on the bus to and from school last week. *Oh, bother! My life couldn't get any worse.*

I hated boarding school, hated being away from my family, and was tired of feeling so stressed all the time.

The boy's name was John Young, and he'd been at Lakenheath since the previous year. He told me he was a junior, and his friend Lee was a senior. I looked at the boy Janet was dancing with–tall, blond hair, handsome. I noticed Jan hadn't hesitated for a second to dance with him, and I decided I was being paranoid. As we danced, John told me that he and his friend were on the football team, they had attended Lakenheath last year also, and it was a great school when one got used to it. For the next several dances, Jan and I chatted with them, and I found I was relaxing for the first time since school had started.

The evening ended, and they walked with us to our dorm. *Maybe I should give this school, this experience, a chance*, I thought.

Then Janet leaned into my ear and whispered, "Whatever you do, don't let him kiss you good night. They've probably made a bet with the other guys on the football team." With that, my paranoia returned with a vengeance.

The next morning, as I was getting ready for school, Miss Rowe, the housemother, made the following announcement over the intercom: "Would the young lady who danced the last few dances with John Young last night please come to the lobby? He is waiting to walk you to breakfast, but he can't remember your name."

I almost died. I added that to my list of things that should not happen to girls who were mortified of attracting any attention. It was worse than my bracelet at Midnight Mass or my choosing the wrong seat at the Woolworth's lunch counter. *It's my stupid name again, and it is, unarguably, my mother's fault.*

I walked down to the dorm lobby, where the boy named John Young was indeed waiting, and he indeed could not remember my name. He told me he was going to write it down so he wouldn't forget it next time, and he pulled a pencil out of the pocket of his letter jacket.

"So," said my father at dinner on Friday evening, "your mother tells me you've changed your mind about wanting to take correspondence courses. I'm only asking because I've sent away for some information." He looked down at his plate while speaking.

I thought carefully before I responded. I was pretty sure it was a trick–I knew my father well. He thought because I had met a boy I liked–I was sure my mother had gone on and on telling him everything I'd told her about the dance–that I would say, "Oh, I've changed my mind. I don't think Lakenheath is so bad after all." And then bingo! I'd have ruined any opportunity I might have had to get out of going to boarding school. On the other hand, things *were* looking a bit brighter, and I didn't want to be hasty. In any case, I didn't think my father would really consider letting me stay home to take correspondence courses, so I decided not to take the bait.

"Oh no, I haven't changed my mind at all. If given the choice, of course I'd rather take correspondence courses than go to Lakenheath. It's dreadful."

He squinted and looked at me. "Oh, good. I'd hate to have wasted a stamp."

I squinted back. Neither one of us could keep a straight face: we both burst out laughing.

Twenty-eight

ANET HUTSON WAS LEAVING. HER FAMILY WAS BEING transferred back to the States; their three years were at an end. I had been dreading that day, and now it had arrived.

It was the last Friday in October. The school bus stopped at Alconbury, as usual, before going on to Chelveston.

"Well, I guess this is it," said Janet. "Just when I was getting to like Lakenheath!"

"Really?" I asked, raising an eyebrow. "Are you sure it is the school you like?"

Janet laughed. "Well, it wasn't as bad as I anticipated."

We hugged, and then, because we were sixteen and girls, we cried.

"I don't wanna go," she said.

"I don't want you to go," I said.

The bus driver yelled back at us, "Ladies! Hurry up, say your goodbyes, and let me get on with me job! Me wife'll have me by the short hairs if I'm late for me tea one more time!"

After another quick hug, Janet was standing on the sidewalk, and I was waving from the bus window. I had always felt that being a brat came with its own unique brand of benefits that, in total, far outweighed the negatives; still, some days felt nothing short of desolate. My best friend was leaving, and I was going to be left behind to deal with the challenges of carving a way for myself in the alien world of boarding school.

Within a week, I had another roommate: her name was Joyce. She was a sophomore, and she had a boyfriend; his name was Roger. I felt relieved to have another roommate—nothing felt worse than being alone in a dormitory room—and I felt lucky to have such a sweet little sister, because not only was she pretty and fun, but she was also neat and tidy. She was the only thing that saved me from a life of detention for having a messy dormitory room. I had every intention of keeping my part of the room organized, but my social life kept getting in the way.

"How hard can it possibly be, Vivienne, to make your bed properly and hang up your clothes?"

"I know, I know, Miss Rowe! I promise I'll do better next week! Honest!" If Miss Rowe, the dorm mother, opened the two dresser drawers allocated to me, I was doomed.

"I'll be back in five minutes." Miss Rowe sighed. "Laziness is not a virtue. Make your bed properly."

We all loved Miss Rowe because she was the sweetest person in the world, and starting that day, I was going to become a model of boarding school compliance, I decided, if for no other reason than to avoid causing her grief.

I told Joyce that I was sorry and that going forward, I would start every day by making my bed first and straightening my part of the room, so she didn't have to sit around and wait. It wasn't fair to her or Roger, I said, for me to make either of them late for breakfast just because of my dereliction of duty. I had decided the term *dereliction of duty* had panache, and I preferred it to *laziness*, which I did *not* suffer from. My priorities were simply skewed, according to my father, and I was going to work on them. Besides, Joyce and I were getting a new roommate, Loray Royall, and I just knew she would add a wonderful balance to our threesome. Hopefully, she wouldn't be nearly as derelict as I was.

It was early November, and the weather was dismal—gray, damp, and cold. The only bright spot was that our new roommate, Loray, moved into the dorms. Like me, she was a junior, and we immediately knew we were going to be the best of friends. By the end of the week, it felt as if we had known each other for years. Loray's family were originally from South Carolina, and like Cissy, she had a charming southern accent. This time, though, I knew better than to try to adopt what, to me, amounted to a foreign language. Besides, I didn't think I could have put up with my father's sarcasm again. The week flew by, and soon it was Thursday.

Thursday was sheet-change day for all five dormitories.

"Do we have to change our sheets every week or every other?" asked Loray.

"Every week, and if you rip them off as quickly as possible after school–because your bed still has to be made for room check on Thursday morning–and run them over to the laundry building ASAP, you will be less likely to get stuck in what inevitably is a long line."

"Wow. Every four nights. Seems excessive."

"I agree. You know, I've been thinking. The only way Miss Rowe would even guess that the sheets were only changed, say, every other week is if the pillowcases didn't look nice and crisp." I wondered, not for the first time, if we could finagle an extra set of pillowcases on Thursdays, which would allow us to simply change pillowcases.

"Well, I did notice there's an ironing board in the kitchen area across the hall," said Loray. "We could maybe see how they look if we iron them."

"Brilliant idea," I said.

It was much easier to run the top sheets across the hall; iron them and the pillowcases into folded squares; and make sure the nice, crisp lines showed when we folded the top sheet down over the blanket just beneath the pillowcases with perfectly ironed creases.

We did Joyce's too, of course, as we all took turns going to the laundry on sheet-change Thursdays. It happened to be my turn. I had to say, the ironed pillowcases looked so good they very well could have raised suspicion.

We wondered if we should tell Joyce, and we gave it serious consideration. We knew she would have agreed that completely changing sheets after every fourth night was overkill; we just weren't sure how she'd have felt about breaking the rules. Joyce was sweet, fun, and smart, but so far, I'd had no indication that she would take rule-breaking lightly. So every other week–when it was my turn or Loray's turn–we ironed the top sheets and pillowcases. On alternate weeks, we–or Joyce, if it was her turn–took the sheets to the laundry. That equated to every-other-week laundering. Eight nights of sleeping on the same set of sheets was perfect, we thought. Soon our concerns about whether we should tell Joyce became less bothersome, and by Christmas, we no longer fretted about it.

Dormitory life had fallen into a nice routine. Between school hours and lights-out, there were a myriad of after-school activities for those with ambition and those who did not spend hours working off demerits every day. Apart from sports, there were the usual academic clubs found in all American high schools the world over: language clubs, the newspaper club, the pep club, the photography club, the drama club, and the yearbook committee. Coincidentally, my father had inquired just last week about any intention I might have had of doing something productive with my free time.

I had mused, albeit not for long, about whether I should consider joining an academic club, but I wasn't sure whether there were any that would be a good fit: I wasn't musical, and I was barely passing Spanish. I had decided to take Spanish instead of French, as I had heard it was much easier. My father was still scratching his head over that one. Anyway, I figured a passing grade was probably the number-one requirement to join that club, and while it was still early in the grading period, things were not looking rosy. I might have liked something to do with theater, but I was mortified of anything that might require me to be in front of an audience. Sports were out. If the school had had a women's baseball team, which it didn't, or allowed girls to play on the boys' baseball team, which it didn't, that would have been something I could have gotten excited about. I decided that on the bus ride home that night, I would think seriously about how best to explain my lack of involvement in after-school activities to my father, who could not grasp academic mediocrity.

"Aren't you interested in *any* extracurricular activities?"

The family had just sat down to my father's favorite dish, tuna and noodles, and predictably, he was asking whether I had any intention of becoming more productive in school.

"I don't have time, Dad—I'm too busy working off demerits."

"Maybe if you weren't so busy getting demerits, you'd have time to get involved in something worthwhile. Why don't you investigate the Spanish club? You're taking Spanish, right?"

"In case you haven't figured it out, Dad, I'm really not cut out for anything academic. I know you'd love for me to be making the honor roll and stuff like I did in Biloxi, but junior high school was easy. Honestly, it's all I can do to keep my head above water. Between the class assignments, the homework, the demerits, and the need to socialize at least a little bit, there is so little time I can devote to excelling in anything. I'm exhausted. Really."

"Still reading into the wee hours, eh?"

I didn't bother to answer. As usual, he was right. School days had settled into a rhythmic pattern, and if I could figure out how to carve out ample reading time, I was happy. During the first week of school, I had run into Bob Peterson as I was walking across the campus, and my joy at seeing my old friend from Phalsbourg had brought tears to my eyes. As we'd hugged, I'd realized this life we lived, this existence of constant change that sometimes seemed an ever-evolving loss—loss of friends, homes, schools, and social life—was not a loss at all. It was the framework of a life that came with its own distinctive type of continuity: a tapestry of people and places solidly woven into our unique community, a community that gave us the supreme privilege of being children of the world.

"Is there anything better than being a brat, Bob?" I'd asked as we sat in the dayroom and reminisced.

"Absolutely nothing," he'd replied. "Wouldn't change it for a million dollars."

"Neither would I."

Now, it was the middle of November, and Grandma Grilliot had again sent the new fall edition of the Montgomery Ward catalog. I was thrilled because I needed to look for a dress for the Christmas dance.

"The dress we bought you for the dance in October is perfectly lovely," said my mother. "What's wrong with it? You've only worn it once!"

I was horrified that she thought I could wear the same dress to the Christmas dance that I had worn to homecoming. It was that darn English thing again. I now knew—from my own experience of attending Flixton Secondary School for Girls—that English schools didn't even have formal dances. After all, there were no students of the opposite sex, so who would the girls have gone with and vice versa?

"Mom, you've got to be kidding! I can't wear the same dress I wore to the homecoming dance to the Christmas dance!" It was unconscionable. If necessary, I'd get my father involved. He was American. He'd understand.

I was not much impressed with the selection of semiformal dresses in the juniors' section of Monkey Ward, so I decided I could make my own dress for the dance. I hadn't sewn in quite a while, but I was pretty good at it. In fact, I wondered why I wasn't taking home economics again that year. That was a big mistake on my part, I realized. It was, after all, an easy A. I would definitely take home-ec next year, I decided. However, that did not solve my current problem of a dress for the Christmas dance. Maybe, I thought, I could borrow a dress from one of the other girls.

Regardless of the general lack of privacy, the restriction of space, and the inconvenience of lining up during peak hours for an available shower, there was one major advantage to dormitory life that far outweighed any of the many challenges: clothes borrowing.

Nowhere on the planet, I realized early on, was there any greater incentive for teenage girls to collectively gather and peacefully coexist than in a setting that offered an opportunity to increase one's wardrobe fourfold. Like majestic bald eagles who could spot their dinner at the bottom of a lake from hundreds of feet above its surface, we girls knew instantly, and from a distance, whose clothes would fit us and vice versa. But the benefit went far beyond the simple task of borrowing a skirt or exchanging a sweater to expand one's wardrobe; it secured a place in the popularity hierarchy, based upon who asked to borrow the jumper you wore yesterday and who was willing to loan you hers. It was a brilliantly executed and flawlessly applied example of democratic socialism: available to everyone but not necessarily beneficial to all.

However, before I invested any time in making, buying, or borrowing a dress, the Christmas dance was canceled.

"How could there possibly not be enough interest?" asked Joyce.

I had to agree; I was sorry to hear it. Still, the lack of a Christmas dance was a mere disappointment compared to the announcement my father made after reviewing my report card. He told me he was going to pull me out of the dorms if my second-quarter report card did not reflect what he thought I was capable of.

"If you don't bring your grades up between now and January, you're out of the dorms for the third quarter of the year," he threatened. Pointing at the report card on the table in front of him, he added, "And you aren't even taking French!"

"I'm taking Spanish!"

"And barely passing it."

"But I am passing it!" I said. "I'm passing everything!"

"I don't consider straight Cs–two of which are C-minuses–as actually passing. I consider them warnings–as in *cautionary* or *conditional*–and therefore, they illustrate a complete lack of academic seriousness on your part. And I can't believe your art teacher actually passed you after that debacle in October!"

The debacle my father was referring to had been a simple error of judgment on my part. I was taking art but had pleaded out of the segment on sculpturing in metal, which required using blow torches and metal cutters. I'd convinced Mr. Franke, the art teacher, at John's urging, that I would work diligently alone in the art room to perfect my skills with watercolors and pastels while the rest of the class went over to the building that housed the shop and tools required for metalwork. It had been sheer coincidence that John's lunch period coincided with my art period, and on the day of the debacle my father referred to, John had stopped by, as usual, to keep me company while I painted.

"Odd that the art teacher saw you making out, don't you think?" asked my father sarcastically.

"Dad! He was simply kissing me goodbye."

"And neither one of you had the common sense not to stand in front of the classroom window while making out. I don't know whether I'm more disappointed in you for breaching the trust of your art teacher or for being stupid enough to get caught!"

On and on he went. One would have thought, with the way he was carrying on, that I had eloped with my Spanish teacher or something.

"If you ever again, young lady," he said, "pull a stunt like that, I will yank you out of the dorms so fast your head will spin. And do not for one minute think that means an education by correspondence! You will ride the day bus every single day for the next year and a half. Do you understand me?"

Oh my God, the dreaded day bus, and he means it! "Yes, sir. I understand."

"Furthermore, you are capable of better than straight Cs on your report card. I expect to see a vast improvement on the next one."

The worst part of having been caught kissing John Young in the art room was the unfairness of the punishment I received. My father was called; I got twenty demerits, the most a person could have at any one time without getting suspended; and the coach of the football team—Coach Mackey—started calling me Hot Lips, though not to my face. I heard he had started referring to me and John as Hot Lips and Huggy Bear in front of the entire football team. John's punishment consisted of extra laps around the football field. He got no demerits, and his parents weren't called. I didn't have to be Einstein to figure out that was the advantage to being the quarterback of the football team.

"It really makes me mad that Johnny's punishment is simply to do what he would normally be doing every day after school anyway! It is not fair!"

I was busy raking leaves on the hill outside the dayroom building, which I hadn't minded doing in the fall, but now it was the beginning of December, it was bitterly cold, and the leaves were six inches deep and soggy from three days of drizzle. Wendy was sitting on the wall, waiting for me to finish my hour. She wasn't allowed to help.

"I know," said Wendy. "But try to put it out of your mind. We'll have fun this weekend! There's a new movie at the base theater that Donna and I want to see, and Greg wants us all to go bowling one of the days."

Wendy and Greg were going steady. They didn't live in the dorms during the week; their fathers were stationed at Lakenheath, and Wendy had invited me to spend the weekend at her house. Donna, Johnny's sister, was Wendy's best friend, so she would be hanging out with us too. I was pretty sure that whatever we did, we would also hang out with the Grove siblings, Gerry and Tom, because they too were seven-day students. I straightened my shoulders; took a deep breath; and raked the wet, soggy leaves, vowing never again to get demerits.

Saturday night was a beautiful, crystal-clear December night. As we walked back to Wendy's house after the movie, I thought about my twenty demerits. I thought about how unfair they were. Just because I wasn't a football player, I had received the maximum punishment. I didn't mind being punished for breaking the rules, but I thought Johnny should have suffered consequences also. When we got to Wendy's house, our group broke up, and Donna and the Grove siblings started to walk back to the dorms. Johnny pulled me aside and kissed me, and while I had to admit that demerits were well worth the cost of getting to kiss such a cute boy, I would have felt much better if he had gotten demerits too.

Late Sunday afternoon, we sat in the living room at Greg's house. I glanced around at the five of us and thought how fortunate we were—how privileged our lives were—to have been born into that amazing, close-knit community of military life. We were brats through and through. Not for the first time, I contemplated what my life would have been like as the child of a civilian couple—could I have possibly coped with living in one place? Even Flixton? I would never know, but I did know I wouldn't have changed any part of that world of mine—of ours. Not for a million dollars. I only ever wanted to be the child of a serviceman, the wife of a serviceman, and the mother of military brats. I loved it all.

"Hey, you know what we should have done this weekend?" asked Greg, breaking in on my daydream.

"What?" we answered in unison.

"Taken the train to London! We could have gone to Carnaby Street!"

Carnaby Street. Of course! We should have gone to Carnaby Street. We had been talking of going to London on the train for months now. Everyone—from my school friends in Flixton to the evening news programs to the *Daily Mail*—talked about the most famous street in Soho.

"We could have shopped at Mary Quant!" said Donna, and Wendy and I agreed.

"Bet if the Rolling Stones were in town, we could have caught them at the Marquee Club!" Greg gave us a shrug that said, "Boy, did we mess up."

I had to agree. This time, I was far more aware of who the Rolling Stones were.

"Well, we'll have to remember to do that next time. Probably in the spring, because now it's almost Christmas," I said.

Suddenly, as though mention of the upcoming holiday had reminded him of something, Greg said, "I know what John bought you for Christmas, Viv!"

"What? Johnny already bought me a Christmas present?" I recognized this was my key to pester Greg to tell me what it was.

"Don't you dare tell her," said John.

"Oh, I won't, and I doubt she'll guess!" Greg said, waving around a yellow slip of paper he'd pulled out of his shirt pocket. "I've been charged with being the keeper of the receipt–you know, just in case it doesn't fit?"

I leaned over toward Greg, and said, "Hmm–let's see. Yellow receipt. Something that must fit. I'll use my ESP to see if I can–grab it!" And I did.

I jumped up and started to run down the hallway and out the front door. I got to the door, yanked on the handle, and Greg reached over my shoulder and tried to slam the door shut as I was pulling it open. It happened so quickly–Greg's hand going through the glass on the upper half of the door–that momentarily, we all just stood still as though in shock and tried to take it in. Then we saw all the blood and the size of the gash across Greg's palm. Wendy ran to find Greg's parents, John and Donna went in different directions to find a towel to place over the wound and apply pressure, and I tried to hold Greg's hand up higher than his heart because I knew that's what my mother did with bleeding limbs. Minutes later, Greg's hand was wrapped in a towel, and Greg's father drove him to the emergency room. Wendy went with them. Donna, Johnny, and I cleaned up the broken glass from the front door as Greg's mom called base maintenance and placed a service request. As an afterthought, I picked up the gift receipt that had fallen onto the floor. Suddenly, I had no desire to see what Johnny had bought me for Christmas.

"Oh, Greg, I'm so sorry. I feel so terrible!" I said, when they all got home two hours later.

"Well, I don't think it was your fault–I was the one waving the receipt around. Anyway, the doctor said he doesn't think I'll have any lasting nerve or tendon damage. No harm done–but in the future, I won't be teasing you about what your boyfriend has bought you for Christmas!"

What my boyfriend had bought me for Christmas was a silver charm bracelet. It had one heart-shaped charm, which was engraved. One side said, "I Love You," and the other had our initials: "*JY + VG.*" John gave me the bracelet before I boarded the bus to go home for the holidays.

"Merry Christmas," he said, and he hugged me. "I'll see you in the New Year."

We all said our goodbyes. The seven-day dorm students were going home for the holidays too, and the dormitories would be empty of students for nearly three weeks. John and Donna were flying to Scotland, as were the Grove siblings—Gerry and Tom—and I was riding the bus for the three-hour journey back to Chelveston. I looked at my bracelet and its silver heart. I looked out the bus window and thought about how amazing that semester at that school I hadn't wanted to attend had turned out. I made a promise to myself to bring up my grades, because I never wanted to ride the day bus and leave that amazing boy for some other girl to "chat up," as they said here in Britain.

If not for Alan Davila sliding into the seat next to me and asking if I was ever going to speak to him again, it would have been a perfect ride home.

On Christmas Day, 1964, at four o'clock in the afternoon, John showed up at our front door.

"How on earth?" I asked.

"I hitchhiked. Merry Christmas."

My dad said, "What do you expect of a hotshot athlete?"

My mother said, "My goodness, you must be starving. Sit down and let me get you something to eat!"

My sister Connie said, "How come you left your house on Christmas? Are you an orphan or something?"

I looked with wonder at the young man who had hitchhiked all the way from Edinburgh, Scotland, to East Anglia on a cold and snowy British day just to spend part of the Christmas holiday with me. For the first time in my life perhaps, I was humbled in a way that defined its truest meaning.

The Christmas holidays seemed to be over in a blink of an eye. John had caught the train back to Edinburgh after spending three days with us, and on January 6, 1965, I boarded the school bus at Chelveston, ready to begin the second semester of my junior year. I walked halfway down the aisle in the half-empty bus and slid into the seat next to Alan.

"Happy New Year," I said.

"Happy New Year. Am I forgiven?" he asked.

"You are if you'll forgive me for being a silly, immature girl who thought her perceived humiliation was more important than our friendship."

"His name is Syd Falk," Alan said.

"I know," I replied. "And if I happen to bump into him, I'll just say hi."

We rode in companionable silence back to school.

Twenty-nine

WAS SIXTEEN GOING ON SEVENTEEN. THE YEAR CREPT forward, and the seasons changed. Soon it was March, and it seemed a lifetime ago that President Kennedy had been assassinated. I speculated often about that event: how it had shocked the world; how it had created such fear and deep suspicion as we wondered who was behind it; and how, ultimately, it had had no tangible effect at all on our sheltered lives.

On March 8, 1965, our sheltered lives took a sudden turn: the United States Marines dispatched 3,500 troops to Da Nang, Vietnam. We knew the decision to send troops into battle in Southeast Asia ultimately would permeate our lives on many levels.

I was sitting in the dayroom, trying to concentrate on my Spanish homework, when Bob Peterson sat down next to me.

"Have you seen the *Stars and Stripes*?" I looked at the headline and scanned the article. We were now at war. Four US ships of the amphibious task force had landed at a place called Red Beach in Da Nang, delivering thousands of marines to fight the North Vietnamese. No longer, explained Bob, was the United States involved with Vietnam from an advisory position; we had now entered into offensive warfare.

"Will your dad have to transfer over there, do you think?" I asked. Bob's father was a marine officer stationed on a nearby air force base. I was pretty sure my father wouldn't have to go–he had been promoted a few months ago and was now a systems analyst. I couldn't imagine someone with that job title having to go to a war zone. Still, he'd been in the Berlin Air Lift, doing something that wasn't office work, so they might reassign him. It was all sobering.

Bob said he didn't know if his father would be reassigned or not. "Anything can happen when you're in the military," he reminded me.

I realized war with Vietnam would not be a simple matter of standing up to an enemy, as Kennedy had done with Cuba. It had escalated to air combat with our air force and navy a long time before ground troops were deployed. I thought about the air-raid shelter on Windsor Avenue that I had played in as a child and of the bombed-out buildings Nanna and I had passed every day when we walked to the shops. I thought of all the families in Flixton and all over England who had pictures of their sons on their walls and on their fireplace mantels–sons who had not come home from the war with Hitler. Just as many–perhaps more–young Americans had not returned from that war either.

I sighed, and Bob said, "Let's go get in line for dinner. There's nothing you and I can do about any of this except pray." Little did we know that for the next seven years, this war would drag on and, ultimately, be for naught.

Within the walls of academia, at least within the shelter of our boarding school, life was relatively unchanged. Soon it was May, and the school year was coming to an end. I had managed, barely, to keep my grades high enough that my father, if not thrilled with my efforts, had not seen fit to pull me out of the dorms and make me ride the day bus. In my mind, that was success enough to make me giddy.

"Why don't you go to the cheerleading tryouts?"

It was not the first time John had suggested I try out for the cheerleading squad.

The Lakenheath cheerleaders got to travel with the school's football and basketball teams for the away games, which meant when our teams played against American high schools in France and Germany, the cheerleaders got to go with them. There was no downside: I could get out of class and travel!

During the week before tryouts, those of us hoping to become cheerleaders practiced faithfully in the gym after school under the direction of Miss Cazebonne, the girls' physical education teacher. I wasn't sure how it worked at other schools, but at Lakenheath, members of the sports teams were called in to watch the final tryouts, and along with certain members of the faculty, they voted on the girls they wanted to be their cheerleaders. It seemed reasonable to me.

Now, I did not think it was anyone else's responsibility to make sure I knew what the requirements to be a cheerleader were, but in my defense, I thought the job description—if there was one—would be based mainly on physical ability: flexibility, stamina, coordination, and so forth. Given the nickname my dad had taken to calling me—Gracie—if I didn't make the team because of failing in one or more of those areas, I would certainly understand, I told myself. However, I thought the tryouts went swimmingly.

At one o'clock, Miss Cazebonne made an announcement over the PA system: "Ladies and gentlemen, the cheerleading squad for the LHS school year of 1965–1966 has been voted on and is as follows ..."

Along with the names of five other girls, my name was broadcast.

Clapping, woo-hooing, and shouts of "Way to go!" could be heard throughout the classrooms and up and down the halls. For someone who was not usually recognized for achieving anything in the academic world—and I realized cheerleading was not specifically academic, but it did take place within the walls of academia—I had to admit it gave me a bit of thrill to hear my name announced.

At two o'clock, Miss Cazebonne's voice came over the intercom again: "Would Vivienne Grilliot and Vickilynn Martin please come to the gym?"

Vickilynn and I are both going to be seniors next year, so perhaps, I thought, *she wants to discuss with us who will be the captain of the cheerleading squad. Vicki can be captain. I don't care about that at all—I have no interest in leadership of anything, as my father can attest.*

"Well, Misses V, did you happen to read the requirements for being a cheerleader? No? There is a minor detail—probably was in really small print–that says you must have a GPA of 2.5." Vickilynn and I looked at each other.

Miss Cazebonne always called me Miss V, but since Vickilynn and I both had names starting with *V,* I wondered if she was talking to me, Vicki, or both of us.

"Miss Cazebonne, which *V* are you talking to?"

Miss Cazebonne was nice, and for a female PE teacher, she was cute. Most of the time, I didn't mind that she chastised me for being out of uniform because I hated wearing socks with my tennis shoes; socks made me claustrophobic. I'd told her that once, and she'd just rolled her eyes and said, "Go get on your mat, and stretch."

Now she rolled her eyes and answered, "Unfortunately, *Misses* V, I'm addressing you both. Vickilynn, dear, you have just barely missed reaching the required grade average. Mr. Chase and I scrutinized your grades to see if perhaps there was a mistake: 2.31 is just not a 2.5. Sorry, kiddo. You, however, Miss V, are so far off the mark we didn't even need to glance over, let alone scrutinize, your grade point average. Any idea what it is? No? It's 2.042. Couldn't even be rounded up to 2.1, not that that would have helped."

"Is 2.0 a C, Miss Cazebonne?" I asked.

"It is. Barely," she said, emphasizing the *barely.*

I let out a huge breath. "Oh, thank goodness! If I drop below a C, I'm out of the dorms! And I know this year is over, but I wouldn't put it past my father to make it retroactive next September!"

Janet Cazebonne rolled her eyes and shook her head, and I could tell she felt bad for the other Miss V.

"Are you OK, Vickilynn?" I asked.

"I guess. I'm just disappointed. Maybe I could be an alternate or something."

"I'll look into that for you," said Miss Cazebonne. "In the meantime, Miss V–and you've probably been told this at least a thousand times before–you really have the ability to be a better student, you know?"

"I guess. But please don't write that in the comments section of my report card–I've pretty much got my father convinced I'm doing the best I can."

Miss Cazebonne rolled her eyes one more time.

John was disappointed, as I'd expected he would be. Although they couldn't have cared less whether I made the cheerleading team or not, my teachers were always saying they were disappointed in me. However, to give him credit, my father was always the most disappointed of them all. Only my mother seemed unperturbed by my consistently mediocre report-card grades. I promised both John and my father I'd study more, because after all, I didn't want to ride the day bus next year.

During the first week of summer vacation, report cards came in the mail. For the most part, none of my teachers had written anything really negative in the comments section–just the usual "Vivienne could try harder" or "Vivienne is not living up to her potential." Mr. Franke certainly could have written something really caustic, but what would have been the use? My father already knew about the overblown art room incident.

"Overblown my behind!" Dad said every time the subject reared its head–which it did only because he kept bringing it up.

One day I sat on the couch, reading all the comments in my yearbook. I flipped a page and was suddenly staring at the faculty pictures. I smiled. Miss Cazebonne had written, "V–Miss 2.042–a pleasure to have you in class on the few days you didn't complain."

I hoped she'd be there next year. Next year, I was going to stop messing around, and I'd wear socks when I dressed out for PE. I was really going to hit the books. I was going to study, bring my grades up, and stay in my dorm room for evening study hall instead of having to go to mandatory study hall in the school building. Next year, I was going to dazzle my father with my academic achievements. Next year, I might even have a conversation with my dad about college. He'd be thrilled. I'd do it around Christmas: that would be an awesome Christmas present for him. That I would actually consider college would put him over the moon, as Nanna liked to say.

The summer of 1965 was a particularly lovely one. Alan and I walked regularly to Chelveston Village. Our days were filled with sunshine and the fragrance of freshly mowed hay, and on evenings when I had no babysitting job, we would sit at the playground and count the stars. It was a summer as lovely as any I had spent in France; and although I, regretfully, no longer believed in fairies, I could almost hear their tinkling voices carried on the evening breeze as Alan pushed me on the swing.

In late July, Alan left for the States. We had been the best of friends for a whole year. Even when I hadn't been speaking to him, we had been part of each other's world—conscious always, I thought, that our friendship superseded our petty behaviors. My circle of close friends was narrowing, even as my world that revolved around John Young was expanding. This school year, I was determined to make better grades; avoid demerit-worthy behavior; and, in short, cause my father less stress. So it was with every good intention and steadfast determination that I began my senior year at our beloved alma mater.

Since my grade point average would determine if I got to stay in my dorm room to study or had to attend study hall at the school every evening Monday through Thursday, I had made an appointment with the senior-class guidance counselor.

"What exactly do my grades need to be for me not to have to go to study hall?" I asked.

"Three-point-oh or better," replied Miss Mirza.

"In everything?"

"Yes."

I couldn't believe my ears. *That must be almost straight As.* I thought my dad had said As started at 3.2. *Good grief.* I hated setting a goal for myself without having had the common sense to check out the parameters that I would have to meet to achieve the goal. *Stupid. Drat.*

"Well," I asked, "how does it work? Do I have to have a B-plus in everything, or would the grades be averaged out? I mean, could I get an A in art, a D in government, a couple of Bs, and maybe—oh, I don't know—a C in something and get them all averaged together?"

I had made the honor roll consistently at Mary L. Michel Junior High School, but I never had bothered to inquire how that was determined. I had never in my life made straight As–I was positive about that–so I knew that wasn't it.

"Vivienne," said Miss Mirza, "I think you are approaching this from the wrong angle. This isn't about seeing how little you can do and still be able to get out of study hall; it's about trying to do your very best in everything. Strive for all As, and if you fall a little short, work harder next time. You will be amazed how wonderful that will be for your self-esteem!"

Great. Now the guidance counselor thought I had a self-esteem problem.

"You know," she said, "your life would be so much easier if you weren't constantly working off demerits and trudging over to study hall every night. Think about it." She was right about that.

"OK. Thanks, Miss Mirza." I was pretty sure she was wrong about the self-esteem thing, but trudging over to study hall really cut into my reading time.

I decided to count my blessings: it was the first week of school, and I didn't yet have any demerits.

Loray Royall had moved back to the States during the summer. She had only been in England for seven or eight months, but in that short time, we had become the best of friends. I missed her and hoped we would never lose touch. I thought back through the years to all the friends I had said that about, and I realized most of us had seldom kept in touch–but that was life as a military dependent. On the flip side, I thought of my friends at Lakenheath whom I had known at other bases: Bob from France and Danny and Janel from Mississippi. The other day, I'd caught a glimpse of a girl I thought I had gone to school with somewhere else too. I was going to look for her in the dayroom so we could reconnect.

In the first few weeks of the school year, everyone was getting settled and learning the routine. I thought about last year–the first week of my junior year–and it made me smile. Janet and I had been determined to take correspondence courses rather than face the horror of living in a dorm with cliquish girls. Those girls had turned out to be awesome, and I wished they were at Lakenheath again this year. Last year, our third roommate, Diane "Baggie" Bagdasarian, who had a bigger-than-life personality, initially had been irate that she had gotten stuck with two newbies from Alconbury. She was in with the in crowd, and her group of friends from the previous year had all been assigned rooms at the opposite end of the dormitory. She had managed to get a transfer and told us not to take it personally. Janet and I had agreed we probably would have done the same thing.

Now it was my senior year. I had not anticipated the overwhelming wave of nostalgia that would sweep over me as Kate Ingram and I walked down the hallway of dormitory one looking for our room assignment on that first day of school. When we found our dorm room, we hurriedly unpacked our suitcases and decided to see who else had arrived, who we knew and who we didn't, and what rooms they were assigned.

As we walked the hall, I pointed out to Kate who had been in which rooms last year: "This was Baggie's room, after she moved down the hall to room with Bev Richardson and Linda Owensby; and this was Ann and Mary Harding's room. Cheryl Ellis was their roommate. This room here was where Loray and Joyce and I roomed."

I was unprepared for the emotions I felt. Logically, I had known who would not be there on this day; still, I felt their absence more intensely than I had anticipated. Many had gone to the American college in Switzerland. Johnny's sister, Donna, and Gerry Groves from dorm number three were gone too. So was Randy Spain. So was Wendy. So were all the other boys and girls who'd graduated last year or whose fathers had been transferred elsewhere. Tom Groves was still there in dormitory three along with John Young, and in dorm one, quite a few of my friends from last year were returning for their senior year: Dee Davis, JoAnn Devito, and Kandy Kinder were at the end of the hall; Joyce was still in dorm one but had different roommates; and Dottie Hoerter and Bente Ericson along with scores of others had returned also. My friend Bob was still at Lakenheath this year; he was like family after all our years together. We didn't play Chinese checkers anymore or trade comic books, but it was comforting to have a friend who'd known me when I was ten and carried a Dale Evans lunch box to school every day.

The first week of my senior year, there was an empty feeling in the halls, as if something vital were missing. As I walked from class to class, regardless of the hum of voices or the chatter throbbing around me, I heard the echo of all those Lancers who had moved on. This time next year, I would be one of those echoes, and I was sure that must have been what the term *hallowed halls* referred to, at least in part.

I was filled with gratitude that despite my dismal end-of-year report card, my father had let me remain in the dorms for my senior year instead of making me ride the day bus, at least for the first nine weeks. Moreover, I recognized, not for the first time, that I had been blessed with a privileged life. I couldn't imagine not being part of this military family! Regardless of, or perhaps because of, the sliver of our lives that was the constant unknown, I thought, we all had learned to appreciate the forming of bonds that we knew would remain throughout our lives. Many of us would never meet again after we graduated and went to different shores, but our bond—of brat life, of travel, of boarding school—would remain in our blood forever.

My friend, and now roommate, Kate Ingram was a year behind me, which was probably a good thing, because Kate could find some measure of trouble no matter where she went. Never intentionally, of course, but if there was any opportunity for a questionable situation to seek her out and grab hold, Kathryn would stumble on it every time, and before I knew it, I would be right in the middle of it! So I felt it was fortunate that I had an extra year of common sense, because someone had to try to stop the occasional runaway train.

Kate and I had no classes together, which was also probably for the best. She had an indomitable spirit that was hard to squelch, and whenever we were together, we couldn't help but have fun. At least we called it fun. For the most part, it was harmless, but I had no doubt that being together in class with Kate Ingram would have gotten me demerited to death.

Across the hall from us were three students new to Lakenheath: Jan and Kathy Chadwick, otherwise referred to as "the twins," and their roommate, Marilyn Saunders. They were pretty and fun, and we wore the same size in clothes. Who could have asked for anything more?

I had made my mind up that year to be more outgoing and less self-conscious. For instance, I was forcing myself to walk into the dayroom to mingle. I realized that people who weren't shy or self-conscious might find it odd to think that was an accomplishment. Also, I remembered how I'd felt a year ago—wanting to stay in my room and even wanting not to be there at all initially—and I was determined to go out of my way to be friendly to newcomers and underclassmen.

John and I, and all the rest of our friends, were preparing to make our senior year the best year of our lives. I would not let my dismal academic performance, which I was determined to try to rectify, put a damper on my social life; after all, not everyone could be an A student.

"I mean, just imagine," I said to my father, "what that would do to the bell curve!"

Thirty

I DID NOT EVER ACHIEVE A GRADE POINT AVERAGE THAT allowed me to study in my dormitory room. In fact, my grades deteriorated further, and my father made good on his threat and pulled me out of the dorms for the entire third quarter of my senior year. I tried to convince him he was splitting hairs, as 1.95 could have and should have been rounded up to 2.0, but he refused to budge. For the weeks that constituted a grading period sometime between February and April, I rode the dreaded day bus Monday through Friday.

I would never have admitted to my father—I would have let someone cut out my tongue first—that it really wasn't so bad, as it meant more than two hours of reading time each way. And occasionally, I used the hours to do my homework so that I had entire evenings free. Since I was not there to accumulate demerits after school, they seemed to disappear into thin air. My mother, bless her heart, felt so sorry for me for having to get up so early and get home so late that for the entire third quarter of my senior year, she cooked all my favorite foods every school day. I did not once have to eat salmon patties or tuna and noodles.

Also, I decided that not making the cheerleading squad was a blessing. It was a bit disappointing not to be traveling with Johnny and the cheerleaders for the away games, but I knew that the practices and the travel would have cut into my reading time. I wondered often if it was unnatural for me to have such a passion for books. I didn't know anyone else who had a need akin to an addiction for reading, to the extent that it obviously encroached on my study time. I blamed it on living in France for more than four years without a television. One could listen to Mario Lanza for only so long before needing a means of escape.

In October of my senior year, I discovered Frank G. Slaughter, who was a medical doctor, according to information on the inside back cover of the book I had just checked out. Dr. Slaughter must have written all day and night, I thought, because there was a list of his published works, and they numbered more than twenty. I was glad he'd written so many, because to me, nothing was worse than reading a really good book and finding out the author had written only that one. I'd read *Gone with the Wind* last year and been greatly distressed to discover Margaret Mitchell just let Rhett ride off, leaving us desperate to know if he ever came back to Scarlett, who, despite her self-absorption and stubborn pride, really was in love with him. Some books were so good that if there wasn't a sequel, I just had to read the book over again. I had done that with *To Kill a Mockingbird*. Next month—the setting of the story just lent itself to being read around Halloween—would be the third year in a row that I had read it, and I planned to read it every year for the rest of my life. It was that good.

It was now early in my senior year, and I had nine weeks to bring my grades up so that I could stay in my dormitory room for evening study hall.

I had decided to look at everything that occurred as being a gift from the universe. Over the summer, I'd read a book different from my usual fare—I couldn't remember the name of it—that talked about the abstracts of metaphysics and how humans, with our principles or lack thereof, interacted with our evolving planet. Its content was way beyond the understanding of someone who barely passed science and who would in no way qualify to take a high school physics course, but I did think it explained why I had been unable to scramble my frog's brain in tenth-grade science lab. (My lab partner, Warren

Strumfa, had had to step up and scramble it for me.) I now had a vague understanding, I think, of universal connectedness. At least that was what I called it.

As I found myself raking autumn leaves one day within a fairly short time of entering the twelfth grade, I thought what a beautiful universe this was and what a spectacular gift I had been given to be outside on that amazing brisk but sunny day, raking leaves. Of course, I would rather have been reading *The Brothers Karamazov*, which I had started over the weekend, but I was determined to remain positive.

It was a glorious autumn, and even though the school itself was devoid of any of the beauty of the ancient architecture found in the lovely villages abundant there in East Anglia, the vividness of the fall colors against the drab exterior walls of the dorms was stunning. Someone remarked that the colder the previous winter had been, the more colorful the leaves would be the following autumn. The leaves had blown into drifts and softened the starkness of the school buildings, providing a lovely contrast against the dormitory walls. I was not unaware of the benefit that positive thoughts brought about, and while I wouldn't have gone so far as to say I'd have volunteered to rake leaves even if I hadn't been working off demerits, I found myself warming to the beauty and the solitude of the task.

An hour later, I was in the dayroom before dinner, waiting for John.

"Saw that you're back at leaf-raking again this year," said Bob, sitting down next to me.

"Can you believe it? Do you ever remember me getting in trouble consistently in grade school or junior high?"

"Nope. You were a model of good behavior. What changed?"

"I really don't know. I think it took that one major screwup last year in the art classroom, which, unfortunately, was almost at the beginning of the year, and it's like every single faculty member has been instructed to watch every move I make. If I forget to throw out my gum, two demerits. If I talk in class, two more. If I am late to class, a demerit for every minute. Oh, bother! What's the use? Any minor infraction, and I get demerits. I can't believe in a school of over three hundred students, I'm the worst one here. The only other person I ever see working off demerits after school is Jamie Hartley! Surely more students than he and I get demerits!"

"I think some of the guys put a bug in someone's ear," said Bob. "Do you ever get KP duty? Do you ever have to wipe down tables in the cafeteria or empty waste cans from the dayroom? Did you ever wonder why you are only ever given leaf-raking duty? And where do most of the leaves end up?"

"On the ground outside the dorms? At least that's where most of them collect."

"One of the guys said something the other day that caught my attention," said Bob. "Last year, the dorm-four guys posted a lookout after school in case Donna Young walked by—you know, even the most mature of us male creatures are still cavemen. Don't you think it's strange that the only task you ever get assigned is raking leaves outside the dorms?"

"Are you saying I'm being watched?"

I had a sudden vision of how I hated to walk into church late and have people look at me. The thought of being watched while I was raking was much worse than walking into church late!

"Look, I know guys. And I remember how they all rushed to the closest window to watch Donna. So if you're tired of raking leaves ..."

The next day, I went to Mr. Radford, the assistant principal, who oversaw demerit-ridden students, of whom, most of the time, I was sure Jamie and I were the only ones.

"I'm wondering, Mr. Radford, if there are other duties besides raking leaves that you could assign me. I mean, given that I have ongoing demerits to work off—and I don't really see much hope that there will ever be a day when I don't—could I perhaps have KP duty or some office tasks? I did take typing, and I'm pretty good—I could probably help your secretary. Or even maybe help Nurse Miller in the sick room. I'm pretty familiar with the routine down there." I probably shouldn't have mentioned that, since Nurse Miller had an uncanny ability to know when I was really sick at sick call, which was seldom.

"Somewhere, I have a note," said Mr. Radford, rummaging through a drawer, "that specifically said you liked raking leaves and being outside–that you would like to request that job if it was available. Hmm, well, it's here somewhere. In any case, that aside, do you think perhaps we might first discuss why you have ongoing demerits? I'm a little concerned at your, well, nonchalance regarding constant infractions. You are not the typical profile of a problem student–well, except for that art room incident last year."

I had been hoping he wouldn't remember that was me. "Well, for some reason, I get caught all the time. I don't mean to constantly be doing demerit-worthy things; it just happens. Once, last year, I got caught sitting in an empty shower in the dorm bathroom after lights-out. I'd carried a chair in there just to finish a chapter in the book I was reading and figured there would be no reason anyone would check in the empty showers after ten o'clock. Because, you know, the house mothers can always tell if someone is reading with a flashlight under the covers in bed! Anyway, I intended only to finish the chapter I was right in the middle of–it was just too cliffhanging not to finish–but I got carried away, and before I knew it, it was twelve thirty, and Miss Rowe found me reading. But usually, it's just stupid stuff. Being late to class, chewing gum, passing notes–you know, things like that."

"I see. Is there a chance you could perhaps make a genuine effort not to chew gum, to be on time for every class, and to adhere to lights-out protocols to maybe, even for one month, see what it's like to be demerit-free?"

"Yes, sir, I will do my best."

"Good. So how many demerits are you currently working off?"

"I think I'm down to seven."

"Very good. Let's say you just worked one off by coming to see me, and that brings you to six. Starting tomorrow, you can report to Mr. Randall in the AFEX and see what he'd like you to do."

"Oh, thank you, Mr. Radford! Thank you very much! I promise I will make every effort to try not to get demerits, and I'll do my best not to read after lights-out."

For the next four school days, minus Friday, I worked for an hour and a half in the cafeteria, wiping down tables and chairs, sweeping the floors, and chatting with the kitchen staff. It suited me much more than raking leaves, and I was determined to remain demerit-free when I finished my fourth day. Much to my surprise, I managed to keep the slate clean for nearly six whole weeks, and it was a lovely feeling–if for no other reason than because I didn't have to work the afternoon of the homecoming dance. Last year had been particularly challenging: raking leaves for an hour and then rushing to get ready for the dance had been stressful.

No sooner was homecoming over than it was Thanksgiving, and then, before we knew it, it was Christmas. My dad asked, "Is that guy who eats us out of house and home coming this year? If so, your mother needs to buy more milk when she goes to the commissary."

My mother said, "I know they don't celebrate Christmas at the Young house, but are you sure he likes turkey? I can do a standing rib roast and Yorkshire pudding if he doesn't eat turkey. A lot of people don't like turkey; they think it has a strong taste."

My sister Connie asked, "Is this the homeless guy who comes here all the time to wash his stinky football clothes?"

My sister Chris said, "I like him. I don't think he's stinky."

Bobby didn't say anything. Except for a couple of baby words, he hadn't learned to talk. He'd just turned one in August, and as infants went, he was happy almost all the time.

I told my mother, again, that John had been just kidding last year when he showed up on Christmas Day–of course the Youngs celebrated Christmas.

"Well," she answered, "I'm not sure about that. He was very hungry, and most people don't pretend that they don't celebrate Christmas. That's a very questionable thing to pretend about."

My mother did not like lies or liars, and her failure to think something was funny caused many a joke to fall flat. So when people she liked joked or fibbed, she had to make it fit within the parameters of what she deemed acceptable—and Christmas was out of bounds. Mostly, we made allowances for Mom's occasional lack of humor: we blamed it on her Britishness.

It was the perfect Christmas Day. There was a light snow falling, Dad agreed to drive to the train station fifteen minutes away so Johnny didn't have to hitchhike to Chelveston, and my mother was in her element, cooking dinner.

Christmas dinner was delicious. It always was, but my mother adored cooking for admiring guests, and as such, John was stellar. As we started to clear the table, my mother waved away offers of help with the cleanup.

"Go relax, play a board game, or do something Christmassy. I don't need help," she said.

I bundled Chris up in her snowsuit and told Connie to put on an extra pair of socks with her boots, and Johnny and I took them for a walk over the bridge that crossed the river, which was frozen solid. We continued down to the little village of Chelveston, which was at least six hundred years old. Parts of the existing church, which was named Saint John the Baptist, dated that far back. Ice-covered tree branches glistened, and the silence that accompanied the winter wonderland, combined with the views of the snow-dusted meadow as the sun glided slowly behind the hills beyond, was spectacular. We turned back, and I stopped on the bridge to take in the view. Just as I remembered the Christmas on Fulton Street and the Christmases in France and at number 7 Windsor Avenue, I would remember that day, that Christmas, for the rest of my life.

I thought of Aurora, Santa Claus on the roof, and my panic in case he didn't know we didn't have a chimney. I thought of Alsace-Lorraine and of going up the mountain with Dad to cut down our own Christmas tree, and I remembered my first taste of French onion soup. I thought of number 7 at the holidays and the scary Father Christmas at Lewis's department store when I was four years old. I remembered the Blackpool lights, Bill the policeman kissing me under the mistletoe, my aunt Barbara, Nanna's knickers, and the fruitcake shot full of brandy. I thought of the New Year and the fact that in less than six months, we would graduate. My thoughts turned to my friend Alan Davila and how lonely Chelveston had become for me without him, and I hoped he was having a nice Christmas wherever he was. I thought of John Charles Christopher, and I said in my mind what I always said: *I miss you so much. I hope you are with Granddad Dempster, and I hope that Granddad has his dominoes and his horse races and that God allows betting. I hope you have Chutes and Ladders. Mostly, I hope you are with Jesus and Mary.*

"It's pretty cold out here," said John, breaking into my thoughts, "and it's getting dark."

"Come on," I said to my sisters. "Let's go get some trifle and mince pie!"

Four days later, John and I took the train to Scotland to celebrate New Year's Eve in Edinburgh. Donna wouldn't be there. She hadn't come home from Memphis for Christmas. Thinking of Donna made me smile.

Last summer, while I had been on holiday in Scotland, Donna, Johnny, and I had decided it was time I had pierced ears. Donna had threaded a darning needle and numbed my ears with ice cubes, and John had held a cork from a bottle of wine to the backs of my earlobes one at a time. After dipping the needle in rubbing alcohol, he'd stabbed the middle of each earlobe–first the right and then the left–pulling the heavy thread through the thickest part. He'd tied a knot at both ends of the thread and said, "Done!" I'd tried not to cry.

"Make sure you pull the thread back and forth every time you think about it, so your ears don't grow shut over the thread," Donna had said.

I'd pulled back and forth diligently, and within three days, my earlobes had become infected, festering and painful. Mrs. Young had been beside herself.

"What have you done?" she'd railed, obviously distressed and angry with the three of us. "She could lose her earlobes! Her parents could sue us!"

"Oh, Mrs. Young, please don't be mad at us! It is my fault–I asked John and Donna to do it. My parents would never sue anyone for something like this. The worst thing that will happen is my dad will put me on restriction for a month–maybe a year. But he'll blame me, not you!"

Mrs. Young had just shaken her head and said, "Come into the bathroom, and let me see if I can clean them up." She'd tsk-tsked the whole time she was cleaning with peroxide and dabbing with mercurochrome.

My ears had healed fine, but if she didn't notice the earrings–little crystal hearts dangling from silver chains–that Johnny had bought me for Christmas this year, I wasn't going to bring attention to them.

John and I went to dinner in Edinburgh for New Year's Eve and then went to a dance at a local nightclub. I thought of my cousins in America and how strange it would have seemed to them that two seventeen-year-olds were out clubbing on New Year's Eve like all the other young people in Britain and probably like all the young people all over Europe. The drinking age was sixteen–at least that was the age at which the pubs served us. Johnny and I didn't smoke, but that legal age was sixteen also, even though I'd have bet fifty dollars that fourteen-year-olds were never asked to show proof of age to purchase cigarettes in Britain. We each had a drink to toast the New Year as a bagpiper in a kilt played "Auld Lang Syne," and old and young alike linked arms and swayed to the melody recognized around the globe. I loved Scotland.

The Christmas holidays–as perfect as they had been–were soon over, and we were back in school, full of anticipation, looking forward to the last half of our senior year.

I had learned recently that I had dual citizenship. I had assumed, like my friends who had been born in other countries and had foreign mothers and American fathers, I was an American citizen only. My mother said that was because those friends must have been born in American hospitals on whichever overseas bases their fathers had been stationed. She reminded me I had been born at Nanna and Granddad's house on Windsor Avenue. That was why, she said, I'd had to go before the judge in Denver in order to confirm I was also an American citizen. I had forgotten about that.

At school, John had received two letters of recommendation—I think they were called nominations—to the Air Force Academy. One had been from Vice President Hubert Humphrey and the other had been from a senator in Tennessee. He would be going to London to complete the entrance examination process, and once he graduated high school, he would be at the Academy for four years. We had talked about getting married after he graduated, but, in the meantime, I was thinking about where I wanted to live.

Nanna had finally moved into one of the new bungalows across the street from number 7, where the air-raid shelter had been. However, it was a council house. The council was strict with respect to who qualified to live in subsidized housing, so living with Nanna probably would not be an option. I could have lived with Auntie Barbara, I supposed, but she recently had gotten married for the second time. She might have felt I was cramping her style, so to speak. Maybe I'd just get a job and my own flat. Then I had a brilliant idea: I would get a job and move to number 7 Windsor Avenue! I'd be right across the street from Nanna. We had known Mr. Levy, who owned the house, for all the years my grandparents had lived there—since Mom, Uncle Jackie, and Aunt Barbara were little. He probably remembered me—he might even be thrilled that I wanted to rent it and move back in, I thought. *Well, perhaps not thrilled, but I'm sure if I could prove I could afford it, he'd let me rent it.*

Still, it was only January, and I had months and months before I had to decide what I wanted to do when I graduated. Suddenly, I felt a twinge of guilt: I hadn't been able to bring myself to tell my father, as his Christmas present, that I was considering going to college when I got out of high school. I could not lie. I had bought him a new billfold instead.

Thirty-one

HE WEEKS AND MONTHS FOLLOWING THE NEW YEAR GLIDED along with relatively little disturbance. I had few demerits, and for those I did earn, I worked in the school cafeteria. I thought my teachers had just gotten tired of reprimanding me, and for my part, I'd given up gum chewing completely. Moreover, there was no point in trying to sneak into the girls' showers to read after lights-out–Miss Rowe had made it routine surveillance on her evening rounds.

The trip my senior class took to Rome over Easter break did not mark the end of the school year, but it might as well have. In the weeks following the trip, I was pretty sure most of us were just going through the motions. In my case, that was certainly true. Since I'd had to ride the day bus for the first half of the second semester, my grades had improved enough that I had little to worry about for the remainder of the year. I did feel a bit guilty, considering I knew I could have done better, but it just wasn't my cup of tea. After all, if everyone excelled, what would happen to the part of the economy that would collapse if there weren't people willing to remain mediocre in order to fill mundane positions? I'd said to my dad recently, "Look, some of us have to feel a sense of responsibility toward mediocrity. We can't all be overachievers."

"Gee," he'd replied, "why didn't I think of that? In fact, now that you mention it, you have elevated mediocrity to whole new heights." Sarcasm ran in his veins like blue blood ran in Queen Elizabeth's.

The annual Lakenheath American High School senior class trip always took place during spring break, and Rome, Italy, had been the destination for several years. Rome was the perfect place for a class trip: Italy was lovely and warm in spring; from England, Europe was amazingly easy to reach; travel was relatively inexpensive; and spring break always coincided with Holy Week and Easter. Where better to spend the holiest week of the Christian year than in one of the holiest of Christian cities? However, there had been some debate and concern last year that the trip might be canceled permanently after an incident in the spring of 1964.

Several Lakenheath boys had caused an international scandal: in the middle of the night, they somehow had managed to climb the walls of the Colosseum and paint *Seniors '64* over the ancient plinth, the supporting stone, above the main entrance. It had been all over the news. It had made the *Stars and Stripes*, of course, and Europe had been shocked at the vulgarity and vandalism perpetrated by the American youths. It was understandable, then, that there was hesitation about whether the school would continue the tradition of the senior class going to Rome, and I was sure there was legitimate concern about whether Italy was ever going to let us back in. Who could have blamed them if they didn't? However, they did, and the school continued the tradition. Going forward, we all knew our behavior had to be exemplary.

If the French railroad workers had not gone on strike just about the time we seniors—and quite a few juniors—were about to embark on the trip of a lifetime and, subsequently, if we had not had to ride through Europe on coaches to reach Rome and had arrived at our destination in two days instead of five, exemplary behavior might have been well within our reach.

After disembarking from the ferry that we had taken to cross the English Channel, we took a short bus ride from Calais to Ostend, Belgium; boarded a train in Ostend; and chugged our way to the

German border, where two private coaches were waiting to drive us through Germany and Austria into Italy. We finally reached Rome on the Friday before Easter Sunday. There had been overnight stops along the way, which had turned out to be a bonus, and while we knew we had to be on our best behavior, we managed to have a grand time in city after city. With only a few exceptions, we wreaked no havoc.

One of the exceptions occurred in a town in northern Italy, where we were spending the night in a lovely old bastion of a hotel that must have been built at least two centuries ago. We American students were not the ones to wreak the havoc. It was not Kate Ingram's fault that she was the only one of us truly fluent enough in French to order at dinner or that the cute Italian waiter also spoke French. Between them, they had a friendly conversation as Kate translated our menu orders. I understood snippets of the exchange, and only once or twice did it cause me to raise an eyebrow. How the cute Italian waiter somehow interpreted Kate's chat with him to mean "Please join us in our room when your shift is over" she had no idea. And Kate was adamant that nothing she had said could possibly have been translated further into "And if you have a friend, bring him along." So things got a bit iffy later that evening when two lusty Italian waiters tried diligently to force their way into our hotel room. So persistent were they that Kate and I had to go out onto the balcony and call across the courtyard for help. Fortunately, some of our classmates who were partying on the balcony opposite heard us and promptly rescued us from the clutches of the two amorous Italians. But that was Kate—all measure of mischief just seemed to follow her around.

Eventually, we made it to Rome and checked into the Olympic Stadium, into the dormitories that had been built to house the athletes during the 1960 Olympics. However, a situation occurred on Easter Saturday that made me realize the frailty of the bond between my self-control and my strict Catholic upbringing, an upbringing in which there was little room—between my father's expectations and whichever priest was currently enjoying Mom's Sunday breakfasts—to give in to temptation.

Of note, my American grandparents in Illinois were financing my trip. They were devout Catholics, and the letter Grandma Grilliot had sent along with her generous check left no doubt in my mind that my not receiving communion from His Holiness on Easter Sunday was not an option. These were the grandparents who had an autographed picture of Pope Paul on their dining room wall, which they'd received as a thank-you for something they'd bought for Saint Peter's Cathedral. I wished I had paid more attention to what it was, because now that I was there, I would have liked to look at their contribution to the magnificent and holy edifice. In her letter, my grandmother had suggested I look for an opportunity to obtain what she called a private audience with the pope. She thought it would be as exciting as meeting the queen, and she could tell all her friends that her granddaughter had been personally blessed by Pope Paul. However, now that I was there, I didn't think meeting the pope was such a good idea. I was pretty certain he had special powers, sort of like Jesus when he'd met the woman at the well and known exactly what she'd been up to. Anyway, on Easter Saturday, I had to go to confession. It was imperative that I be in a state of grace when I received the body of our Lord Jesus Christ on Easter Sunday.

Kate, John Childress, John Young, and I arrived in Vatican City early on Saturday, and we spent the better part of the morning touring the magnificent walled area—the smallest city in the world, someone said. There were thousands of tourists from all over the globe, and most were there to attend Mass tomorrow, on the holiest day in the holiest week of the Catholic year.

After we toured the cathedral, I announced to my friends that I had to go to confession in preparation for Easter Mass. I steeled myself for the ordeal. I always had disliked confession, even back when I'd had to make things up because I hadn't committed any good sins, but now, in that holy place, when I certainly didn't have to make any up, I dreaded it even more.

"We'll wait outside," said Kate. "Do you think it will take long?"

"Probably. Do you see the lines outside all these confessionals? And they don't look like they're moving very fast. But I'll try to pick a short line."

Inside the massive cathedral, there were a dozen sets of confessionals. Each confessional—as was usual in Catholic churches—had a center cubical and two sides. Each side had a door by which the penitent entered and then knelt inside to confess his or her sins. The priest sitting in the middle between the two listened alternately to the confessions of the sinners in each side booth. Looking now at the lines of confessors waiting for their turns, I tried to pick out the shortest line. The lines were moving at a pretty good pace, but as soon as someone came out and someone else went in, there were more people—like me—joining the lines. Each confessional had a constant stream of people moving in and out, right and left.

Once faced with having to get in line, I abandoned my plan to try to find a short line and picked instead a line that looked as if it had a lot of sinners in it. In my experience—and the short lines with mostly elderly ladies seemed to support the fact—little old ladies were not particularly major sinners, which was why those lines moved more quickly. I based my theory on my grandmother's saying that missing Sunday Mass was the worst sin of all—it broke Our Lady's heart that we would choose not to devote one hour out of the week to worship her Son. I bet that happened to be the sin du jour of these little old ladies. I decided to join a line with what looked like younger people and quite a few men who looked really sinful. I hoped that by the time I worked my way up the line, my worst sin might somehow pale in comparison—or at the very least, I wouldn't rise to the level of Mary Magdalene.

The line I chose seemed to be moving a little slower than the others, so I might have been spot-on in my assumption. I used the time to work on my phraseology: *Forgive me, Father, for I have sinned. I let my boyfriend—no, no, no! Forgive me, for I have sinned, Father. My boyfriend and I—nope! Forgive me, Father, for I have sinned. I'm guilty of committing heavy petting with my boyfriend.* Yes, that was it! With any luck, the priest wouldn't ask me to clarify that; he wouldn't want to come across as being creepy or voyeuristic. I was still dreading going into the confessional, but I felt better now that I had a plan. Nevertheless, there were times when I wished I were still Church of England, and this was one of them.

I knelt in the confessional box. I heard the priest murmuring to the person on the other side, and eventually, the little door covering the grille on my side opened.

I said, "Forgive me, Father, for I have sinned. It has been one month since my last confession."

"Ja, mein Kind, Deine Sunden Sind?"

He was Dutch—or German—and he didn't speak English! I was faint with relief—giddy, in fact. *Oh, thank you, God! Thank you, Jesus! Thank you for this gift!*

"Well," I said, "my boyfriend and I are traveling—in fact, a whole bunch of us are traveling. We're on a school trip, and it was supposed to be by train, but there is a rail strike in France—you might have heard—so now we've been on a bus for days on end. So you know, heavy petting. And believe me, I'm sure it's not just us—that is, my boyfriend and me. It's probably the whole bus. In fact, probably both buses are filled with couples engaged in heavy petting. Just a guess on my part. I mean, we've been on these buses since Germany because, you know, the strike and all. Otherwise, we would have been here in one day, or two at the most, which wouldn't have presented such an opportunity. Anyway ..." In my profound relief, I was babbling.

The priest interrupted me. *"Sie sind freigesprochen, sagen wir drei* Hail Marys."

Drei? How many was that? "Excuse me, Father, but is *drei* two or three Hail Marys?"

"Tree," he said.

I said an Act of Contrition, and in my profound relief, I meant every word of it. I exited the confessional, knelt immediately, and said my penance of three Hail Marys.

Outside, Kate, John, and John were waiting patiently.

"Whew," I said. "I'm glad that's over!" I felt as light as a feather as we drifted toward the Sistine Chapel.

"You know, the chapel has the second-most-famous painting in the world on the ceiling," said Johnny Childress.

"What's the first?" the rest of us asked in unison.

"The *Mona Lisa*, of course! And if we get to spend a whole day in Paris on the way back, we might get to see that too!"

For twenty minutes, we looked with awe at the splendor of the interior of the most famous chapel in the world. Finally, Kate and Johnny Childress said they'd had enough; they would meet us outside. I told them we were ready too. John Young said, "Hold on a minute. I want to look at something over here behind this statue."

And that was how I ended up having to go to confession again. My Protestant friends shook their heads.

I took a deep breath, let my eyes adjust again to the gloom of the cathedral, and then joined the line in front of the confessional with the German priest–or Dutch, or whatever he was. Eventually, I entered for a second time.

"Forgive me, Father, for I have sinned. It has been thirty minutes since my last confession."

"What?" asked the priest–in English, with an American accent. "Did you say *thirty minutes?*"

For a split second, I thought about saying, "Oh, sorry. I meant thirty days." I didn't but only because I was sure God would have been tempted to strike me dead, particularly at that moment. "Oh. Well, it's like this, Father ..."

"You did what?"

And that was how it came about that I had to say a whole rosary as penance before I could receive communion from His Holiness Pope Paul VI in the holiest church in all of Christendom on Easter Sunday in 1966.

Thirty-two

THE REST OF THE YEAR PASSED WITH RELATIVELY LITTLE turmoil. I got few demerits; my grades stayed at an acceptable-enough mediocre level for my father, though my bell-curve postulation had fallen on deaf ears; and my friends and I cherished every minute of this life that we knew was a gift few young people around the world were privileged to experience.

In the end, I graduated from high school. Mr. Ackerman, the history teacher, wrote on my report card that I was graduating on his generosity. My father read that out loud at the dinner table three times. My mother said, "Really, Robert? Do you really think her future husband is going to ask about her final report card, let alone quiz her on her knowledge of history?"

"So," asked my father, "any chance you'd like to go to college?"

"You're kidding, right?" I responded.

"Well, I just thought you might like to see if you might like college. You know, just give it a try?"

"Dad, I've been to boarding school for two years, and I really liked it but not enough to want to immerse myself in more boring subjects. I think living on a college campus might be a lot of fun, but I really am not cut out for all this cerebral stuff."

"So what do you think you want to do as a career?"

"Well, I just finished my first week as a waitress at the NCO club. I loved it. I'm really good at it, and I got great tips."

My father just sighed. My mother said she thought that would be a perfectly good job until I settled down and got married.

My father shook his head.

My mother said, "Really, Robert? As long as she can manage her housekeeping money, what does it matter? And she'll be a wonderful little mother–look how she is with her siblings!"

I decided to change the subject and, for once, not be a smart aleck. "Today I met a young sergeant who just came back from Thailand. He sat at one of my tables. He's an aircraft mechanic."

Suddenly, conversation about my lack of career aspirations veered to more serious matters.

"Really? Usually, after a tour of duty in Southeast Asia, the military assigns staff to a base in the States. Did he say how long he was there and what it was like?"

"He said the base he was at was mostly where our fighter jets were–the ones that fly over Vietnam and fight with the North Vietnamese. I don't remember the name of the base. He got injured somehow and was sent to Walter Reed in Washington, DC, and then was reassigned here. Dad, Bob Peterson and I were talking about Vietnam and who would have to go. His father is an officer in the marines, and he's pretty sure sooner or later his dad will be sent over there. Will you ever have to go, do you think?"

"I doubt it, Gracie. I'm a systems analyst, and while I'm sure there are computers at all our bases, in most settings, an analyst wouldn't be much good in day-to-day operations."

"How long do you think the war will last, Dad?"

"I can't imagine it will go on too long," he answered. "We have the best fighting forces in the world, and our fighter pilots are second to none."

"Some of the boys who graduated from Lakenheath last year and the year before were drafted, and we know for sure some of them got sent to Vietnam. Frank Kelley told me today that a boy we went to school with was killed in combat."

We finished our dinner in silence–my lack of interest in furthering my education suddenly seemed a petty topic, even to my father.

A few days later, following another argument between my parents, I realized again that they were poles apart not only in their expectations for their children, or at least for me, but also in many other ways. Lately, I'd found myself wondering how they had ended up married.

They were very different. Dad never had learned ballroom dancing, and Mom never had learned to like country music. Their senses of humor never met at any crossroad, and they were, as Nanna would have said, as different as chalk and cheese. Being home again full-time after being at boarding school for two years, I realized how much more conflict there seemed to be now than in the past.

My parents had arguments. They never got physical when they got angry–well, except for my mother and the occasional swat to my backside with her wooden spoon when I was younger–but they got verbal. At least my mother did. Dad rarely ever raised his voice. Most, if not all, arguments were over my father's drinking. If he went to the NCO club after work and forgot to come home in a timely manner, dinner was ruined. Dad would say it wasn't ruined for him; he could eat anything, even K rations. That would catapult my mother from angry to livid. She had a temper–one she was often quite proud of–and she would throw dinner into the garbage. Of course, we kids had already eaten, but Mom's temper would rise to a point where she would not eat, probably to make my father feel bad. Dad would say she was cutting her nose off to spite her face, and his lack of engaging in an argument over his inconsiderateness would only add fuel to the fire.

When my father drank at home–which wasn't every day and not even every week–he would sit in his recliner, put country music on the record player, and turn up the volume. Hank Snow was his favorite. The more annoyed my mother became at my father's drinking, the more he drank, and the louder Hank sang. "There Stands the Glass" was Dad's favorite. That did not go over well with my poetry-reading, ballroom-dancing, opera-loving mother. I paid little attention to any of it; there were never any lasting ramifications, and it never affected the warmth and closeness we otherwise shared as a family. Still, occasionally, a fleeting thought would cross my mind: *Dad had better pay a little more attention to how his drinking is affecting Mom. With her beauty, her personality, and her fabulous British accent—now I wish I still had mine!—someone might come along and sweep her off her feet one of these days. Then what would we all do?*

The drinking-related argument I most remembered happened when I was in my midteens. It happened because my father had no sense of smell—zero. We all knew that his nose had been broken twice when he played football for the Freeport Pretzels as a senior in high school. Because he had been a quarterback, he had suffered a lot of injuries, and both the injuries and the suffering had made him popular with the girls. Sometimes, I thought, he forgot he wasn't still in high school.

It was a shame, I used to think, that he couldn't smell the turkey on Thanksgiving, the lovely scent of the Christmas tree, spring flowers, or anything.

"Can't you smell how great the ball field smells while you're mowing the grass, Dad?" I would ask.

"Nope. Cutting the grass just makes me sneeze," he would say.

"That's because you drink too much while you're mowing, Robert. You sneeze when you've had too much to drink," my mother would reply sharply.

That was true. Too much of any kind of alcohol made Dad sneeze.

When my mother wore her favorite Shalimar perfume, Dad never said, "You smell nice." Mom would have known he was lying; still, it was a shame he couldn't make it up occasionally, I thought, even if he'd just said something like "I think I can smell your perfume tonight. It's very nice." Then he could have put his face in her neck and said, "I can. You smell lovely!"

He was a lot like me—he found it difficult to tell even white lies.

On the evening of what might have been his most catastrophic inebriation—and the one I most remembered my mother's anger over—they were at a formal dance of some sort at the NCO club. A young female friend named Jane joined them at their table. They had drinks, they danced, and they had more drinks—at least Dad did. After dancing a second time with Jane and returning to the table, Dad leaned toward Jane, inhaled a long breath, and said, "Jane, I don't know what sort of shampoo you use, but your hair smells absolutely wonderful!"

"Prell! Can you believe it? Every last one of us air force wives use Prell!" railed my mother afterward. "I even wash you girls' hair with Prell! Do you ever recall your father saying any of our hair smells wonderful? 'Oh,' he says, 'I can't smell anything. My nose got broken in football, and after surgery, I had no sense of smell ever again.' The problem with your father, Vivienne, is that he still thinks he's a bloody high school football hero!"

I was never sure what my mother wanted my answer to be when she was that angry with my dad.

"If you think Dad's drinking has become an albatross," I said, "we could move to England and live with Nanna."

"I don't know how to drive," she answered, which was her standard response whenever she got that angry. Not knowing how to drive was always the reason she used to remain in a situation that obviously caused her grief. Secretly, I knew she was proud of Dad, was proud of being the wife of a military man, and loved her life as an air force wife and mother.

I did worry a bit that someday she might decide she'd had enough of Dad's drinking and—although I rarely witnessed it—his flirting and decide to call it quits. Although I acted as if I'd have loved to move back to England, I'd have wanted to do so only if we went as a family. Dad needed to pay a little more attention to his behavior; after all, he couldn't cook, and even I knew he'd soon get tired of cereal, chicken noodle soup, and K rations.

The months turned to years, and the war in Vietnam labored on. My parents' marriage limped along. Martin Luther King Jr. was assassinated, and less than two months later, Robert F. Kennedy was too. We left England when my father was transferred to Luke Air Force Base in Arizona, and eighteen months later, he was transferred to Eglin Air Force Base in Florida. In Arizona, he again offered to send me to college–his tenacity was admirable; my lack of ambition wasn't. In Florida, I decided waitressing probably would not be a fulfilling lifetime career, and I took a mind-numbing office job. Just as I was beginning to think I should at least look at local junior college programs, I met my future husband.

For several years after my father retired from the air force, life was grand. My parents moved back to Dad's hometown in Illinois, where he took a job as a systems analyst with a national insurance company, and my mother finally had the house of her dreams.

It came as a stunning shock when Mom announced they were divorcing

Thirty-three

Indianapolis, Indiana
March 1975

Y MOTHER JUST TOLD ME THE SECRET SHE HAS KEPT
from me all these many years: my father is not my
biological father. She was single, unwed, and living
with her parents when she got pregnant with me, and they supported
her completely in her decision not to get an abortion. Finding out
as an adult is a shock, and I wonder that I never guessed—there have
been so many clues, I now realize, all through the years.

My parents are divorcing, so my mother feels it is as good a time
as any to tell me the truth: my biological father was British. He died
some years ago. She showed me the obituary notice from the local
paper in Urmston, which my grandmother sent to her: it reveals that
I have five half siblings in England. *Funny*, I thought as I read the
obituary. *I am an only child. I am the eldest of ten children and the only
child of my biological parents.* Suddenly, I realized, *I am British*, and
everything fell into place. With equal surprise, I also realized I was
the child of the man who adopted me; we were alike in so many ways.

It is strange the things one thinks about at moments of emotional
shock. I think about myself as a child, struggling to be more American,
unable to understand why all those other brats who had foreign

mothers seemed never to have to try. With clarity, I have a flashback to the courthouse in Denver, Colorado, and I now understand our visit that day was not just to confer upon me American citizenship but also to finalize my adoption by my mother's husband, my American stepfather. At least I now know why Dad didn't put his foot down and demand I be given a cute American name–it turns out it wasn't his fault after all. I smile as I think about a long-ago conversation between us.

"I just do not understand why you gave Johnny, Connie, Chrissy, and Bobby such nice, ordinary names, and you let Mom stick me with the awkward name of an old movie star! What were you thinking?"

He grinned and said, "Well, I wanted to name you after my favorite female singer, but your mother adamantly refused. Guess I should have persevered, eh?"

"Wait–who is your favorite female singer?" I asked.

"Eartha Kitt, of course! You know that!" he responded.

I never again complained about my name.

My mother's anguish is understandable. Her home and family are her pride and joy, her life's mission. She has never worked outside the home, she has never written a check, and she has never learned to drive. She never thought she would need to. She has lived in America–or lived an American life–for too many years now to consider going home to England. Her parents are gone, and her children and grandchildren are all here. It will be difficult for her, but she will survive. Her indomitable spirit will see her through.

I don't tell her what is in my heart this day, because her emotions are too raw, but I think of what an amazing father this man has been to me. Through all these years, not one time has his grief over losing Johnny turned into resentment that he lost his beloved son, when it would have been much easier for him to lose a stepdaughter: not better, but easier.

Somehow, our mother will survive, and our father will end up regretting his decision. I know this because I am, regardless of the lack of his DNA, the product of his profound influence in my life.

~~~

Freeport, Illinois
July 1999

My father died two weeks before his seventieth birthday.

A gentleman named Jack introduced himself to me at the wake.

"Did your dad ever tell you about our train ride to Chicago the week after we graduated from high school?"

He had not, I replied.

"There were four of us: Don, Billy, Bob, and me. The Chicago Cubs were having open tryouts, and we hitched a ride on your grandpa's train from Rockford to Chicago. Back in those days, it was no big deal for local kids to ride for free for a short distance. Your grandfather would give a nod to the conductor, and away we'd go. Anyway, that particular day, when we were as free as jaybirds, with big dreams and no money but lots of confidence, we headed to Wrigley Field. We didn't know whether we'd get a chance to try out, but we sure were gonna try."

He stopped for a minute and gazed into the distance, as though he were recalling the events of that early summer day—reminiscing, I supposed.

"One by one and then all together—you know, with other guys from other places—we were put through a variety of skill tests: pitching, batting, and fielding. Your dad was a great catcher, but he also played shortstop. I'll tell you, for a bunch of kids from Freeport who had grown up rooting for the Cubs, reading about the Cubs, and hitching a ride on the train to see a Cubs game when we'd saved up enough money by washing cars and cutting lawns, well, making it to the tryouts and being on that field where some of the greatest players in history had played—that was something."

"I bet!" I replied. "What an awesome opportunity–and a great memory!"

"That day, when it was all over, your dad was offered a position on the farm team. He was handed a contract and told he needed to get a signature from one of his parents because he was only seventeen. And you know, while the rest of us were disappointed, we all knew Bobby had real talent, and we were pleased as punch that he'd made it. One of us guys from Freeport, Illinois, was going to play for the Cubs. We felt it in our guts."

"I love this story, Jack. But what happened? How come Dad never talked about that? Was his career short-lived? Wasn't he good enough after all for the farm team?"

"Well, we all liked and respected your grandfather, but he could be real strict in some ways," Jack said. "We got back on the train, but of course, your grandpa wasn't the engineer on the one going back to Rockford; he'd gone on to New Orleans, his regular route. Maybe if he'd been on that train and seen our elation–boy, were we excited. Three days later, when your grandpa got back to Freeport, your dad showed him the contract. And according to Bob, his father said, 'Well now, I think playing baseball is no real job for a grown man!' and he wouldn't sign. The very next day, your father went to the recruiter down on Stevenson and enlisted in the Army Air Corps."

I thought about a picture I had of six-year-old me that had been taken in Muncie when Dad was teaching ROTC at Ball State. In the picture, I was wearing catcher's headgear; the metal grid and leather straps overwhelmed my small head. I was holding the catcher's mitt out in front of me, waiting for my father to toss me the baseball, heeding his instructions on just how to crouch and on the angle at which to hold the glove. With a full heart, I now wondered, *How amazing is destiny, and what would my life have been like without him?*

Epilogue

At the time Dad died, he was divorced from his second wife, and my siblings and I buried him next to our brother John in Freeport, Illinois. Eight years later, our mother died. She would be buried on the other side of John. She had clipped her favorite poem out of a magazine many years prior to her death and had reminded us often that when she died, she wanted her headstone engraved with her two favorite lines from the poem "The Soldier" by Rupert Brooke. As Dad had only a small gravestone provided by the Veterans Administration indicating his military status and Johnny likewise had only a small marker embedded over his grave, when Mom died, we decided there should be one large granite stone placed at the head of the three graves, listing the name and birth and death dates of each.

The lines our mother had requested would be engraved on the back of the granite on her side of the headstone. That left my siblings and me to decide on an excerpt or quote to be engraved on the back side of the headstone for Dad. We wanted something Dad would have chosen. Most nights in the 1960s and '70s, he had stayed up to watch the late news and hadn't turned the TV off until after the recitation of "High Flight," the poem written by John Magee Jr., a Royal Canadian Air Force pilot. Dad had loved that poem, especially the part about reaching out and touching the face of God. But Dad's favorite poem, "Casey at the Bat," was the one whose lines he'd most often quoted. We decided on the latter and submitted the information to a monument company in Rockford. It would take weeks to be fabricated, and we would not see the marker until a return trip.

A little more than a year later, Connie, Bob, and I returned to Freeport and made a visit to the cemetery.

The beautiful stone had been placed at the head of the three plots and was engraved with names and dates. The back of the headstone was engraved with the excerpts from the poems, and they perfectly reflected our mother's love of England and our father's love of baseball.

> If I should die, think only this of me:
> That there's some corner of a foreign field
> That is for ever England.
> —Rupert Brooke, "The Soldier"

> Oh, somewhere in this favored land the sun is shining
> Bright;
> The band is playing somewhere, and somewhere hearts
> Are light.
> —Ernest Lawrence Thayer, "Casey at the Bat"

As I stood with my siblings, reading the back of the beautiful headstone with the perfectly chosen lines of poetry, I was misty-eyed. Our parents, with all their foibles and their failures, were together again, and I hoped that in the perfectness of their new lives, they were as happy as they had been many years ago. I hoped there were drive-in movies with heroes in white hats, and I hoped they were watching them with Johnny. I hoped there was baseball up there, and I imagined Dad was again playing, umpiring, or coaching his favorite game. I hoped Mom and Dad were dancing as they once had—the jitterbug, of course, but maybe Dad had finally learned to tango. Mostly, I hoped Dad had his sense of smell back and could finally smell Mom's perfume.

Then Connie said, "Hey, look at that! Mom's poem is on the back of Dad's side of the headstone, and Casey is behind Mom! The granite people screwed up!"

We all looked at one another, and we knew wherever they were, our mother was not amused, and our father was grinning from ear to ear.

Afterword

I am aware of what a great privilege it was to have lived and traveled in Europe for most of my childhood; that this richly diverse world was served up so wonderfully dressed and colorfully presented still astonishes me. The plethora of sensations I experienced constantly in my youth–love of travel; love of history; love of adventure; and love of reading about travel, history, and adventure–were a heady elixir. Unfortunately, love of studying did not, to the dismay of my father, ever stumble its way into that concoction. On the other hand, my mother was so charmingly nonchalant about my lack of academic brilliance that, if nothing else, it created a tolerable balance in my life: where education was concerned, I could count on Mom to side with me in any altercation centered on my dismal academic record, while I could count on Dad to come to the rescue and solidly assert my Americanism and its traditions when necessary.

My mother was the most vivacious person I have ever known, and she was an amazing storyteller. She was completely confident in her recollection of all things: the England she grew up in, the poverty the Dempster family experienced between the wars, and her vast knowledge of people and events in World War II. She had immense pride in being both British and, later, an American citizen, and what she lacked in formal education she made up for in her astonishing knowledge of European history and her love of literature and music. If I had to pick one word to describe the mother of my childhood, it would be *dazzling*. Throughout her life, she was a woman who lit up every room she walked into and charmingly dominated every conversation she ever held. I thank her every day for being an amazing mother and for choosing life for me.

Mom must have been supremely confident that I would turn out OK. Her nonchalance at my lack of serious application to subjects that bored me was the antithesis of my father's determination that I would become, if never brilliant, more than mediocre in my studies. I think he must have seen, somewhere betwixt my passion for reading and my loathing of math, a glimmer of something that led him to think I might someday amount to something. Not that there is anything wrong with being a waitress—he would have been the first to say that. But he would also have insisted—and he did—that I make an informed decision to do so, which required at least a rudimentary exploration of other options.

That I never guessed that he wasn't my biological parent still amazes me and speaks volumes about his character. It fills me with wonder that he was so much a part of my physical world as a child: instilling in me a passion for baseball; taking my sister Connie and me on weekend drives in France to visit nearby sites of interest; and sitting with me in the evenings after getting home from umpiring a baseball game, tired though he must have been, until I got my long division and, later, my fractions right.

I like to think that perhaps I inherited the best of both my parents: my mother's love of history and literature and my father's sense of humor and understanding that a solid résumé matters. I believe that was what he wanted most for my siblings and me: for us to be our best selves and achieve whatever our dreams were.

Sometimes, when I'm having a particularly difficult day, I hear him in my ear, asking, "So, Gracie, compared to fractions and conjugating French verbs, how difficult is this?"

I smile and say, "Not difficult at all, Dad."

Acknowledgments

It's hard to know where to begin or end the recognition of all the help I have had in writing this. So many people have contributed so much.

To my children, Jim and Jonathan, you are my inspiration. I love you beyond measure: your belief in me and your support of everything I have ever attempted fills me with awe. To my grandchildren, Tayler, Yanni, Christopher, Jordan, and James, this is for you. You already know these stories—well, most of them. I hope that my putting pen to paper paints for you a picture as vivid as my childhood remains in my heart. For your individual contributions over these many months, I thank you all. To Christina, Jon, and Yanni, without your technical help, considering my complete hopelessness with anything but a manual typewriter, I'm sure the publisher would have paid me to just go away!

To my siblings on both sides of the pond: how diverse we all are! I am, being the eldest of ten and the only child of my (our) biological parents, in a unique position to embrace you all, and I do so with my whole heart. I hope this memoir gives you a glimpse into the familiar and perhaps not-so-familiar world in which I lived.

To my cousins in England: you are my Dempster family. You were my first family. You are also the family who knew our grandparents, Gladys and Jack, and I count on you to remember always with me number 7 Windsor Avenue.

To my family in Freeport, Illinois: thank you for welcoming that little English girl with wide-open arms so long ago—and for being so wonderfully American! You all—aunts, uncles, cousins, grandparents—have given me so much joy through the years, and I love you.

Many people have contributed to ensuring this memoir made it to production. Frank Kelley, your talent with graphics and your skill in repairing and restoring both the cover photo and several of the interior photos in this labor of love are much appreciated. I am indebted to you; moreover, I thank you for the years of friendship and for all you have done to keep our Lancer family connected.

Dr. Don Osborne, friend and Lancer, I cannot thank you enough for sharing your personal experience as an author and for your support and guidance during the earliest draft of this memoir. Tom Bernakis, also friend and Lancer, thank you for your help with my rusty French. Honestly, one of these days, I *will* take my French seriously, and my father will do a happy dance in heaven! John Bakshis, LTCR, USN retired, your expertise as a navy guy saved an entire chapter that otherwise would have suffered awkwardly from air force jargon. I owe you a bottle of Crown Royal for the rewrite, my friend!

Sarah Northard, what can I say? Thank you ever so much for allowing me to revisit my childhood. It is indeed a rare person who will let a total stranger wander through her home, and I am touched by your generosity. And thank you, Charli Henning, for arranging that.

To my friend and confidante Glenys Berns: to be able to share these memories with a fellow Brit (a fellow Lancastrian at that!) in real time, weekly, and over Gin and Its has been invaluable, not to mention your unique perspective and your spot-on British vocabulary: it's not a pantry; it's a larder!

I can't begin to list you all, but to our many friends at Applebee's, know that your encouragement and friendship have touched my heart in ways you cannot imagine, and a special thank you to Ted Martin, whose interest in my first book led to my writing this memoir.

To my reviewers (girlfriends all!) Kathleen Banas, Glenys Berns, and Diane Bagdasarian Schmidt: you ladies are, quite simply, the best!

To my English sisters, Kathryn Carr and Naomi Jackson: thank you for your enduring patience with all my queries regarding England in the 1950s and '60s: What were grades in British primary schools called? How did we write out money (e.g., five shillings and sixpence)? Where exactly was the queen's farm that was in the vicinity of Chelveston? When did Chelveston become a village? My vivid memories, alas, sometimes lacked specificity.

There are people in our lives with whom we have no idea how we were so blessed to cross paths, and for me, one of those people was Robert Peterson. I am filled with gratitude to Bob for a lifetime of friendship, for teaching me Chinese checkers in France, for giving me the inside scoop on comic book trading, and for not dropping me from the top of that human pyramid in the sixth grade. I miss our frequent morning chats as he finished the night shift at his police department in Ohio and I drove to Gainesville to do rounds at the medical center. You were my friend in France, in England, and here in America, and I miss you.

Finally, Paul Worthington, there is an Irish colloquialism: "You are the side of me." (Because I would never be so corny as to say, "You complete me.") Without your unflagging encouragement and support and your limitless patience, this memoir would never have been written. You are the better part of me, and I love you.

Printed in the United States
by Baker & Taylor Publisher Services